BE A N

BE A MAN!

MALES IN
MODERN SOCIETY

Peter N. Stearns

HOLMES & MEIER PUBLISHERS, INC.

NEW YORK • LONDON

First published in the United States of America 1979 by
Holmes & Meier Publishers, Inc.
30 Irving Place
New York, N.Y. 10003

Great Britain:
Holmes & Meier Publishers, Ltd.
131 Trafalgar Road
Greenwich, London SE10 9TX

LIBRARY OF CONGRESS CATALOGING IN PUBLICATION DATA
Stearns, Peter N
    Be a man! : Males in modern society.

    Bibliography: p.
    Includes index.
      1. Men. 2. Sex role. 3. Masculinity. 4. Social
history. I. Title.
HQ1090.S73   1979   301.41'1   79-11847

ISBN 0-8419-0435-9(c); -0587-8(p)

MANUFACTURED IN THE UNITED STATES OF AMERICA

Cover photo: Rolling black sheets in
tin plate works, Pittsburgh, Pa. (*photo
courtesy Carnegie Library of Pittsburgh)*

For Carol, who teaches me
and, yes, sustains me

Contents

Acknowledgements   ix

1. Introduction: Manhood as a Social Construct   1

2. The Tradition of Manhood   13

3. Manhood and the Challenge of Industrialization   39

4. The Emergence of the Working-Class Man   59

5. The Emergence of the Middle-Class Man   79

6. Manhood and the Contemporary Era   113

7. Themes in Contemporary Manhood   127

8. Conclusion: *Vive une différence*!   169

Notes   199

Selective Bibliography   225

Index   227

Acknowledgements

I am grateful to many people for insights and suggestions concerning the writing of this book. Among academics whose comments have been particularly valuable, I wish to thank Philip Greven, Patricia Branca, Natalie Davis, J. Devine, Carol Stearns, Elizabeth Pleck, Kermit Kynell, William Coles, Susan Van Horn, and Julie Jeffrey. My beloved children, Duncan and Deborah, continually teach me something of what it is all about; my parents, Raymond Phineas and Elizabeth Scott, at least tried to. I must also express my appreciation to many new nonacademic friends who have given me such important understanding; they know who they are. And, lastly, thanks must be given to upwards of a hundred undergraduates at Carnegie-Mellon University and thirty at the University of Houston who made my first efforts on this subject a precious experience.

1. Introduction:
Manhood as a Social Construct

The plight or glory of men in modern society is open to an amazing array of conflicting interpretations. Macho man, artifically and oppressively virile, asserts himself over hapless women and in fields of aggression ranging from big business to war, from the raising of sons to the domestic cloistering of wives.[1] Man the henpecked, dominated by untamed shrews from mother through wife, cowers in a dangerously matriarchal society. A generation of female vipers challenged men for household dominion a few decades ago.[2] Now a new wave of feminists threaten men in business and government, making further inroads on the beleaguered male.[3] Man the tender-hearted has developed in the twentieth century a new sentimentality that reduces, if it does not yet eliminate, the stern patriarchalism of the past.[4] Or man the surpassed, already outsmarted by women who develop a more satisfying diversity of roles, live longer, survive the death or absence of a spouse better, and in general put the work-hounded, overstuffed male to shame.[5]

The images are bewildering, and so are their implications for remedial action. If the most articulate comment on sex roles has recently come from women critical of male claims, real or presumed, some analysts now point to the need for reasserting a specifically male role in family and society. It is easy to find appeals for a greater emotionality among men, a nurturing supportiveness, counterbalanced by laments for a tougher male persona of a century ago. Ultimately, the only common currency among the diverse interpretations of manhood now available is a sense that masculinity is sorely troubled in modern society, both in concept and in practice. What we need, clearly, is a more explicit effort to determine what this trouble is and what has caused it. In fact, maleness has long been in crisis, for the advent of an industrial society challenged some key canons of manhood and made the fulfillment of others increasingly difficult.

It is past time to study how males and modern society interrelate with the historical forces at work on each. Much of what is now heard about men in society comes indirectly, though not necessarily incorrectly, as a counterpart to what is asserted about women; men are often urged to change, with only the most cursory examination of what they are already. Men badly need more gender self-knowledge, and women can profit from the results as well.

There is a slim body of literature on men in society. The best of it uses some anthropology—male characteristics in primitive societies and what these suggest of essential maleness[6]—and the worst uses little of anything save verbal facility and goodwill. Overall, the literature is present-focused and moralistic; the real or presumed situation of men today is sketched and then assessed according to the author's value system, sometimes bolstered by the traits of a primitive island people who are put forth as a model for contemporary America.[7] There are two weaknesses in this approach. First, it lacks a sense of history. In cross-sectioning the present it is impossible to distinguish among features that are new and important, new but shallow-rooted, old but fading, old and fundamental. Second, the typical argument for modern man's salvation is simplistically attractive yet profoundly pessimistic. Modern man has gone wrong; perhaps even premodern man went wrong. History here need only be invoked, not studied, because history is the villain. All we have to do is reverse the tide of the past.[8] Western society, not just the American West, has rendered men incapable of feeling. The solution is obvious: start feeling. What is called for explicitly in the "men's liberation" literature is a revolution in behavior and emotional stance. Although we may need revolutions, it would be far more encouraging if we could think of using the past, not casting it off, if only because behavioral revolutions are so difficult to achieve. This use of the past requires historical analysis to sort out what is old and new in the condition of men.

This book, then, represents a history of maleness oriented toward present social concerns. It is not an elaborate or detailed history devoted to capturing the past in its entirety. The novelty of the subject, and the gaps in our knowledge of it, call for speculation and probability analysis. But as history, the book warrants a brief bow toward a professional introduction. Why do we need a history of men? Don't we already know this history? Can it be known?

Manhood—the concepts and behavior associated with being a man—is of fundamental importance to understanding modern life. These concepts and behavior have changed over time. What a man is and what he should be in contemporary society differ from the social expectations and reality of a hundred years or, even more dramatically, two hundred years ago. Men look different: they are taller, heavier, and have bigger feet. Similarly, the proofs and badges of manhood have changed, though not completely. Manhoood is an evolving social construct reflecting some continuities but many more changes. In talking about manhood, we are inevitably talking about history.

There is relatively little about man that is biologically determined, though that "little" is vitally important.[9] Men are biologically bigger, physically stronger than women, possessed of distinctive hormonal balance and, of course, a y in addition to an x chromosome. (Very young males are generally less healthy than their female counterparts because only the x chromosome carries a full set of defining body characteristics; a man's single x chromosome may be defective, whereas a woman, who has two chances, seldom falls short; hence the vastly different infant-mortality rates for each gender. But the distinction does not, as a result, carry into adulthood.) Men are naturally more aggressive, raucous—witness the differences in infant behavior patterns, with the male infant invariably more obstreperous—and, some would add, violent. Some anthropolgists would argue that these traits not be carried too far into determinism, citing tribes of nonviolent, household-tending males. But it seems fair to view these instances as culturally induced aberrations, interesting in revealing a society's ability to channel even fairly fundamental biology. Overall, the male of the species seems designed for purposes similar to those of the big apes: provision of sperm; the size and bluster vital to frighten enemies and, if necessary, fight them; and the establishment of territoriality within the species for breeding and residential purposes. Differing from the other primates—and also from most big cats—the human male *may* also "naturally" hunt. (Among the apes the question does not arise since they are vegetarians; among the cats, females normally gather most of the food, which seems "naturally" true of primitive peoples *except* for hunting.) But here we already blur the distinction between what is instinctive to humans and what may have been conditioned early on, a primitive role division between men and women reflecting humans' peculiar ability to eat both meat and fruits or vegetables. (One cannot forebear to note Freud's explanation of the division: once fire was invented, males could not avoid urination competitions to quench the flame, a sport for which women were not equipped; so women had to stay near the hearth, leaving the hunting to men.)[10] Lionel Tiger, an anthropologist, has asserted that a "natural" male bonding developed as a result of the need for cooperative hunting, one that still lingers in distinctive patterns of male association.[11] I will return to this, but here I would note only that with bonding we are clearly drifting into cultural, not biological, attributes of maleness, however deeply rooted, and to attributes whose precise expression depends on the culture of an area and period.[12] Aside from basic sexual functions and the size/activity differential, male biology tells us little about what we want to know. It predisposes, forms a vital background, but does not predetermine effect.[13]

Men are always born of women, almost always nurtured by them, and usually suckled by them. All have to carve out some distinctiveness from women, most commonly from the mother, to achieve identity as males. This process is always complicated and will vary in success in individuals as in cultures. It is, however, a biopsychological given. But what form the definition of male identity takes depends far more on cultural than on biological factors; moreover, it changes substantially over time. Basic male psychology is thus a historical province to which we cannot apply present psychological precepts with any assurance of accuracy. Relations between sons and fathers in the upper middle class were, as we shall see, at a peak of difficulty around 1900, precisely when Freud, working mainly with this class, devised his complex of complexes; Freudianism is thus more the result of a particular history of men than a theoretical framework readily applied to that history.

Does biology determine male superiority in human society? Here is perhaps the basic question, far more important than questions of intrinsic hunting instincts or reactions to parents. Mammalian life dictates a division of functions between males and females that can be interpreted as male superiority. The male, physically larger, must penetrate, while the female yields or at least receives. The female normally nurtures and, if she lactates, undergoes hormonal changes that shape some measurably maternal behavior; it would be difficult to argue for an innate paternal instinct of any magnitude or consistency. Hormones dictate that men will, on the average, be more aggressive than women; this is a natural function. But to go from a biologically rooted division of functions to a natural superiority is a needless leap. Men, as products of history, are certainly not always sure of the worth of their function, much less their superiority, and degree of self-esteem is itself a significant cultural attribute. Superiority is a subjective word, here deriving from the assumption that certain kinds of physical powers and freedom from the hearth are better than female receptivity and nurturing functions. There is no way to avoid this circularity.[14] In sum, issues of dominance and superiority, while significant, do not lend themselves to easy or programmatic statements.

Division of function is itself part of human society, preconditioning, but not precisely shaping, personal relationships; it has been worked out in an impressive variety of ways historically, with the version developed in Western culture probably the most nuanced. The very fact that in contemporary society so many men and women can take seriously pleas for a major reshuffling of functions reveals the importance—some would argue, the possible transcendence—of social function over the biological base. We do not know much when we know biology alone; hence the need to know the history of the superstructures we have constructed upon our mammalianism.

The recent comment on maleness from the social sciences readily grants the low importance of biology in determining what we think of as male traits.[15] Margaret Mead,[16] among many others, says that most "male" traits (particularly those objected to by liberated women) are just cultural artifacts.[17] I would caution that, first, biology cannot be written off; saying that it does not determine precise function should not obscure its basic presence. Second, saying that a trait is a product of culture must not lead to the assumption that we can easily get rid of it. Cultural predisposition, such as the impulses associated with hunting, runs deep. A major task of a historical study of the male past is to find the roots of maleness and determine how profound they are.

Feminist historians rightly point out that until recently most history dealt with men. But it did not deal with ordinary men, nor with the private spheres of male existence. We are seeking definitions of the male gender, expressed in familial as well as in public life, over the past two hundred years, and understanding of the forces that determined these definitions. There is but one serious history of male roles, covering developments in the United States since 1900, which I will cite at appropriate points.[18] Social historians, concerned more with groups than with "great" men, have talked a lot about men, which is why we can venture the present essay using much established information; but rarely have they discussed their subjects as cultural or historical expressions of maleness. Their divisions have usually been based upon class, region, or ethnic group. While women are often given short shrift in their analyses, neither are features of maleness explicitly established. Recent efforts to use age groups as significant social divisions in the past have also focused primarily on males, notably in the case of histories of youth, but the same peripheral attention to gender attributes largely applies.[19]

Gender is a valid, though not exclusive, means of social analysis. But efforts at gender distinction have thus far focused almost entirely on women and female roles. The result is a considerable lack of knowledge of things male, a lack both undesirable and unnecessary. Discussions of the history of sex in our time, for example, have focused almost entirely on women (who also, in producing babies, leave the most concrete records).[20] Males are assumed to be completely sexual animals, who therefore need no sex history—an assumption that, at the very least, needs testing, especially since pre–nineteenth-century Western culture assumed that women, not men, were the insatiable sexual aggressors, with men as vulnerable creatures in need of protection.

A history of men is necessary, and no adequate study presently exists. We have the materials in at least as great an abundance as do the historians of women. Babies can be records for men, too, as can patterns of family structure, child raising, mortality—all the records of the basic rhythms of life. Since men are more likely to join organizations—trade unions are a prime modern example for the working class—certain materials on aspects of maleness outside the family are available. Of course, there will be unknown areas: How common was male masturbation in the nineteenth century in the face of public defenders of health and morality? How pervasive was the practice of homosexuality in past time? Similar questions are encountered in virtually any field of sociohistorical inquiry precisely because the investigator's intent is to uncover human acts and intentions so basic or so feared that the records have been obscured.

Is it time yet for a study of men? We do not have a host of scholarly monographs to underpin any general statement. The subject has rarely been taught, much less explicitly researched. This essay is not based on extensive or exhaustive research into primary materials. There are no startling new statistics, few statements about masculinity heretofore unrevealed. I will largely use social histories and contemporary social-science analysis of activities in which men engaged—work, family, leisure—and analyze the elements that most clearly reveal what men, as men, were about. Research I have done on closely related subjects—work, business, aging—give me some personal confidence in the data I will use. The results justify, in my opinion, a general survey with a high probability of accuracy. I hope this study will stimulate new work and, even more, that it will give readers the broad outlines of the historical evolution of an aspect of human existence that all of us, male and female, are currently involved with, and in so doing inform this involvement directly. Historians need not always be cautious, letting other disciplines carve out a field and then creeping in carefully after mental sets are already established. Here is a field that needs defining, that we can define, which is why I am writing now, and at a high level of generalization. Professional potshooters are duly warned.

As a history, this book has at least three other features that demand preliminary notice. One followers rather obviously from what has already been said: The essay does not have an elaborate scholarly apparatus. Footnotes indicate key references, most of them from solid social histories of other relevant subjects or, somewhat more haphazardly, from primary materials, on the one hand, and contemporary social science, on the other. I am trying to be useful to a scholarly audience while not being bound by its conventions. I will be applying history to a large area of public concern, of which scholarly interest forms only a part.

The present study deals with Western society—roughly, the peoples inhabiting North America and western Europe. Illustrations are drawn almost exclusively from the United States, Britain, France, and Germany, but in theory the Low Countries, Scandinavia, and Canada can also be included. The approach is not primarily comparative. I am concerned with broad trends, although precise comparison would be interesting and profitable. From a pragmatic standpoint, inclusion of a number of countries permits the use of a more extensive historical literature, containing abundant and diverse examples. More significant, however, is the conceptual framework. I argue that Western society, with its combination of classical, Judaic, and Germanic cultures, developed a distinctive definition of maleness. Developing first in northwestern Europe, and distinct from the gender culture of the Mediterranean world, it spread in due course to North America. What is Western about us in this sense shapes us more fundamentally than what is American or French. Western society has recently undergone a common process of industrialization, occurring at slightly different times and in slightly different ways from place to place (from region to region, actually, rather than from nation to nation). Again, the general patterns are more interesting than the particular varieties. We know that some national stereotypes relating to men are simply not true; Frenchmen, for example, are not fantastic lovers on the average, though it may be important to their maleness that they are told they are.

More serious regional variation may have resulted from the frontier experience of North America. I will deal with the image of the cowboy and the more subtle attitude toward women that arose in a female-short society. But the cowboy is a recognizable kind of folk hero in Western society, which is why French boys play cowboy almost as avidly as do American youth; cowboy and police shows are our most popular TV export. Nineteenth-century American attitudes toward women were at most a special brand of

Victorianism.[21] General process overrides national peculiarity. Even if national distinctiveness is asserted, the broader pattern is essential as a measurement. Most of our strengths and weaknesses as men are modern Western ones, not subregional, and can best be understood in this context.

My chronology is fairly obvious. This is not a detailed history of men before the modern era, but an analysis of what was distinctive about Western men and why. I will make brief soundings into ancient and particularly medieval history, whose purpose is not a step-by-step survey but generalization necessary for an understanding of our present culture. More attention is paid to what manhood consisted of in the seventeenth and eighteenth centuries (early modern Europe, colonial America) because these definitions remain partially in force today even if the possibilities of measuring up to them have become increasingly difficult.

The first historical argument, then, is the statement that Western society provided a distinctive balance of functions between men and women within the framework of agricultural society in general; and an even more distinctive complexity in the definition of male and female characteristics. A discussion of Western traditions of gender bears directly on contemporary problems of gender, for in reacting to change both men and women have appealed to traditional criteria, often exaggerating them, in an effort to provide some continuity of identity.

My principal focus, however, is on the broad process of change associated with industrialization and the rise of cities, and the development of modern society and a modernized outlook from the late eighteenth century to the present. The crisis of masculinity, which means, simply stated, a new uncertainty about what it took to be a man and a new difficulty in meeting the most common definitions, essentially began with the modernization process. Modern society questioned conventional notions of masculinity, ranging from physical strength to property ownership. Perhaps in the long run we can see modernization as moving men further away from their biological nature— their natural aggressiveness, for example—than agricultural society had done, though it is vital to recall that manhood in any organized society flowed more from the culture than from innate gender characteristics. It is not clear that being a man in modern society is less satisfying than it was in days when gender criteria were clearer; indeed it may be more so, for premodern society was in many ways a bleak place. But modern society both complicated the definition of manhood and made it less certain—witness the current glut of manuals on how to be a man, an artifact never before explicitly required.

The impact of modernization on manhood has been something of a two-stage process, a fact that is reflected in the organization of the bulk of this study. Modern society initially provoked an increased rigidity in the definition of sex roles for men and women. The resulting gender ideals and images, themselves adaptations of gender tradition, have left their mark. For example, aspects of working-class male culture, developed in the first decades of industrialization, describe a type of male behavior still recognizable today.

The twentieth century introduced additional challenges, including dramatic changes in the position of women. At the same time, men sought to modify the extremes of the initial gender reaction to industrial life, and to find a richer role for themselves in the family as well as at work.

Aside from what is inherently male in biology and psychology, I deal with a fourfold overlay: first, the implications of any organized society on manhood, for all social structures must deal with and build upon some rather primitive traditions; second, a specifically Western amalgam of characteristics that established something of a male ambivalence, albeit in many ways a fruitful one; third, the sweeping challenge of the industrial way of life, which contained dramatic implications for male aspirations and expectations while severely constraining male behavior; and fourth, what seems to be the dominant contemporary trend, the search for a more flexible definition of maleness.

In all of this I seek to deal both with functions that are distinctively male and with perceptions of what the male character should be; of what were held to be distinctively male virtues and vices by society at large, by women, and, above all, by men themselves. We may consequently gain some idea of what man is in relation to what he has been and perhaps even of what he can become.

Although I am stimulated by the early development of a new branch of sociohistorical inquiry, its potential contribution toward a better understanding of the past, and the vigorous application of the historical consciousness to an assessment of our present state, I am spurred by a strong personal element as well, namely, the effort to articulate a gradual understanding of a subject that has enthralled anyone growing up male: what it is to be a man.

I have never felt totally at ease with certain "manly" attributes touted by our culture. I have not merely a dash but a mile-run of physical cowardice. I was never much interested in cars (unwitting ecologue versus manly boy). I have spent long periods of time without close male friends, though when subjected to company in numbers I have always preferred men to women and do communicate well with individual men in sports. Malely male gatherings confuse me a bit; they leave me feeling out of place. Gratuitous obscenities strike me as an unilluminating form of speech, and I cannot hold my own in skirt-lifting stories. I have, in sum, always viewed manhood with a bit of perplexity, which may be useful in producing an essay on the subject. Just a warning, in any event, that I cannot pretend to write as a men's representative, though this study is not a shy boy's revenge against he-men, a kick of verbal sand at Charles Atlas.

Furthermore, I write after two confusing and fascinating years during which I had to think rather explicitly about what kind of man I wanted to be, years in which certain possibilities surfaced that I had never dreamed of, never even wanted. Is tranquillity a virtue? I had thought storm and stress were indelibly linked to real manhood. Some of this personal assessment has to be suggested in this book, because I cannot write history quite as I did before. I am indulging myself here, explaining a bit of me to me, though this is not my primary purpose. I also believe that a broad consideration of the place of men in modern society is an extraordinarily revealing path to male self-awareness. If this book imparts a glimmer of self-understanding to men and to those who must deal with the mysteries of being male from the outside, as well as some knowledge of possible links between past and present definitions of maleness, its purpose has been well served.

This is not a book about women. It is not a book designed to explain what men did, and do, to women, though it can, of course, be used to gain a partial understanding of this issue. Too much recent feminist history has treated men as stereotypes, backdrops for, or villains in the anguish of females. I hope I can avoid repayment in kind and examine intergender reactions with some understanding of women's history, but I do not pretend to present a balanced treatment. I have definitely not sought out juicy quotes in which women put men down as cloddish, insensitive creatures—though they often do—which would be the debased-male counterpart to woman on a pedestal. I think one could write a plausible history of Victorian images of men that would be fairly sickening, by making women seem bent on male degradation.[21] This would not capture much of real interactions, any more than outrageous statements about women (which women make just as readily as men) tell a lot about how women were actually treated.[22] Changes in female roles have affected men, sometimes adversely, and this is a vital point to establish. But there is no search here for villainesses.

Some remarks about feminism are necessary because feminist rhetoric shapes so much of the current debate over the nature of men. Feminism has played some role—and not just recently—in affecting male behavior, though this can be easily exaggerated, and so feminism must be considered as a factor in the male social environment. However, the recent history of maleness has not been fully illuminated even by sensitive, altruistic feminists whose urgings that people be people posit a solution to the problems of modern manhood. Radical role redefinition is not so simple, and it creates problems of its own. We have to know what modern Western males are about before we can fully judge the consequences of giving women "their share" or of merging male and female characteristics to produce "people." Some women's advocates—male as well as female—have not been particularly sensitive in commenting on the male role, tending to view men as faceless encumbrances and making scant effort to understand them.[23] I do not attack, but I definitely do not conciliate. In this respect, the present study does not adopt the tone of much recent comment on masculinity.

One of the fascinating features about some modern men, beginning in the nineteenth century and most obvious in the men's liberation literature of today, is an almost masochistic sense of guilt about the real or imagined woes of women, a desire to be in the forefront of the fray against "maledom." I grant the reasonableness of many specific goals and some specific accusations. But I am a bit weary of the bombast; I do not claim that some of this sentiment does not creep into this book. Men have listened patiently to an amazing array of claims about their own callousness to women's historical condition. For various reasons, including male masochism, that I will seek to explain, men have reacted more in terms of mutterings than by an articulate examination of the nature of their behavior and of their past. Callousness is at best descriptive, not explanatory. The main point is that a history of men must be conceived on its own terms, not as support for, or point-by-point rebuttal of, the feminist vision. I have necessarily written with feminism in mind. I have (I think necessarily) disagreed with some claims by feminists concerning men.

A book on men must, of course, talk about women quite apart from feminism, and from an academic standpoint it is to be hoped that increased study of manhood will complement women's history, thereby contributing to an understanding of gender itself. I seek to establish relationships between men and women as they affected men, and differences between men and women when they existed, not superiorities or inferiorities. Women's life expectancy, relative to men's, has increased steadily with modernization, thus widening the slender biological advantage. Does this mean that women are doing something right that men should imitate? Or does it mean that men have shouldered heavy burdens that women have managed, or been allowed, to avoid? Or—heretical thought—is longevity not all that important to the quality of life? Comparisons of this sort must be made in order to obtain a realistic measurement of men's past and future prospects. Beyond establishing clear differences in behavior, such as comparative longevity, I seek to explain without denigrating either sex. Sometimes explanations must remain inconclusive: Do women feel thus-and-such less acutely than men? Is concern about breast size among women more or less acute than comparison of penis length among men? Did measurements of this sort change in value as sexual attributes became more important with modernization, and as opportunities for measurement against hordes of peers grew more abundant? It is easier to raise comparative questions than to answer them. Yet in an ultimate sense I am not trying to be comparative in that I do not study women here for their own sake. Being a man has become increasingly difficult in modern society. This is not to say that manhood is therefore more difficult than womanhood. Historically, as gender differentiation was more sharply drawn, fulfillment of both the male and the female role became more complex. Each gender, trying to meet new criteria, complicated the efforts of the other. The fact that we focus now on about half of humanity does not make the other half's efforts less important.

Be a man! What a strange order, yet it runs through so many human societies. We do not rush out to daughters and urge them to be women. The signals we give are more subtle, though they can be just as constraining. For a boy, manhood is at once desirable and mysterious, a state demanding achievement. One does not just become a man. A natural passage such as sexual maturation is not enough. In most societies, including our own, boys require a more extensive, arduous transition to manhood. Somehow being a man needs special prompting. *Don't cry. Don't be a sissy about pain. Keep up with the other boys. Compete. Be a good sport. Win. Don't, for God's sake, be gay. Be kind to women, treat them rough, and don't tell them nothing.* What a jumble it is to have two different types of chromosomes and to have modern society build rather explicitly on both at once. It's time to find out how we got here.

2. The Tradition of Manhood

Western man is faced with a fascinating dilemma. There is within him an impulse toward toughness, a hard self-sufficiency, but also a gentleness, a desire to love and be loved. The hard, aggressive strain was essential to virtually all men in a hunting society. Western culture has carefully preserved a selective memory of hunting traits to support a belligerent upper class, a fighting aristocracy whose values could not be avoided even by that majority of men usually far from the military battlefield. But as hunting gave way to agriculture, a gentle man emerged, a man open to the risk of expressing and seeking affection. Certain cultures, such as those on the Indian subcontinent, opted for this type of individual. The West tried to incorporate both. It tended to categorize the male principle as one of strength and the female principle as one of docility. In a related fashion, it had an unusual revulsion against the effeminate male. Western man can be embarrassed by the tenderness within him. He yields to women with a knowing wink at other men in order to show that he is not ensnared; but ensnared he often is.

Western man is not an expression of unbridled machismo. He is tempted toward it, and individual men yield entirely. But the man can be embarrassed by his tough strain, too, wondering what harm he has done if he indulges it too fully. Gentleness and compassion were found in men at the inception of Western society, and it was, and is, cherished by both genders. Western man, created in God's image, judges but also may try to save. He tries to rule and to love simultaneously. The hero is wrathful toward the enemy, proud and silent among men, compassionate toward the weak, nurturing to the young. What will impress women? Brute strength yet also deep sentiment. Does art demean a real man or ennoble him? How much fear, loneliness and yearning must be hidden from other men? How much can bind men together? Western man must choose between the hard and the soft, or some subtle combination of the two, in trivial situations as well as in the basic course of life. The West produced vicious dictators who cry at the sight of children,[1] and ordinary men who struggle between love of women and proud solitude. It harbors men—and women—who inevitably waver in their understanding of what a man should be.

The traditions of manhood have evolved over an immense range of human experience. We still like to think of ourselves, in part, as hunters, and to some extent we really are, through inheritance as well as physique. But the more important attributes of the manly tradition developed in the specific Western variant of agricultural society, a variant resulting from the forces that exploded classical society and introduced a Christian culture. Modern manhood is thus a transformation of a special kind of agricultural model of manhood, itself a major mutation from the manhood of the hunt. Before dealing with the more recent pressures of modernity, we must sketch a vital and complicated Western gender tradition that involved pressures of its own. Modern man differs greatly from the European or North American man of 1700 in his personal values and certainly in his social context, but he can still recognize the proofs of manhood that had developed before the advent of industrialization and, indeed, he still builds upon their tensions.

The dilemma of Western masculinity effectively begins with Christianity. Europe was then still tied to a hunting past; more than most advanced civilizations, we still recall a variety of hunting values and myths. Traces of hunting society remain for men in any society, for man's physique was designed for the hunt, notably in its capacity for running, and must find some expression. Military activity, necessary, to some degree, in any society, also reflects manly traits that, if not innate, were at least acquired for the hunt. But Western society—rather loosely organized as compared with the irrigation-based agricultural civilizations, and until recently rather sparsely populated—kept men particularly close to the hunt. Its leadership opted for the hunting and military virtues to a greater extent than was true in most Asian societies. (Relatedly, these leaders were less polished in some of the more civilized arts than other elites until modern times.) So we must briefly begin with what the West retains from hunter-warriors, a memory fed by recurrent contact with other hunters—most recently the American Indians—who could not be scorned (as the Greeks, for example, scorned barbarians), despite enmity and immense cultural differences, because the Indians embodied so much that the West regarded as intrinsically male. As we killed these hunters and sapped their spirit, we honored their physical bravery and their independence. We thought we saw a simplicity in their definition of men and their freedom from women. Whether or not we remember rightly, we begin with the story of society in its infancy in our own effort to build boy into man.

Anthropologists have found no society in which women dominate men, none, in fact, in which male activity is not regarded as more important than female.[2] Why? We can avoid some of the silly imagery of the dominant penis and the yielding vagina, the man on top and the woman on the bottom, which still fascinates some men and women, and focus on three intertwined factors: size, nurturing, and psychological differentiation. Men are, by nature, generally taller and definitely heavier (as a result of their bone structure) than women. A distressing degree of their alleged superiority is owing to their size and resulting intimidating strength, as is the case among all mammals. Their greater size is functional for purposes of defense. Tree-dwelling primates, having few enemies, show fewer gender distinctions than land-based groups, including man. Add some differential male aggressiveness to size and it is difficult to see how men and women could have assigned themselves coequal roles in early human activities.[3] At the same time, the human child, with its large brain and relative lack of instincts, requires an unusual amount of care. The importance of a natural maternal instinct can be played down, but women carry children and they alone can nurse them. (Nonhuman feeding of babies became possible only in advanced agricultural societies.) They were thus logically assigned primary infant-raising tasks. This substantially reduced their ability to operate at any distance from home. It left men freer not only to defend but to form ideas and power structures based on general social relationships rather than those of kin and hearth alone.

Did men envy women's reproductive power? Early religions certainly stressed fertility, the female principle, over the fascination of the phallus. Possibly men not only had the freedom and the strength but also the functional need to define tasks for themselves that were different from those of women and, by male definition, more important. Men may have been driven to assert their superiority because of a nagging sense that they were inferior. Certainly, aside from the possibility of womb envy, men had a natural need to assert a distinct gender identity. Male and female children cannot be treated identically by their (usually female) nurturer. A mother, from cave days to the present, has to separate her male child from herself earlier than she does a female. The male is more active, his teeth biting harder on the nipple; and his sexual characteristics are visible. So the mother distinguishes him by holding him less and weaning him earlier than she does a female. The female, in fact, can grow up never entirely separated, in a psychic sense, from the mother, although she need not. The male can never have this psychic security or stultification. He naturally searches for a different identification, usually finding it in the adult males present.[4] Without an immense amount of compensatory socialization, then, of a sort never yet undertaken in any human society, the male has to be different from the female, and he will bend his strength and his freedom from primary nurturing to convert difference into superiority. The first main human arena in which he did so, with durable consequences, was in hunting societies.

As a boy I spent a not inconsiderable amount of time wondering exactly how my courage would be tested and how I would fare. A physical ordeal of some sort seemed quite likely. I was grudgingly attracted by stories of the tests imposed upon Indian boys and, later, by accounts of Masai tribesmen, but more real to me were books on the warrior bravery of chieftains like Robert Bruce. With a good bit of boyhood passed during World War II, an updated military test seemed quite likely. I thought about the air force and the navy—the dull danger of the infantry had no appeal—less with a sense of opportunity for heroism than with a not entirely unpleasant apprehension before the inevitable. I certainly wondered how I would stand up to physical torture. I cannot recall whether I really believed I would face this, but I certainly found it possible, not out of line with the experience of a man; and I was convinced I would do badly. All of this was too awesomely private to discuss with anyone, but was wrapped up in the mystery of growing up male. For in a variety of individual ways, growing up male involves sharing, sometimes fearfully sharing, values and anxieties developed in the childhood of mankind. We have a cultural appendix of no mean a size, and unlike its physical counterpart it defies complete excision.

No one can know when the mysteries of manhood and womanhood began to be sensed in any articulate fashion. Some kind of specialization of function followed from mammalian biology, but in a fashion unique to humankind. Females, the food gatherers in almost all mammalian species, in addition to being breeders and child rearers, were limited initially to supplementary productive activities among humans, providing only the vegetarian portions of the diet—that which is basic for the apes but not for carnivorous humans in a hunting society. In contrast to the big hunting cats, human males were the game killers, not just defenders and decorative studs.[5] Probably because of the special demands of human child rearing, woman did not hunt. Male aggressiveness was transferred from mere defense and sexual rivalry to the killing of game, and a deep association between maleness and hunting remains in modern Western society, constituting one of the areas least likely to be breached by women, a test of manhood even amid the flanneled paunches of middle-aged males and a framework for almost exclusively male conviviality. Associated with the original, unique division of labor were devices such as fire, which built on and intensified the need to link women with the hearth.

Yet perhaps because hunting was a late, almost contrived, development among primates, certain special values and fears were bound up with it. Lacking a particular physical appratus for the kill itself, human males had to group together, a clannishness not unknown among other primates but in humans extended beyond sexual ordering and defense. Males could rarely be successful lone hunters. Yet grouping involved constant tension among natural sexual rivals. The bull male patriarch, the archtypical father figure so common among the big apes, had to extend his dominance in hunting, not just assert himself in a sexual hierarchy. Patriarchal maleness thus early involved a kind of economic leadership, a mastery of key skills. Yet youthful insurgence was greatly facilitated by the strength demanded in hunting. Father-son competition, the aggressiveness of each type of male, was built in from the species' inception. But the group bonding was vital as well. A sense of fundamental common enterprise, of a distinctive male sharing apart from women, took root early, in contrast to the big apes, where the sexes spent much more time together.[6]

As almost self-created hunters, physically feeble save for their ability to run, men needed an array of virtues designed to test and toughen. Obviously, rituals promoting a passage to manhood were associated with hunting and fighting skills. Indeed, the transition to manhood was only loosely linked to the actual age of puberty, since its direct importance was as much economic, in hunting and defense, as sexual. (Defiance of the patriarch could not be sexual alone, lest skills and leadership vital to successful hunting be jeopardized; the age hierarchy among men, inherently stressful, had to be carefully arranged, and graded tests of manhood played a vital role here as well.) The man was brave, tested against the animals and the elements in almost every hunting society. Physical courage, the self-discipline needed to withstand pain, the patience needed for the hunt—even, one might argue, the quality of silence, which was less important for women at the hearth—all were taught by example, then probed. One was not born a man. One learned to be a man, acquiring characteristics that exaggerated some natural attributes and re-pressed others, such as the desire to run from danger. Not all boys could make it. In few later societies could all males fully become men; in few did all males not worry and wonder if they had the potential to do so.

With the development of the specialization, the grouping, the sense of manhood needed for hunting was the need to articulate some image of women as rivals or underminers. What was involved here was less a reaction to real women than an abstraction of women, complement but also contradiction to the manly principle.[7]

Women had to be kept at the hearth not simply to fulfill their part in the division of labor and to breed to the maximum in a highly sexed species, but to defend by contrast the list of virtues exaggeratedly male. Which is to say that gender roles in a hunting society functioned adequately but that they were not innately determined. Neither males nor females were so naturally pure hunters or pure hearth tenders as primitive culture dictated. The roles caused anxiety, and men could not measure what they were, or were sup-posed to be, by absolutes so much as by the absence, real or imagined, of the male attributes among women, from whence an exaggerated tendency to attribute soft, vulnerable, nurturing qualities to the females.

What of all this remains significant in discussing contemporary men? It is highly misleading to attribute the values of a primitive society to a complex modern one. This is but a step away from biological determinism. Men are no longer primarily hunters. Primitive society has twice been fundamentally altered, each time greatly increasing the range and diversity of appropriate male behavior. There is no effort here to follow the simplistic path of some zoologists who mix perceptions of the present with a knowledge of man the primate with no intervening history. This distorts the nature of both primitive and modern man. The contemporary manager is not an ambulatory ape in pin-stripes. Yet traces do remain, for the characteristics of maleness so painfully established for successful hunting have rarely been cast aside by society as a whole. The prevalence in boy's literature of accounts of primitive manhood rituals clearly links individual childhood with the childhood of mankind. We associate manhood with bravery, with physical testing. Hunting directly appeals to the culture, though there are many other manifestations.

Nostalgia for the manly past, the sense that some remnant of the hunting virtues should be transmitted to new generations of boys, makes sense only if certain male characteristics have been directly carried forward. Lionel Tiger saw current forms of male association as such direct carry-overs of the bonding necessary for a hunting society, itself an evolutionary elaboration of male grouping found among animals, especially primates. Building on an attraction, not necessarily erotic, of male to male, hunting societies solidified a normal desire for exclusive channels of male companionship, given the fact that women did not hunt. Men became accustomed to their associations apart from the hearth, and war long served their needs. (Tiger ignores the fact that in post-hunting societies most men did not serve in wars.) In more recent times, secret societies, fraternities, sports teams, even politics have performed the same function. Perhaps most consistently, post-hunting societies have normally organized male work groups, not always from a specialization conducive to economic advantage, but because the social need to perpetuate the male hunting group is so keenly felt. And apart from formal groups, there are all-male card games, drinking parties, the nights out with the boys.

Tiger encountered a good bit of opposition to his views. The implication that male bonding is special, that females cannot match it, is not necessary to the argument here, which holds simply that, from hunting societies on, men have perpetuated the need for frequent contact with formal and informal associations confined to their own sex. Women may well have the same need. The obvious problem would arise when the needs conflict. To the extent that certain areas of socially important activity, notably work and politics, have been substantially defined in terms of male bonding, women who express a desire to penetrate these areas rouse resistance or confusion because the areas are significant to precisely that part of manhood, first honed in hunting societies, that defies description simply in terms of economic or social privilege. Men acquired a set of attributes in hunting societies that they wanted to show off to women but not all the time, attributes that could also be enjoyed in a different way in the company of one's own sex. Here was a pleasure, a necessity for some, that was passed on even as the specific need for grouping in a hunting society waned. Hence the development of activities—not only fraternities but also mining and sailing—where the presence of women was considered unlucky. Men needed a place, apart from the nurturing power and sexual attraction of women. Hence the joy of team sports, where companionship is exalted in coordinated physical effort, so much like the hunt, where man can be happily torn between the poles of his own culture— the desire to excel in individual prowess and the joy in merged comradeship.

Most fundamentally, hunting societies provided models for personal identification that long survived their economic basis and remain valid simply because some models are needed. All children emerge from their mother with no idea of self and encounter great difficulty in separating self from mother. The mother must, to some extent, be rejected for the self to emerge. Some rejection inevitably occurs as a child learns that mother does not, cannot, satisfy every felt wish. And, quite definitely, various societies encourage and tolerate varing degrees of self-definition anyway. But a hunting society demanded more than what must occur in theory. In men, above all, economic specialization depended on weaning the male child, physically and psychologically, from the woman. Female children could be allowed a partial self-definition, for they were to reproduce the mother's roles. But the male had to be brought to the father, and training for the tests of manhood often involved a quite literal lack of contact with the mother and with females in general. This is much like military service or attendance at male boarding schools and colleges in our day, where occasional sexual encounters but not emotional involvement with females are tolerated. As the hunting father had to have attributes of strength and some degree of physical courage, the boy, coming to separate himself from his mother, did so by adopting these qualities.

Societies usually perpetuated something like this self-definition long after primary reliance on hunting had ended. Western society definitely has done so. Social need was often involved—no large society has been able to dispense with some specialization in military service, usually supported by encouragement to display bravery and physical prowess. But the process was, to some degree, self-sustaining. The son, in order to be a person and not just a man, had to approximate the same attributes of the father. Here, clearly, is why the tests of manhood of the hunting societies still echo loudly in boys' stories and games. Impulses are taught and conveyed that we do not need any longer for division of labor, though this may have some bearing, but rather to define a masculine type for its own sake, to allow males to identify themselves apart from the mother and to allow women some means of knowing that the different creatures they are supposed to love are men. To the extent that hunting society's definition of men has been maintained, even as a means of personal identity, it has become increasingly artificial. We simply do not need the virtues of hunters and warriors and, indeed, could well do without some of them. But their artificiality rests in terms of economic, not personal, need, so they simply do not crumble when their inutility is pointed out. Men face human problems not always much different from those of women, but many are inclined to try to figure out what their proper response is as men—what would a real man do? This inevitably colors and often complicates their reaction, for although the "real man" is variously defined, an essential ingredient is a standard of raw physical courage and the moral resources necessary to sustain that courage.[9] Some part of most modern males would like to be a great hunter, some part seeks to transmute the hunting attributes into actual life in modern society—work group as hunting group, for example—and some part will resent female incursion into realms that have served personal identification.

The legacy of the hunting society is vital, but that society did not persist. It was replaced, with unrecorded difficulty and pain,[10] by agricultural systems that considerably altered the male role and greatly increased the options both in male behavior itself and in the functional relations between men and women.

Women could have considerable power in hunting societies through their control of the home base; differentiation of function should not be equated with corresponding differences in power.[11] Agriculture, however, was built on skills readily available to women, on tasks that they had carried out frequently. Greater reliance on agriculture simply augmented the women's share in the total economic product. Warrior bands, like the Germanic tribes that overran the Roman Empire, when accompanied by semisettled agriculture in the hands of women, concentrated significant political authority in individual women as well. For their strict economic functioning, agricultural societies could afford a substantial reduction in the distinction between gender roles. The principal barrier, apart from personal and group identification with earlier hunting attributes, lay in the need for some available military defense. Where defense needs were not paramount, where hunting or fishing as ancillaries to agriculture were not complex, and where agriculture itself was not terribly burdensome physically, role differentiation could fade substantially. Men could be gentle, sharing household and childrearing tasks with women. Specific examples, dear to those who urge a change in Western sex roles on the grounds that men do not have to be patterned after Western men, are drawn from some of the Pacific islands, where these conditions prevailed. Males might maintain separateness, in other cases, around a warlike and occasional hunting role, but in ordinary times they served as virtual drones around the industrious agriculture of women; this prevailed among some of the Amerindians.[12] Or a society's "maleness" might be class-based, concentrated on the military and related hunting prowess normally limited to a warrior caste, as in medieval Europe. Military values would penetrate the rest of society to some degree, thus contributing to the maintenance of a valorous measurement of male worth, but the bulk of peasant producers would abandon the old tests of manhood.[13]

Agriculture tamed men. When a frontier society revived the possibility of the hunting male, his disdain for the humdrum virtues of the nesting male would be vociferous and violent. Yet agriculture was so much more productive and reliable than hunting for support of society that it had to triumph, leaving certain kinds of men unsure how their manhood could be proved and defined. Although men were tamed in function, value systems changed less than did normal economic methods. Again, with brave men needed for combat and with men eager to have their sons trained in their image, both society at large and familial transmission of culture were served by the perpetuation of part of the hunting ethic. In Europe, young nobles trained for combat as their ancestors for the hunt, while peasants, though fearful of war, taught their sons codes of self-discipline and manly honor.

Nevertheless, with greater resources and social complexity, a diversity of male roles became not only tolerable but desirable in agricultural societies. One has to wonder about males in a pure hunting society who were, quite simply, cowards. Many died or were killed. Some hunting societies institutionalized a place for unmanly males. Most seem to have provided for a period of homosexuality for adolescent males, who often served as the passive partner in a homosexual relationship with an older man who was himself bisexual. This kind of relationship was believed to heighten the prowess of warriors in Japan. But a few men preserved the passive sexual role into adulthood, often as transvestites, such as the *berdaches* of North American Indian tribes, who were only wiped out in the present century through concerted white pressure.[14] These men were tolerated—they could even prove valiant fighters in emergencies—but they were certainly less than equal. What would happen to a timid but thoroughly heterosexual soul is anybody's guess.

Most agricultural societies tolerated adult homosexuals to some extent, but developed far more widely accepted models for nonhunters and non-fighters. The priestly role was the primary example. Agricultural societies, though in a variety of ways, developed a dual elite, both parts of it vigorously male but only one directed to explicit physical aggression. Priests might express virtues similar to those of the warrior caste, in courage, dominance over the unknown (if not over physical nature directly), but they were permitted an emotional range far greater than anything articulated among men before, including a sense of ecstasy and beauty. They could be passive, reflective, even loving in their relations with an awesome divinity. They tended to diversify, possibly to complicate, the attributes acceptable for manhood. Women might share some priestly functions, but important gender distinctions were usually maintained, with women specializing in purity, certain kinds of religious ecstasy, and some magical healing. Tension between priest and warrior there was, and it could be embodied in an individual male trying to choose which set of attributes to adopt. But the possibility of diversity has enriched the male experience, just as it enriched civilization itself. In some Asian civilizations the contemplative role predominated. It particularly benefited the older male, who could now prove himself on nonphysical grounds; the bull male and the patriarch could at last be dissociated.

Typically, agricultural society arranged itself into social strata which differentiated among priests, warriors, and farmers. The latter group included the vast majority of men. The peasant male might distinguish himself by being particularly valorous or particularly saintly, but most peasants could not define their lives in either terms. The day-to-day manliness of the peasant was more prosaic: doing work away from the home, spiced by occasional hunting or the broader forays of migrant labor (and of course assuming major responsibility for military service if necessary); tending the staple crops, though not necessarily undertaking the heaviest physical labor; providing the more complex craft skills such as butchering, construction, or fine metal work. This economic specialization was far less rooted in necessity than that of a hunting society, which is why women were found taking over most male jobs in family crises and often sharing substantially in local governance. Peasant society, touched by the warrior and priestly virtues of the larger culture, defined the male role primarily in terms of ranging a bit farther from home, dealing with the highest production skills or those, like butchering, which involved strength and a certain bloodiness, and maintaining prime public responsibility for the economic survival of the household. Not a particularly glorious role, but one that could be stubbornly maintained. And it could be built up, so that in some peasant societies accession to manhood became equated with the assumption of the full duties of a farming peasant. As with all good tests, some people would fail.

In most agricultural societies—and in all of those complex ones we call civilizations—gender roles are at least as differentiated in principle as they are in hunting societies, even though the economic basis is reduced. Some of the reasons for this are not hard to find. Agricultural peoples inherited gender distinctions from their hunting ancestors and passed them on as part of childrearing. Few human phenomena yield so slowly to change as do child-raising norms, for one naturally tends (even when educated otherwise) to pass on traits that one's parents conveyed. Insofar as agricultural societies long retained a part-time hunting role, the old norms made particular sense. Women's concentration on childrearing might increase, for population grew under the aegis of agriculture. Most important, however, was the appeal of territoriality, newly necessary to agriculture, to the male impulse.[15] Hunting societies had, of course, roamed. Men, like all male mammals, instinctively inclined to defend turf and thought in terms of group defense. Agriculture, however, required settlement, and this meant group and family property. Now the turf was tangible, which is what escalated the male function in defense. Maleness and property are naturally—some might say, tragically— intertwined in agricultural societies. Married women move to the male property, disrupting their kinship bonds and putting themselves in their husband's thrall. Some analysts add that with family property men acquired a new need to determine their paternity, to know it was their children to whom their goods would pass. (Matrilinear inheritance modified but did not dissi- pate official male supremacy in the family.) Certainly, with the establishment of family and property came a strong, often overriding tendency simply to include women in the bargain, to hold them as chattel along with the land and the tools. And women had little choice but to yield. Physically weaker, they also saw in agricultural society a precious aid to their childrearing functions, with more abundant nutritional sources and possibly a useful domestication of their men. For agricultural society did involve a taming of men, just as women had earlier been tamed to the hearth in order to raise children. It probably reduced the level of purely physical violence between men and women; it definitely elevated the military and political functions of men, functions which only men had time to perform and which translated defense and manipulation of property into larger terms. Only much later might some women wonder if the inevitable bargain had been a good one.

Almost all the complex agricultural societies relegated women to a separate, inferior sphere. Religions progressively stressed fierce or fatherly male gods, owning gods, and phallic symbolism over the still-important female fertility principle. Systems of law typically excluded women from access to defined rights of person or property. Agricultural cultures stressed women as the origins of evil—Eve, Pandora—and the bearers of weakness.[16] Women might wield immense informal power because of their domestic and economic importance. They might thrive under separate gender cultures. But agricultural men had no trouble knowing what a man was, or knowing that in manhood lay superiority.

Western civilization, born in parts of Europe but now embracing North America as well, is a particular, somewhat unusual variant of agricultural societies in general, not necessarily better than others but decidedly complex. The West's conception of manhood was not inevitable, but rather was shaped by its peculiar combination of barbarian and Christian culture. We are not interested here in a general survey of Western civilization; what we seek is the extent to which the Western pattern added to the definition of manhood derived from biology, the heritage of a hunting society, and the general framework of an agricultural civilization. We need not linger over classical Greece and Rome, which were typical of the more general run of agricultural societies in terms of gender roles and contributed little to a distinctive Western mix with regard to manhood. There are, however, a few salient points.

Facing the inevitable problem of any agricultural society in balancing priestly and military functions, classical civilization leaned toward the military. Maleness in Greece as well as Rome was associated with valor, prowess in sports, even physique. Of course women were considered inferior, as was true in most complex agricultural societies. Greek women, for example, were publicly scorned. Pericles put it this way: "For a woman not to show more weakness than is natural to her sex is a great glory, and not to be talked about for good or for evil among men." Roman law granted women no legal rights as either plaintiffs or defendants in court: "The husband is the judge of his wife." Privately, however, women might have great power, through their family role and even as property owners.[17] More important in the legacy to later Western civilization was the association between definitions of the male intellectual style in terms of rationalism. Formal Greek thought focused on rational inquiry, and this was acceptably male. Here was a linkage of great importance, particularly with the rise of science in recent centuries. In Greece itself, the rise of rationalism hinted at a new form of male intellectual dominance over nature, different from the more mysterious priestly style. There was some correspondence between the structure of the physical universe and the structure of men's minds—not women's minds, for the classical philosophers credited the female with scant mental power.

Subsequent Western culture honored both the military and the rational strands of classical manhood. The athletic competitions of Greek males were of course directly imitated. More generally, boyhood stories repeat the tale of the Spartan youth who let a fox eat his belly rather than show pain as something odd, but admirable, along with the stories of manhood tests in purely hunting societies. Prometheus, who suffered for the sake of knowledge, is also admired, if somewhat later in life. The gentle male, open to love, except perhaps in the patriarch softened by age, did not receive much support in classical culture. The passions of the Greeks were active, even violent. Predictably, the gods disported themselves in overblown masculine fashion: they drank, they wenched, they fought, they trumpeted their power. Here were clues about what real men should be like even for common farmers, remote from the gymnasiums and military legions of the mighty. These elements of masculinity were retained or imitated in later Western culture.

Judaism added a vital ingredient, a father of fathers. A single, awesomely male God. Wrathful, stern in his omnipotence, quick and physical in his vengence, the Jewish God was masculine authority writ terribly large. There was no feminine softening here, no multiplicity of male roles among a variety of gods. Manhood, in God's image, was authority and it was overwhelming, even ponderous responsibility. It could be proved, also in God's image, by fathering itself, not merely in the contribution of seed but in the provision of a stern, male-dominated household. Here was a quality readily assimilable to the kind of peasant society that subsequently developed in Europe. We can often see played out in seventeenth-century France or even colonial America the drama of sons forced to submit to their father's will, yet, ironically, presumed also to be ready to take on the patriarchal role when the old god died.[18] A tension was built into Western masculinity—the dutiful son tempted to rebelliousness, the patriarch wearily seeking to maintain his moral ascendancy as his only remaining trapping of manhood—already enacted in the stories of the Old Testament.

It is by no means fanciful to see a prototype of Western man in the combination of classical and Judaic masculinity. Males in the prime of youth would learn most from the Greeks and Romans. They could test their bodies in games and war, grouping with other men. Love of women, as opposed to the physical use of women, was not a major theme; in the classical context, widespread homosexuality, which usually involved the linking of a young man with a bisexual older man, added an erotic element to male grouping. With age, raw valor shifted from physical courage to the responsibility of leadership and ownership and, with the Jews, fatherhood, the dominance of a powerful patriarch over his growing sons in the image of God. The combination, not achieved until Christianity brought the Judaic strain to the classical West, built obviously on the attributes of the hunting male, but it blended well also with dominance over property. The male might of course succeed in priestly functions rather than as warrior, particularly in Judaism serving as a channel between people and an aggressively male God. He might in Greece claim dominance over rational thought, fathoming the order of the universe. The father figure was not primarily now the leader of a hunting band, though he would prove valor as well as leadership in the field of the battle as required. He was stereotypically an owner and he had domain, which gave added power but also new responsibility. He was training his sons in the skill and will needed to control, to take over the family patrimony. He was a ruler not in the hunt but, appropriately to an agricultural society, in his own house. Valor for the sons, stern governance from the father—a picture Western society would construct on the ashes of classical civilization.

Yet Western masculinity was not only the fusion of classical and Judaic attributes. The real Western history of manhood begins with Christianity and the culture of the Germanic invaders of Rome, played against the background of classical values. This new combination made it more difficult and challenging to be a man than ever before, and produced men far more interesting aesthetically and morally than those of classical society. No other civilization, though several were more advanced by normal standards of measurement for centuries to come, developed such a complex or stressful amalgam.

Germanic culture, the culture of a hunting and warring society, was tied to a rather primitive agricultural system, and naturally heightened the emphasis on heroic virtues. The gods called for war and demanded military valor. Germanic chieftans, bands of hunters and warriors, epitomized an aggressively masculine role.[19] Medieval culture, established on the ruins of the Roman political and economic system, enshrined the crude warrior-huntsman as the new aristocracy. An emphasis on lusty virility, the hunt, and military prowess would remain traits of the European aristocracy in later centuries, even as it acquired great polish and sophistication. As in classical Greece and Rome, ordinary peasant men were remote from this. Aristocratic privilege could indeed challenge their masculinity, as well as threaten their fragile agriculture, as when the nobles claimed exclusive hunting rights. There is no sign that most peasants assimilated the aristocrats' professed zeal for fighting. Indeed one of the bases of the medieval system was a concentration of military chores in the hands of the new upper class and its immediate retainers. But aristocratic values inevitably colored the image of masculinity of the whole society, and directed it away from the gentle, contemplative male. In Mediterranean areas, aristocratic codes of honor, expressed in duels over trivial insults, easily invaded the peasantry by the late Middle Ages, adding a vengeful defense of the family name to the list of obligations of masculinity in Spain and southern Italy.[20] Beyond a refined, if misguided, sense of honor, medieval civilization associated manhood with the lusty indulgence of the senses. Of course, only the aristocracy could afford this with any regularity, but the standard was set for the wider society.[21] The ideal man made women bend to his will—it is hard to argue that Western masculinity includes a particularly subtle approach to sex. He ate mightily and drank hard. He indulged in quick, repeated and rather gluttonous satisfaction of his senses. Western man still appears thus to a more fastidious (effete?) Asian.

Christianity qualified this picture even in the early Middle Ages. Here was an important alternative to aristocratic and peasant culture, one stressing self-control, asceticism, prayer, and contemplation. At the least, Christianity served as an important outlet for men who shunned the more popular Western definitions of manhood. Furthermore, it influenced all but the most callous, bawdy warriors, causing them to wonder if their expression of masculinity was totally awry. Moments of prayer and contrition, increasing as age dulled sensual pleasure and physical prowess—for mainstream manhood in the West originally worked best for the young—expressed a real dualism in the concept of masculinity. Maybe the priestly way constituted genuine manly heroism after all. And later, when the Reformation reduced the separateness of the priestly function, still more men might wonder if self-domination, not self-indulgence, expressed true manhood. Collectively, Western men are still wondering.

Christianity brought the omnipotent father to the major part of Europe and, later, to the New World. The apotheosis of patriarchalism was central to Christianity. The father was final authority, omniscient, stern, and inflexible in judgment. Recurrently, with varying success, earthly fathers tried to act in this image. The words and symbols of their religion encouraged them. Control of states or estates, in the upper classes, or humble plots, for the peasantry—for Western society was a property-owning society in principle— made sense of patriarchalism and also gave it vital support in the inheritance, the earthly heaven, that could be withheld as a final weapon against a rebellious son. It was admirable, in a society based on property control, to seek to imitate God the Father, and the system perpetuated itself. Sons must be disciplined, prevented from rebellion, yet enticed by the idea that they would become fathers in their turn. Valor and physical strength—in battle, in ability to till the land—were tested, but true manhood came with the assumption of the mantle of paternity, in God's image and with the support of the Christian Church.

Yet it was hard to be a godlike father, even leaving aside the host of human frailties that so removed any patriarch from divinity. It was hard to discipline the sons, to obtain the unquestioning obedience that men, in turn, owed to God. Hence, as the God of the Old Testament was a wrathful God, so Christian fathers turned to physical punishment to keep their sons and their women in line. Erik Erikson has pointed out how shocked American Indians were at the sight of beatings of children by the Western intruders.[22] Paternal power in Western society was often based on fear, not moral supremacy. Western man established authority without full maturity, raising submissive sons who in turn became domineering fathers. God the Father subdued men to His will, and earthly fathers enforced their own will with some of the crudest weapons available.

But Western society was not simply another male-dominated agricultural society. Christianity was far more complex than this. In the image of man it conveyed, and in the introduction of the feminine element it created, a unique model of maleness for subsequent centuries to pursue. Patriarchal Christianity was of course a man's religion. Men were its principal priests. Men were not only the leading but the most numerous church members in societies such as seventeenth-century New England which emphasized the relationship of the will of men to that of God. But for a total religion, undiluted patriarchalism was normally too tough to take. Christ, a man—but also a suffering, gentle man—had to mediate between humankind and the Godhead. Appeals to the passion of Christ in no way diluted divinity but removed it from a realm of unendurable fear and authority. Christ did as his Father told. He suffered courageously. It is important to realize that Christ was not *in principle* a man to balance the Father, but complete unto himself. His message was of strength, not weakness: "I come bearing the sword." His meekness was the meekness of one who need not fight, not of one who cannot. Ezra Pound captured something of what can be considered the gentle essence of true masculinity in *The Ballad of the Goodly Fare*:

> . . . and no capon priest was he,
> Why, I ha' seen him cow a thousand men at Galilee
> Wi' eyes like the grey o' the sea.
> The'll na' get him in a book I think
> For a man among men was he.

Christianity elevated the possibility of the gentle man: loving and wanting love, compassionate to the weak, touching. It praised men, in fact, who had many of the virtues more commonly assigned to women, which complicated the definition of both genders rather substantially. It can be argued that the characteristics of the gentle man, the man who opens himself to his own and others' emotions have been too difficult for most men in Western society to emulate. Certainly Christianity did not obliterate the patriarchal image, the image of a harsher but simpler man. But Christ served as corrective, a pervasive reminder that the stern man might be deficient, indeed unjust. A tension was created in manhood that could neither be avoided nor readily resolved.

By the later Middle Ages, Christianity added other mediators, often a definitely feminine element inspired by the passions of female mystics. Mary, the mother undefiled, could be appealed to against the burden of overweening maleness.[23] Here was an infinite source of mercy. Saints, male and female alike, furthered the mediation between human kind and the Father. Christianity was a religion both for the angry, forceful man and for those, male and female, who feared such men.

Countless domineering fathers and harsh, belligerent priests (one facet of Christianity was the warrior-priest) reflected and furthered the image of the Father. But this image was directly challenged by Christianity itself. Gentleness, love, and compassion were virtues. Christianity not only provided a role choice for men between the warrior and the priest. More important, it provided a dualistic image of what men were supposed to be: stern, forgiving; tough, gentle; authoritarian, vulnerable—the juxtaposition of opposites is multifold. Western society clearly favored the image of the Father, so suitable for a warlike, property-controlling civilization. But individual men could not escape doubts about this image, wondering if a son possessed of soulfulness and tenderness might also be manly.

Christianity also granted an unusual place to women and the attributes of women. It did not, of course, grant women equality. Men ruled the church as they did the state. Men dominated theology, leaving women's Christianity more starkly passionate, with scant rational structure. But among the world's major religions, Christianity, in a sense through the gentleness of Christ, gave a strikingly ambiguous role to women.

Women were human beings with souls, in an ultimate sense, as valuable as those men. With some qualifications, they worshipped alongside men. The contrast with Islam, which utilized God the Father with far less complexity, is obvious. They were not relegated to a distinctly separate sphere. Men and women were all creatures of God, and men could not prove their authority simply by dismissing them.

One result has been an extraordinary diversity, in Christian culture, of concepts of the female. Women as a potent source of evil, the emasculator of man, was distinguishable from man but a fearsome threat. She might be a witch, in confused times, such as during the later Middle Ages: "And it should be noted that there was a defect in the formation of the first woman, since she was formed from a bent rib . . . bent as it were in a contrary direction to a man. And since through this defect she is an imperfect animal, she always deceives. We have already shown that they can take away the male organ . . . those witches who in this way sometimes collect male organs in great numbers . . . and put them in a bird's nest."[24] But woman was purity incarnate, essential to the comfort and ennoblement of sinful man, as in the increasingly revered image of Mary. This ambiguity in the woman's role has continued in modern times, and compounded the problem of defining what a proper man should be; for confirmation could not come from a secure contrast to an inferior world of women.

Presenting conflicting images, failing to separate women decisively from the spheres in which men operated, Christianity vastly strengthened one cultural artifact in defense of fragile manhood. It anathematized homosexuality. Christian Europe, and later the New World, became the only large society to take this step, though the degree of receptivity to homosexuality varied among the other cultures.[25] Judaism, in the Old Testament, stigmatized homosexuality, the sin of Onan, and possibly the stigma had been put into practice before Christianity. But classical civilization accepted homosexuality, as did Islam, Asia, the African cultures, and Amerindian society in varying degrees. The Christian West alone stood apart. And its condemnation bore primarily on men. Lesbianism was rarely suppressed, not even officially illegal, for women were sexually nearer a state of nature and less in need of the special restraints demanded by manhood. Men, trying to maintain an emphasis on virile bravery and dominance amid clashing values, could not endure the challenge of a different sexual culture. And so homosexuality was reviled and persecuted, though less in Italy and possibly France than in northern Europe. Homosexual subcultures had developed in Europe's larger cities by the seventeenth century, with contacts possible in bars and "molly houses." But penalties for apprehension were severe—the death penalty in many cases—and efforts to find partners in parks or latrines were dangerous indeed. The discovery of homosexual activity within military forces such as the British navy led to extreme severity (though the serious consequences of a successful accusation inhibited the frequency of arrest and trial), for here homosexuality's subversion of the proper male virtues was particularly intolerable. The eighteenth and nineteenth centuries, though they reduced the legal penalties for homosexuality and deemphasized the Christian prohibition, still viewed it as stemming from an unnatural mentality, to be treated as a mental illness.

Homosexuality in Christendom became more than a reproved practice against which men could measure their manhood. It was corrosive of true masculinity. But one must wonder what was so fragile about the good that it could yield so readily to evil. Christians bitterly fought homosexuality wherever their aegis spread; this was one of the basic cultural attributes of colonialism. The cancer had to be excised so that men could be men.

Western man's visceral fear of homosexuality reflected the complexity of the masculine image. Men were schooled to recognize the validity of certain compassionate and emotional values, attributes that they were simultaneously schooled to fear. Can a man share a woman's appreciation of beauty and still remain masculine? In the formative years of early puberty, when some homosexual affection is natural in almost all males, although severely restrained in Western culture, what conflicts about basic maleness develop? Is it abnormal or weak to wish to stop being aggressive and self-sufficient, to prefer the spiritual son to the omnipotent father?

Even normal sexuality had serious implications for the Christian man. There is no basis for arguing that Western men were inherently less active sexually than their counterparts in other cultures, although for an important period of time they undoubtedly were. But the Christian approach to masculinity could easily heighten the fear that sexuality jeopardized a precious maleness. The ascetic standard of the priesthood, not held to be generally applicable but suggesting a hierarchy of manly virtues, prevented an absolute association of sexual prowess with masculinity. Conflicts between gentleness and aggressiveness could easily intrude into the sexual arena. In addition, Western manhood, unique among the major civilizations of the world, involved a battle against nature, a sense that nature should be bent to man's purpose. Sexual nature was included in this struggle, for man's duty, particularly in the role of father, was to control himself.

Western manhood extended the common societal role of man as prime human agent in dealing with physical nature, and Christianity heightened claims of human superiority over the brute world. But man's dominion was not easily won, and there could be no distractions, no yielding to animal influences. It was here that women were most readily seen as a threat.

Hence the idea that excessive sex was harmful and the widespread belief (until the nineteenth century) that women were far more avid for sex than men. From Elizabethan England came the statement that sexual intercourse "harmeth a man more than if hee should bleed forty times as much."[26] Women, closer to nature, free from man's special responsibilities, had lustier appetites, as Robert Burton lamented in his *Anatomy of Melancholy*: "Women's unnatural, unsatiable lust . . . what county, what village does not complain." Of course, Christian men engaged in sex beyond the need for procreation; temperaments differed widely in practice, as they did in matters of homosexuality. The undercurrent of bawdiness in Chaucer or Boccaccio involved men fully. But the elements of hesitancy, even of fear, were significant; sexual expression did not necessarily confirm one's manhood.

Western man did not talk of outright emasculation in love, and he spoke more of sex than of woman in his fears. Religious aversion to undue sexuality was combined with sound economics: too many children, the fruit of uncontrolled sex, could ruin a whole community. Western society had balanced the need for children with definite limitations by the end of the Middle Ages. Deeper anxieties were not merely arguments to justify material necessity. By the seventeenth century informed medical opinion held that a single male orgasm was equivalent to the loss of forty ounces of blood, and this belief persisted well into the nineteenth century. The notion that sex is debilitating to manly strength remains even today. Why else do coaches try to isolate their virile charges from women on the eve of a big game? And why, even when Western man engaged in sex, was he tempted to flee from it as quickly as possible, to turn from woman before any mutual pleasure lest he be weakened?

Western society thus made a distinctive set of adaptations to the hunting male. Alterations in some areas were surprisingly small. Physical courage, aggressiveness, and displays of prowess ranked high among the virtues. Man the father can be seen as only a slight modification of the patriarch of a hunting band, providing wisdom along with a firm hand, with control of property now thrown into the bargain. Intimidation and actual physical punishment were crude methods of masculine control, most often of children. The Western male was childishly quick-tempered. Yet contrition was present as well. Compassion was a virtue, and childishness could fuse into childlikeness, the gentle male. Women, the measurement of men by contrast, were themselves so hard to define that the criteria for manhood were inevitably confusing. Not slotted into a distinct category, they could be seen as voracious or passive or souls of beauty and mercy to whom men, the fearful dominators of nature, had to repair.

Efforts to blend the various strands of manhood have been numerous. The culture of chivalry of the later Middle Ages was highly elaborate.[27] The physical competitiveness of males was recognized, but it was expressed at a partial remove in the form of individual contests rather than pillage or war. Love, carefully restrained by a code of honor and a sense of beauty, could be expressed. The problem of what women were was resolved by making them the aesthetic mentors of men, inspirers of a pure affection interestingly free from sexual taint. Habits of courtesy developed—the strong male doing deference to the woman—that still affect gender relationships in Western culture. But chivalry described only a small part of behavior in practice. It did not really cover the vital role of man as father, save in invocations of a gentle authority. Chivalric honor could easily degenerate into the petty and brutal defense of the family name, the defense of female purity into quick reactions to real or imagined abuse of sister or daughter. Chivalry did not really resolve the conflicts of manhood. And at the top of society, among the aristocracy for whom the code was initiated and most fully developed, chivalry quickly became a hollow game, a fat Henry VIII prancing about on the Field of a Cloth of Gold, troubadors crooning of love to men bent on power, knights making harmless runs at each other with blunted lances. The medieval stage of Western civilization might dwindle with the hollowness of chivalry—for it is hard not to think of chivalry as decadence, involving games that real men would not play—but the more durable impulses of men in Western society were not profoundly touched.

Within the formal cultures that applied to manhood, the majority of men, most of them faceless peasants, had to hack out their own manner of life. Not for them the luxury of gentle asceticism or, if they could avoid it, a call to arms and military valor or the details of chivalric etiquette. Yet codes of honor could apply to peasant life. Backs to the wall, few peasants could deny that men had the responsibility for physical courage. Uncertainty about sexuality was widespread;[28] the popular mind certainly assimilated the revulsion against homosexuality. Priests and monks were widely visible as images, however imperfect, of asceticism and compassion. So the general framework of Western masculinity had applicability to the real life of most men. But "most men," of course, had a particular responsibility to define economic manhood. As heads of households they continued to assume the most difficult physical burdens of supplying the family, which they dominated in law. They controlled most of the more elaborate skills, in farming but even more as artisans and in mercantile activity. In all of this the image of man the father had particular relevance, man providing for and controlling the lesser beings—women, children—in his personal world. Nascent capitalism of course picked up the aggressive strand of Western maleness, though this was still muted in the security-conscious Middle Ages.

Certainly the image of man the lord of nature deeply permeated the fabric of Western manhood. Christian men faced nature—physical nature but to an extent their own nature—as a force to be dominated. Of course the worst ravages of nature, such as disease or storm or famine, would not be controlled, and religion was a vital solace here. But manliness required that nature be viewed as something to be conquered, not appreciated or upheld in superstitious awe.[29] Nature was not a friend. Nature was not beautiful. Aesthetic values have combined only uneasily with manhood in Western culture. Nature was not peopled with gods to be propitiated. Nature was to be faced, on a day to day basis, by men unaided, armed with tools that were only tools.

Trees had to be cut down, and there was no worshipping their spirit to soften the task. Axes were axes, not objects of religious power. How painfully did Western men, descended from fearful worshippers of the spirits of nature, learn to face the nights and the forests unaided, responsible for their dominance? Western man, assuming a role so close to the godhead, capable ultimately of such massive technological achievement, was close also to the nameless fear of a creature set unaided in a hostile land.

Economic man experienced fully the ambiguities of Western culture with regard to women. A segment of popular opinion sought a strict division of labor between men and women, more a division of tasks than an unequal allocation of power. Men did the work and women had to care for the children, so vital to the family's economic survival. A French peasant proverb summed it up: "It is the husband who carries the stones, but the wife who makes the house."[30] But men and women were economic partners as well. The family economy may have captured women more thoroughly than men in the sense that their tasks were more closely bound to the house, but it was a joint venture. A man was not alone in working for his family. Here was solace but also challenge: How, then, did he know he was a man? Only a small part of the answer lay in formal legal responsibilities, for women made crucial decisions in practice. The major explanation resided in the identification of certain tasks with manhood: The exclusively male guilds consecrated manly pride in being an expert weaver or toolmaker or baker. Physical strength as well as pleasure in working with other men, including one's sons in the field, might satisfy the farmer's needs. But part of the question, as in Western culture generally, was unanswered and unanswerable.

Two developments at the eve of the modern era complete the picture of how Western man modified agricultural man, a modification of hunting man, who in turn was descended from biological man. These modifications occurred before industrial society altered manhood yet again. Both developments sharpened key characteristics of Western masculinity. The Reformation substantially purged Christianity of its feminine elements, leaving men and women alike faced with a starkly masculine religion.[31] The central ambiguity of gender remained, for women gained in many ways in the reformed churches. They could be full church members and were no longer excluded in any part from channels of sacramental grace. The Reformation and other trends in Western Europe actually heightened an interest in women's education, though it was as a result of the Renaissance in France and Italy that women began particularly to assume roles as patrons of culture. Important debates began about the nature of women's intellect, foreshadowing modern times yet maintaining the Christian tension about women as human equals. Yet, in the Reformation God the Father was now installed in virtually unqualified majesty. The mercy of Mary no longer mediated; even Christ's gentleness played a lesser role in ritual and theology alike. The Protestant male image was simple, less balanced and attractive than the Catholic. Martin Luther wrote into the new religion the intensely ambivalent feelings he had about his own father. The feelings were not necessarily unusual for the time, but Luther was exceptionally explicit in translating them into religious attitudes. Hans Luder, a miner of peasant stock, was a harsh father—cruel by modern standards—meticulously overseeing his son, beating him frequently, yet ambitious for the boy's future.[32] Luther resented his father's authoritarianism and may well have transmitted this into his rebellion against an authoritarian church. But his God, though possessed of elements of mercy, was paternal authority all over again, omnipotently disposing of the everlasting fates of mankind. It is probable that Lutheranism and Calvinism, even sterner in its patriarchal image, appealed in part because of more basic reinforcements of fatherly rule. Men taught to obey their fathers might be tempted to a rebellious outlet, but like Luther they sought a perfect father in an omnipresent God. Certainly Protestantism helped justify a pattern of childrearing in which paternal authority was transcendant. Even more than before, the righteous father was armed with moral authority and the image of God, responsible for enforcing obedience for the sake of his child's immortal soul.[33]

However, the most general expansion of paternal power occurred in Catholic countries like France as well as areas that were to become Protestant. Toward the end of the Middle Ages, land in Western Europe became free of the most oppressive manorial controls. A peasant could think of his plot as his own in almost the modern sense of property ownership. Probably for this reason, family patterns altered to further and preserve the ownership role, and the definition of manhood was inevitably affected by this change.

People, men and women alike, began to marry later, in their mid- to late twenties, in order to reduce the birthrate and to relate family formation to accession to property.[34] A woman could not marry in peasant or artisan society until a dowry was available, nor could a man until he came into land. This gave fathers immense control over their offspring, particularly their sons. A son denied inheritance could not normally marry at all. A son who offended might at the least be punished by a father's refusal to retire early or indeed yield any of his property until death. Tensions between generations could be sharp, but there was little recourse against paternal power. Where land was relatively abundant, as in colonial New England, most fathers worked out a peaceable accommodation with their sons.[35] But the father's authority remained predominant in the family, and obedience was expected. A man was an owner or, among urban artisans, possessed of a recognized skill. Full manhood in Western Europe and North America became inextricably intertwined with fatherhood, and fatherhood was linked to ownership and disciplinary control. Thus, in Western society the Christian Godhead reached as full a secular translation as was possible.[36]

From an American Evangelical Protestant ethic in the early nineteenth century there emerged an intensely responsible father: "The right of the parent is to command, the duty of the child is to obey . . . Obedience (the first law of children). By this I mean that the relation between parent and child obliges the latter to conform to the will of the former because it is his will."[37] Boys needed the special attention of the father because they were less tractable than girls, but the goal was the same for both: to break the will. The result? At best, a pious son, devoted to his father's memory in later life—for docility resolved the conflict created by rage against authoritarianism—successful in this world and not unlike his father in what he expected of his own offspring.

And what, overall, was a man in Western society by the seventeenth and eighteenth centuries, before the winds of change began to blow fierce? A boy was male, not a man. He was not rigorously differentiated from girls, except that he joined his father at work in fields or in the shop.[38] Most notably, the dress of a young male was distinctly feminine, and would remain so in many social classes well into the twentieth century. (As I write this, I stare at a photo of my father, aged six or so [whom my son so resembles], taken around 1910 at a farm in Illinois: hair cut short, but wearing a dress with woolen stockings.) To be sure, there was in boyhood more than a reminder of the range of values applicable to men in their prime. With work in the fields, increase in strength and size could be a source of manly pride. Skill, for artisans, could be closely associated with manhood. Hunting could occupy a young man occasionally, though tests of masculinity in hunting were uncommon save on the frontier. Sexual prowess was also difficult to demonstrate. Marrying late (though in the early twenties in colonial America), men had few other outlets for sexuality. Nonmarital, or even premarital, intercourse was amazingly rare; the economy of property ownership was too fragile to be disturbed by unwanted births, and not only religion but close supervision by family and village limited sexual experimentation.[39] Homosexuality was scant, insofar as we know, outside big cities and within the military. How common masturbation or bestiality were one can only guess, but while they might relieve sexual tension they could hardly feed a young man's pride. Youth was allowed some latitude for rowdiness and aggressive games. Village tugs-of-war, sometimes pitting unmarried against married men, could turn into outright brawls.[40] Beyond this, stories of military valor could fire the imagination, though only a small minority of unfortunates or misfits actually served in premodern armies. Enough was recalled or transmitted from the ruling classes, where lustiness and combat were more real possibilities, to orient young men when youth became freer.

For most young men, particularly in the countryside, youth (extending well into the twenties) was a time of waiting and learning, more than of testing. Swaddled and confined in infancy, lectured, hectored, and physically punished as children, boys did have a good bit of their will drummed out of them.[41] They were to work in assisting capacities and obey. Real manhood required a certain maturity; a significant number never matured, though they lived to adulthood. Some, of course, chose, or were pushed into, an alternate career in the priesthood or the ministry, maintaining some link to those qualities of spirituality and gentle contemplation that could be manly, preserving the link between manhood and religious guidance and rational activity also. Far more males, younger sons or offspring of desperately poor or unfortunate families, never amassed the property needed to marry and form families and had, particularly if they remained in the countryside, to spend a lifetime serving a relative or a wealthier neighbor. Still lacking a sexual outlet in most cases, seldom possessed of significant skill, barred, above all, from the kind of independence and authority associated with heading a household, up to 30 percent of all adult men in Western Europe (far fewer in North America) never attained full or independent manhood.[42]

But most men could wait, with varying degrees of good grace, to come into property, or the full exercise of skill, and marry. A few murdered their fathers—older men comprised the largest category of homicide victims in rural society.[43] More chafed until they assumed the independent control of property, which was the real badge of manhood. "And then my father died, and I became free to act as I wanted," a French peasant noted casually in his diary.[44] For being head of a household meant a certain freedom combined with power. The father was a legal authority, controlling both his children (until they established independent households) and his wife in the eyes of the law. He was the basic, though by no means exclusive, economic mainstay, notably governing the work of those sons who remained—dutiful, calculating, or simply lacking alternatives—to work by his side. He was in principle the moral authority, responsible here too for guidance of wife as well as children.

There was, of course, more than a small chance of failure. Famine or disease could ravage a peasant household and make a mockery of male authority. The fortunes of peasant families fluctuated wildly, in part depending on the talents of the male; this was a stable society only on the surface. The principle of male responsibility, however qualified in fact by the important female role, was burden as well as privilege. It is hard to play God when one is in fact not, and in premodern Western society men were often tempted to do so. To whom does the god of the household tell his troubles? Does the stern patriarch admit them even to himself? From Christian asceticism, from the legends of warriors, from the striving for moral self-sufficiency of the household head, all combining to this end, it was easy to believe that one should not admit pain. But that did not mean that pain was not felt.

Even so, there is a comforting sense, in part the illusion of a simplified past but in part truth, that at least men could know what it was to be a man. One ruled, if only a very small world, and one was responsible. Some, more often through accident of birth than anything else, could not qualify, but the goal at least was clear. It was rather pompous manhood, perhaps, not the stuff of heroic tales, but consecrated by many centuries of a developing Western society. With patriarchalism, particularly in the Protestant countries, even some of the basic ambiguities of Western manhood might be glossed over. Fathers might be gentle or harsh in their authority; the key point was that they had authority. Some of the hesitations over sexuality loomed less large simply because sexuality was less important. Even in marriage, apart from the aristocracy, there is no evidence of frequent, much less imaginative, sexual intercourse. The more basic problem of women was not resolved. Were they almost coequal or distinctly subordinate? The extension of patriarchal authority in sixteenth- and seventeenth-century Europe was to some degree offset by new claims for the equality of women, virtually an intellectual feminism.[45] Even in humble families, economy and household allowed a large number of variations on these themes, but no basic resolution. Still, there was, in the century before industrialization (the later seventeenth century was in many respects a quiet time)[46] considerable agreement on the trappings of manhood. Whatever the adequacy of the criteria for manhood, they did seem established. The next age might prove a more exciting time to be a man, but it was inherently disturbing because so many settled principles were challenged, even invalidated, for large numbers of men. Many men chose to meet that challenge by asserting that the values of the previous centuries had been essential to a definition of manhood. The importance of sex-role definition increased markedly as an early and durable response to industrial society. As it became harder to be a man—by criteria valid in hunting, agricultural, or specifically Western society—it became vital to prove one's manhood, especially to oneself.

The bases of patriarchy may have been eroding in the upper and middle classes even before industrialization's challenge. The eighteenth century, particularly in England, saw a loosening of the strictest discipline over children, a reduction of mechanical constraints, such as swaddling, and a growing delight in educating and guiding one's offspring. Fathers and mothers alike became somewhat more affectionate and permissive. Between husbands and wives patriarchalism was modified by a growing interest in love and companionship. These changes were fed by the spread of market relationships that heightened individual emotional potential and, possibly, emotional need as well, thus making people more eager to express themselves through affection. They related to the new Englightenment ideals of equality. But the precise cause and extent of these ideals are difficult to ascertain.[47] The strictest patriarchalism was hard to maintain in terms of the tensions of the basic Western tradition. But for most people, its ideals and its certainties were not jettisoned, which is why, with industrialization, the patriarchal values yielded slowly and why men, even as they sought additional satisfactions—greater love, for example—readily fell back on patriarchal definitions of their relationships within the family and toward the broader society.

Just as the hunting culture has left its traces on modern manhood, so has Western agricultural society. Ownership equated with independence equated with manhood remains an obvious impulse, yielding only grudgingly. Urban men can enjoy a garden as some contact not only with nature but with control over nature. Even more, craft skills such as furniture-making, no longer relevant in manufacturing, constitute popular male hobbies, a quiet but significant retention of a masculine tradition. Control of animals may also serve, though this is no more an exclusively male realm in the cities than it was in the preindustrial countryside. More basically, ambiguities about sexuality, including homosexuality, and about women have been transported bodily into modern times.

Patriarchalism, of course, remains the most vivid remnant of recent Western male culture. Agricultural society bequeathed this most specifically to adult males, leaving hunting values more for youth. Few fathers fail to sense that they should be an all-wise and powerful patriarch even if they neither can nor want to be. My father, far from the farm of his youth, assumed the role more than occasionally. We had no property to serve as base, though he did hold out a prospect of higher education, a gentle but important surrogate. More significant was his moral authority. And when that authority faltered, or I faltered, there was physical discipline, followed typically by tearful apologies which confused me about what either he or I, as males, should be. I could not figure out why just punishment, merited apology, and my father clearly could not figure out whether toughness or gentleness most became the patriarch—the classic Western dilemma. It was hard being a latter-day patriarch, for modern society forces the child, the extension of one's will, into situations beyond paternal control, and this can be agonizing. But the Western male tradition, certainly the patriarchal tradition, said nothing about an equation of manhood and happiness. Pride, yes; occasional fierce joy; but a cloying happiness could be positively dangerous.

The sense of a past when standards were more certain and manhood more definite—for to be a man one had above all to be a father—is part of the legacy of patriarchalism. As patriarchalism weakened or proved inadequate, as it had to do in the modern world, it left more than one generation confused. For if a man could not be like his father, even a father he detested, could not measure his achievements against his father's standards, when did he know that he was a real man? Modernity complicated personal and public judgments of manhood while making a distinctly male role more important than it had been in premodern society. "Be a man!" increased in urgency just as men could have legitimately claimed that the task was beyond them.

A number of feminist historians have bemoaned the passing of preindustrial society as a downgrading of women's power. As a result of a loss in productive function, they supposedly lost status.[48] This is not the place to review this claim fully, save to note that property, not productive labor directly, engendered status in preindustrial society. The work ethic implies rather more modern standards of status. What is true about preindustrial society is that it set definite standards of gender, which could be of advantage to both men and women. While the Christian ambiguity about the exact relationship of the two sexes remained, most men knew what it took to be a man, and women had the same advantage. There was indeed no sense of evolution in gender relationships—they seemed given, by God and by history—and certainly no basic criticism arose of the patriarchal structures. Periodically, preindustrial culture, like many other cultures, played with gender inversions. Men would dress and act like women, in pictures and stories, in processions and outright protest. On a number of occasions peasant men dressed like women before attacking government agents; more rarely, women assumed men's garb and roles.[49] The reasons for this need not unduly concern us here. Brief gender reversals may have relieved the tensions of sex roles. They definitely allowed men to be irresponsible, to do things "as women" that sober men might undertake reluctantly if at all. Again, the use of gender reversals is common in many societies. What is important is their indication of relative *security* in gender roles, if some stultification as well. Men could occasionally act like women, for particular purposes, because they knew they were men (or, in the case of the more transitional adolescents, because they knew they would become men). Feminine garb for children was similarly appropriate in a patriarchal world because masculinity was so clear that it could be acquired. A child, no more than a woman, was not a man. Industrialization destroyed much of this clarity. It was as important as before to be a man, but much less certain how to become one. So the old excursions into role reversals largely ceased. Only in the twentieth century was there an occasional revival of transvestite comedy, and only secure male worlds, such as those of Harvard or Princeton in the first half of this century, used female-garbed male performers. But in saying that the establishment of gender identity became more chancy with industrialization, we may also be saying that it became more interesting, potentially less confining. In the long run, men perhaps will not need to dress as women to break free from the ordinary fetters of being men.

3. Manhood and the
Challenge of Industrialization

Men's places. The dark shaft of a coal mine, one of the real tests of nineteenth-century masculinity. Fearful men, rightly afraid of the mechanical descent into the pits, the danger of asphyxiation, or burial at the pitface. Men exceptionally conscious of their rights, in response to the risk they took, readier than most workers to protest and to seek compensation. But men proud of being men. The traditional exclusion of women from the mines was upheld with only rare exception. The great miners' strikes were strikes by men, backed by their wives and families in most cases but acting above all as a male mass. And the miners' sons, particularly after a generation or so of acclimation, dutifully followed their fathers into the mines at a rate of 90 percent or more. Lured by relatively secure pay, to be sure; poorly educated in isolated mine villages and so lacking a sense of alternatives; but also convinced that mining was the only choice a man could make, that to avoid its fearsome challenge would be the worst cowardice.[1]

Men's places. The administrative offices of a factory were beginning to grow in the mid-nineteenth century; they were staffed by men trained in chemistry, engineering, or accountancy, the new skills of the male middle class. Here there was nothing like the miner's fear of women as bad luck. Many a factory office started in the early nineteenth century as a husband-wife operation, with the woman doing the books in the traditional manner of the business class. But now the wife was gone; only small retail shops retained the traditional male-female cooperation in the workplace, and when women were reintroduced into offices after 1870, they came as subordinates.[2] The offices offered none of the physical challenge of the mines or the machine shops. But they offered a kind of mental challenge: the male as aggressive business competitor (a new image which retained traditional hunting or warlike qualities, though in a sublimated fashion) and the male as master of rational knowledge, an old image in Western society which now became increasingly important.

The present chapter deals with some of the basic forces that have transformed the male role and image since the advent of industrialization. Specific patterns of male behavior depended heavily on social class; the following two sections deal with working-class and middle-class men. Both groups faced certain common problems, themselves the product of increased industrialization throughout the nineteenth century. Patriarchy, most notably, was everywhere challenged, and men had to grope for compensatory mechanisms and identities. In the nineteenth century, the traditional male roles were fundamentally changed. That century, and the early part of our own, saw the most concerted efforts to adapt existing male traditions and even to hark back to earlier images of the fighting and hunting male. We deal, then, first with some broadly common pressures encountered by men throughout Western Europe and the United States in the first hundred years or so of industrialization. We can start with a somewhat anomalous, but vital, reaction: industrialization heightened the importance of gender; for men, it heightened the importance of defining the criteria of manhood and of fulfilling those criteria.

We know that women were greatly affected by industrialization and not just as passive victims. It caused them to initiate a host of changes in home and family of vital importance, some of them relevant in the long run to employment situations as well. (An openness to household technology has, for example, been associated with the early female monopoly of paid typewriting, against the resistance of tradition-minded male scribes.)[3] But for a full century industrialization steadily converted nonagricultural production to a male sphere. Women and children worked in the textile factories, of course, and whenever cloth or metal goods could still be produced in the home, women were employed in large numbers. In largely household economies such as that in France, by 1900 some 30 percent of the manufacturing labor force was female. But until the rise of chemical industries the key growth industries were almost wholly male. Textile industrialization primarily involved putting labor in factories, not creating new labor, and its workforce steadily decreased as a percentage of the whole. Not only mining but also metalwork and metallurgy, construction, railroading, and shipping were predominantly male.[4]

Furthermore, outside the workplace, gender distinctions also increased with the advent of industrialization. It became increasingly important to make sure that boys knew they were boys, and girls girls. Changes in children's costume eroded the unisex of preindustrial childhood; the skirt, for men, was now confined to infancy alone. The decline of the wig emphasized different gender hairstyles in adulthood. A growing female concern with slenderness accentuated different bodies.[5] The male domination of most nineteenth-century trade unions was less novel, for earlier producer guilds were typically grouped by gender. But division or new leisure activities by sex was revealing. Working-class bars, race tracks, and sports were heavily masculinized, and there was little male-female contact in leisure apart from courtship. Middle-class patterns were more complex, but the rise of men's clubs shows the increase in gender distinction of leisure activities.[6]

The advent of industrialization saw an effort to categorize people in a number of ways that seem debatable now, and gender divisions were part of this process. Age groupings, for example, were isolated with growing precision, and peoples' associations became increasingly circumscribed by their age peers. The categorization impulse was in part bureaucratic. To deal with new urban masses, groupings and grades seemed essential. The industrial mentality—and I think we maintain this today—had to seek keys to identify strangers, and the effort extended from phrenology to handwriting analysis.[7] Sex-role stereotypes were a convenient way to categorize strangers. People deceived themselves about the uniformities of male or female nature just as they eagerly seized on notions that bumps on the head or facial expressions revealed the whole soul.

The combined impact of early industrial technology and demography explains in part the increase in gender distinctions, for more was involved than a conveniently visible categorization. Many of the early machines did not significantly reduce the need for physical strength, and in few cases they even enhanced it. Women had always been able to spin by hand, and they could run the smaller new machines. But the largest spinning machines required, until the 1840s, the manual activation of heavy machine parts, and were almost uniformly reserved for men. Still more important, the early technology did not significantly apply to many production areas of growing importance. Rails helped haul coal, and in England girls did mine work alongside boys for a while; but there were no new machines at the pitface for hewing coal. The construction industry was unchanged by mechanization until electric and gasoline motors allowed power saws and, even more important, lifting equipment; the same applies to dockwork. In metallurgy, the growing size of blast furnaces and new skills such as puddling actually increased demands on physical strength.[8]

Western society had long reserved, or claimed to reserve, some of the heaviest physical jobs for men, particularly in manufacturing (manual weaving, traditionally a male trade in contrast to the lighter spinning, is a case in point). Early industrialization increased the number of jobs requiring heavy labor, such as metallurgy or construction. Pride in physical prowess was at least as great in nineteenth century labor as before, an important aspect of working-class masculinity. Relatedly, working-class families carefully concentrated protein intake among the all-important male earners—when there was little meat, men got it—so that the male strength and size advantage over women probably increased. (In the higher classes something of the same effect occurred as a result of the growing popularity of the slender, sylphlike female image.) In the long run, developing technology would lighten tasks and open them to women. Presently, we are probably engaged in the kind of gender reshuffling that follows the new round of technological change. The collective confusion, and the considerable male anguish, at this largely twentieth-century shift away from the need for brute strength reflect in part the fact that early industrialization deceivingly attached men to productive roles more exclusively than ever before.

Of course, the explanation cannot be so neat. Men moved to predominance in areas where strength was not always required by the available technology. Mechanical weaving, introduced after 1820, lightened the task, and boys and young women were extensively employed to operate the new looms. Later technology increased the speed of the looms but not the physical strength required. Nevertheless, men quickly took over as machine weavers except in the United States (where, presumably, there was a lack of available, sufficiently cheap male labor).[10] The reason? Men had always done weaving-for-sale, from the time of the hand looms. They insisted on extending their traditional mastery, now far removed from its initial basis in strength requirements, into the factories. Even the timing of mechanization was related to gender. On the whole, traditional areas of female manufacturing were mechanized earlier and more quickly than areas of male specialization. In part this was coincidental; in part it reflected the fact that, in manufacturing, males had done the more complex as well as heavier tasks, which were in turn harder to mechanize. But in part it reflected bitter male resistance to technical change and a desire to retain jobs on the basis of continued association of strength with production, from mining to construction work. In weaving, further technical change was resisted more firmly than in thread spinning because the latter was a female preserve and therefore considered less important.[11]

Further, the whole gender division of labor in the middle class, the increasing male monopoly of business management, along with the continued male hold on the professions, was not based on technological necessity at all. Business, and particularly professional men, could point to the long-standing association of maleness and rational knowledge. As medicine became more "scientific," for example, supervision of childbirth passed from midwives to male doctors, while there was simply no question of women's entry into fields of applied mathematics such as engineering; the importance of traditional male claims to rationality in setting industrial tasks should not be minimized.[12] Clearly, however, gender economics was not the exclusive product of technological determinism or of male customs more broadly construed. Demography also played an important part in increased gender distinction.

Early industrialization occurred in a period when families in most social classes had a growing number of children surviving early infancy, compared to the situation before c. 1750. This resulted either from a decline in infant and child mortality, as in the middle class, or primarily from a higher birth rate (working class). The nineteenth century itself did not witness further gains in the reduction of infant mortality (though child mortality declined), but the century did preach, particularly for the middle classes, the need for increased care for children.[13] With childrearing demands actually rising, both objectively and subjectively, a family specialization of labor became virtually a necessity, and of course it greatly heightened gender differentiation. Middle-class and working-class families alike developed a belief that married women should not work outside the home.

No mystery, then, in the gender distinctions, no particular plot, just good sense in context. The new technology did not greatly increase female employment because it came at a time when home duties were particularly compelling. So, logically, men and women became increasingly separate. Of course, the ideas and practices associated with the functional differentiation could easily outlive their initial usefulness. The special responsibility of men for breadwinning made sense in the early nineteenth century. It had partial sanction in tradition, it followed from the demands for physical strength and dealing with strangers in the new industrial setting—both male roles by custom—and with the exacting functions of women in the home. Men had to be trained, with new emphasis, in their special responsibilities, and they were given to understand that some specially male rewards accompanied them; hence, perhaps, the importance of distinguishing male from female at a very early age. But by the late nineteenth century, the gender ethic of male superiority had taken on a life of its own. Men barred women from jobs the latter could perfectly well handle. Working-class wives continued to sacrifice their own comfort, even their basic diet, to make sure the male was sufficiently well fed and psychologically bolstered to go out to work in the outside world, a functional division that may have given some sense of purpose or satisfaction to both parties but one that had no basis in objective necessity.[14]

Even during the first half of the nineteenth century we can assume that gender roles reflected not merely technology and household but a refuge, available really to both sexes, from dealing with the impact of change on maleness and femaleness. People reacted to a new economic and social structure, new even before the advent of the first factories, by providing themselves with gender measurements of self-worth. The generations that moved to the cities, abandoning agriculture for business or manufacturing, could not have the satisfaction of knowing that their lives fit into the mold of their parents' and ancestors' lives. The traditional social fabric was rent, and while there was great new opportunity in this, there was also strain.

Enhancing the sense of disruption was an uncertainty about generational transmission from father to son. Many sons still followed their fathers; the working class actually reestablished a generational sequence after the disruption of moving to the cities, while the middle-class father could use control of property and educational choices to the same end. But many men could not impel their sons to follow them, for alternatives grew steadily. Many businessmen, for example, found their sons yearning for the greater prestige of professional life, and while they could restrain and prod, it was hard to say no. Many men, blue- and white-collar alike, were taught by a new ethic of mobility that they should *want* their sons to be different from them, better than they were. Each generation saw improved educational levels, which guaranteed that many sons would know more than their fathers did. Finally, many fathers realized that their own work was becoming obsolete in a changing economy, that they would not guide their sons in their footsteps. Adult men, in large numbers, thus could no longer confirm their own lives through their sons' actions. Sons might find uncertainty as well as independence in hacking out their own identity. Here, obviously, was one source of the new insistence on criteria of manhood that could be achieved apart from direct generational succession. Young men had to know who they were; mature men wanted to be able to find something of themselves in their sons.

Working-class masculinity was most directly challenged by the rise of market manufacturing and then by the factories themselves. With the rising population in the second half of the eighteenth century (even in North America, tension increased over the problem of inheritance), access to property became immensely difficult. Rather quickly, Western Europe headed toward a situation in which half or more of the adult population would never own property. However, the spread of tenant farming, sometimes made more productive by new techniques, manufacturing in the home, and factories allowed masses of people to survive and some to prosper modestly. But not owning property hit at the essence of masculinity, as it had been defined in Western agricultural society. Patriarchalism was severely affected. A propertyless worker might rage at his son, try to dominate him physically, but the vital hold was gone: the son could walk out without great damage to his economic future. A propertyless man in preindustrial society, and there were many, was not fully a man at all, prevented usually from marriage, from normal sexuality, condemned to dependence. The nascent working class was now, for all intents and purposes, entirely propertyless; it was indeed dependent, each worker directed by a supervisor, his motions watched and regulated. How could workers be manly?

The answer lay in stressing those elements of masculinity that were still valid, and adding a list of new male attributes. Sexual conquest took on new importance. The working class began to engage in sex at an increasingly early age—around eighteen or twenty in a society that previously had reserved heterosexual intercourse for between the ages of twenty-five or twenty-six. One result was rising rates of illegitimate births throughout Western Europe and North America from 1780 onward.[15] Sex was available earlier for men than before, and for a larger majority of men than before, in the working class. Clearly, this provided some compensation for the loss of patriarchal property: where this property had been a tiny holding of land, a man could emerge with a feeling that his bargain had been well made. He could, in any event, form a family, and marriage rates rose in most areas. But a sense of loss, of uncertainty, might linger, and working-class males could be impelled to use sexuality, particularly during the critical period of youth and young adulthood traditionally spent in expectation of inheritance, to prove that they were men. The change in working-class sexuality involved not only more and earlier activity, but possibly greater male assertiveness, with proof of maleness not just in begetting children but in dominating the female partner.

Once married and the father of children, the working-class male was, on the whole, inclined to define his masculinity in terms as close to tradition as possible. The authoritarian father, so pervasive in working-class culture until after World War II, clearly harked after the patriarchal image. Of course not all workers even wanted to be authoritarian, and most definitely not all of them could be. But the image was there, and it was passed from father to son. Its exercise might help still doubts about masculinity.[16]

The breadwinner role was the classic male obligation in the working class. Again, men might prove unable to fulfill the role, might resent it. But there was widespread pride in being able to provide for one's family amid the difficulties of a new economic environment. Hence, among other things, the pervasive belief, lasting well into the present century, that the man had failed whose wife had to seek employment outside the house.[17]

Many workers clung to an association of manhood and skill (plus strength, of course). Here was perhaps the most direct substitute for property ownership. Craftsmen fought to maintain their skills in printing, metalwork, or carpentry. Machine workers could derive pride from mastering their equipment, and machine building, metallurgy, railroading and the like involved new skills of real complexity. Many a peasant's son could feel upgraded by the skills he learned. The association between manhood and skill came closer together whether the trade involved had traditional sanction or not. Workers who struggled to reserve job training for their sons, a practice soon as common in the factories as in the crafts, were not looking for family economic security alone. They wanted to justify their manhood by making sure that their sons followed the same course, their uncertainties impelling them to seek proof of human worth through repetition by their progeny.[18]

Nineteenth-century definitions of manhood, in theory and in behavior, worked. In both their working-class and middle-class versions, they had substantial roots in reality. With our twentieth-century hindsight, as we struggle against the real limitations of continued adherence to patterns of the past, we can readily poke holes in the adjustments our forefathers made. But these adjustments had a substantial base in tradition. Where tradition was breaking down, notably when a majority of men could no longer expect to acquire the prime badge of preindustrial patriarchalism, the ownership of property, with its sometimes deceptive promise of economic sustenance and moral authority, adaptations were made that compensated to some extent. The propertyless male could increasingly claim freedom from control—if not at work, at least outside the job—whereas his preindustrial counterpart could not. Freedom and manhood were intricately intertwined. Frederick Douglass thus described his feeling when, as a slave, he first offered resistance to his master: "I was *nothing* before, I WAS A MAN NOW." This is why protest and manhood were so frequently—and newly—associated, and why so many men could not see freedom for women in the same light. Freedom was very fragile in the industrial world. Few people were their own masters. But some men could see a chance to struggle for what they did not have, and most could, for a time, enjoy proofs of manhood that had been more difficult to acquire before. The new enjoyment of sexuality was one such proof. How imaginative this new sexuality was may be open to question. Manly sex, in its nineteenth-century Western version, required female partners but not necessarily female pleasure. But many a young man, vaguely aware that the full proof of traditional patriarchy would elude him, found sensual diversion and psychic satisfaction in his sexuality. Significantly, a revolution of sexual behavior also occurred among the new hordes of propertyless people in the countryside, even before massive urbanization. Here too young people were less restrained by parents who had no promise of property inheritance to hold over them, and they saw no damage to their own economic future in having more children, earlier than before and often without sanction of marriage.[19]

Sexuality, providing pleasure, a sense of independence from parents, and possibly a feeling of dominion over women, was related to two other demonstrations of manhood, not new but more widely available than before. The steady increase of marriage rates in all classes was supplemented, in the working classes, by a drop in marriage age. Even without a guarantee of property acquisition, though this was still associated with marriage in the middle classes, a man could have his own household and father children. Although a father's ability to care for children became more difficult as work was separated from the home, the desire to sire children, to prove manhood through potency, did grow until midcentury or beyond.

In preindustrial society a large minority of males could never prove they were men. Propertyless, they could not demonstrate sexual prowess—their desires were slaked, if at all, by masturbation and bestiality, which left little opportunity for self-satisfaction and none for public congratulation. They remained personally dependent, usually on relatives, for their entire lives. Now, with independent money earnings through production for a market economy often available by one's late teens, the nineteenth-century counterparts of this group had new vistas open to them. Even men who had a direct sense of loss, who perceived that in the olden days they would have had a shot at patriarchy in the more literal, propertied sense, might enjoy their new facility in passing the simpler tests of manhood, particularly in their early adulthood, when so many key decisions were made.[20]

The increasing awareness of gender that accompanied industrialization made functional sense in a number of ways. Division of labor, not new in any event, seemed imposed by early industrial technology and the concomitant demands of a rising birth rate. Men had to be readied to go out to work, in contrast to women who, our images of factory girls notwithstanding, mainly confined their labors to a domestic setting as servants and wives. The new importance of dressing boys as boys owed much to work, for trousers were much safer than loose garments in the factory or mine. Attention to the schooling of men, their disproportionate advance in literacy, technical training and, in the middle classes, higher education, so pronounced in the first two-thirds of the nineteenth century, had its base in the increasingly distinctive economic roles of the two sexes.

There was also a psychic aspect to the new importance of gender, a significant hedge against the pressures of industrial life. Arduous, dangerous work might be endured as a demonstration of manliness, pitting one's strength against matter, one's brain against the complexities of machine design or bridge construction. Certainly there was scant time to think of alternatives when the work was done alongside one's fellow men, when complaint might seem unmanly. Women had their own stake in manliness. Their own sustenance, and that of their children, depended on the male breadwinner. Their standing in the community owed much to the manliness of husband or father. Quickly and durably, manhood drew new strength from the forces of industrialization.[21]

Resentful women or beleaguered males in the twentieth century might wish that another path had been chosen less than two hundred years ago. With property increasingly risky as a bastion of patriarchy, with new opportunities for women's work and a new technology attacking many male skills and diminishing strength itself as a requirement for work, why did men not relax the difficult quest for manhood, and settle for a common humanity? Economics aside, the reorientation would simply have made no sense. The attractions of manhood, of a special masculine role in continuing contact with tradition, remained too great. Manhood had to be adapted, without question, but there was no felt need to redefine it.

Yet it is not misleading to stress the fragility of early industrial manhood. Industrialization was challenging and difficult for women as well as men; ultimately the dilemmas of modern society are human ones. But men were impelled to make some exceptionally risky choices as men, and these deserve brief comment.

The link of manhood and work was not new, but the work involved was. Men staked a lot in defining themselves in terms of particular skills or even as breadwinners in an uncertain economy. Their decision was not courageous; few saw or had any choice in the matter. But they did run great risk of failure— and failures among new businesses, at a rate of 50 percent or more, must be counted along with the injuries and bad luck of working people— which would, in their own eyes and that of their families, be their fault.[22] Manliness at work involved not only adaptation to rapid economic change but responsibility for economic security that too often was beyond any mortal power. Here, of course, was the penalty for assuming independent manliness in a world where independence was no more available than it had ever been. Yet the facts seemed clear. Men alone involved themselves centrally in the new economy. If disaster struck they could rarely blame familiar enemies like war or weather; the sicknesses of the industrial economy were at once more remote and more unfathomable. Even God seemed an increasingly lame excuse to men who, far more rapidly than their women, lost their active religious sense. New abstractions—most notably capitalism—were invented to explain the disparity between a man's labor and a man's reward. But new doctrines of socialism or trade unionism or middle-class anticapitalism (most commonly in the guise of anti-Semitism) spread unevenly. Women, less open to formal ideology, were frequently skeptical of the new excuses and even hostile to them as possible impediments to the man's work. It was difficult to escape a sense, when the work went bad, that it was the man's fault.

Men did not of course realize how fully they were identifying manhood and work. Most would have defined manhood in terms of family as least as much as in terms of economy. And family, in turn, with the addition of an early period of sexual freedom, was seen in terms of a masculine tradition little more adapted from tradition than the male association with strength and skill. Before the late nineteenth century, the image of patriarchalism lingered tenaciously. Yet, never automatic or easy, patriarchalism was harder than ever to attain, for several reasons.

Family expectations of men changed and helped confuse a patriarchal role. As courtship became freer of economic criteria, particularly in the working class, a man just might fall in love with his wife and modify patriarchal dominance over her for romantic reasons. A desire to see the family as a refuge and the woman as a haven, articulated most clearly in middle-class literature, suggested a family that a man might choose to rest in rather than to rule.[23] More immediately, the same division of labor that made the man breadwinner outside the home gave the wife increasing control of the family. A man might seek and claim dominance, but he was simply not present for day-to-day decisions ranging from allocation of money to raising of children. Patriarchalism in this situation would be rather hollow, though man and wife might both, for their own reasons, pay lip service to it.[24]

Two changes were particularly crucial, one involving kin and the other children. Particularly in the working class, the network of relatives surrounding a family switched from a male to a female base.[25] (The nineteenth century was the first century of the mother-in-law joke, a stock-in-trade of British music halls by the 1880s.)[26] In village society in Western Europe, relatives had typically formed around the man, as property owner. A bride had traditionally gone to her husband's home and kin when she married. The urban working man lacked not only property but also the time to spend at home with his relatives. Women took over the task of organizing networks of relatives who provided the family with social life and with economic assistance in bad times. Newlyweds in the new working class, if they could not afford their own apartment, typically went to live with the bride's parents. Even more uniformly, aged parents, needing support from an adult relative, went to live with a married daughter. This change was immensely significant for the man's social horizons, for his home could be filled with people with whom only his wife had real bonds. A female-based kinship network—which we reflect to the present day in assuming, against most of Western history, that it is normal to honor a wife's ties to her relatives over a husband's to his—clearly reduced the effective authority of the husband in the household. The clan no longer belonged to the male, if it ever had. There is no need to suggest a great deal of explicit strife over this. If jokes reveal some tension, the change was in many respects almost unperceived. But it added to the gap between lingering patriarchalism and social reality.

Most important of all was the growing tension between fathers and sons, for this relationship lay at the heart of successful patriarchalism. Working-class fathers did preserve something of the older pattern when they could arrange jobs for their sons and direct their early training. Middle-class fathers still had the hold of property or, more commonly, support for higher education over their offspring. Papa could still be boss, and the nineteenth century offered an array of brutal fathers and benign authoritarians. It was not hard for a son to see his father's worldly achievements as a clear model, against the prosaic domestic tasks of his mother; hence an autobiography such as John Stuart Mill's, which focuses on his father's educational role and makes a single, demeaning reference to his mother. Overall, however, relationships between sons and fathers deteriorated from about 1750 onward, reaching their nadir around 1900. A survey of literary autobiographies—not a conclusive form of evidence but the best we have to date—traces growing hostility to fathers (and attachment to mothers) throughout this crucial period.[27] Too many fathers were asserting authority that they no longer really possessed. Too many sons could blame their fathers for providing inadequate patrimony, for acrimony roughly paralleled growth in family size and eased only a generation or two after family size diminished. The father who asserted a dominance that was not compensated by the prospect of economic security really courted tension with his sons. Working away from home, the father was an intermittent boss and authority model at best, at least until a boy reached working age himself. The sense that the younger generation was out of hand, defiant—a staple lament of industrial society since the early nineteenth century—was initially a reflection of a patriarchalism that was still expected, perhaps by sons as well as fathers, but which no longer worked.[28] When, as was the case from 1850 to 1900, sons were typically better educated than fathers, tensions could be exacerbated. The son who pulled up stakes or refused to follow the father's career was all too familiar. More common still was a strained relationship, in which ties were retained but with a feeling on both sides that something was wrong.

Women as well as men had dilemmas during the first decades of industrialization. Most men coped without feeling themselves complete failures. But there was a male dilemma, involving an effort to preserve too many aspects of the traditional definition of manhood, an unwillingness to rethink this aspect of self-definition in what were in fact radically new circumstances. Enough elements of the traditional gender role seemed to function, including patriarchalism, or even to be essential, such as the male association with work, that men were tempted to measure themselves against standards of masculinity that could not fully apply. To the extent that a masculinity recognizable in custom could be preserved, it could be a real comfort, not necessarily to men alone, in an otherwise changing world. But the gaps, beginning with the near impossibility of being a real man at work and a real man in the family simultaneously, were troubling. They might lead to complaints about the world being out of whack, about the younger generation, uppity women,[29] or machines. And this could lead men to a sense of failure.

It is not surprising, in this situation, that the definition of manhood tended to rigidify for a time. It was too vulnerable to challenge in practice to be very flexible in theory. The unmanly man was detested at least as vehemently in the nineteenth century as before. Homosexuality, increasingly shorn of religious proscription, became a mental illness; there was little relaxation against it in community custom. Hostility toward men who opted to become poets or artists increased, though a larger number of men could now choose these roles. In middle-class tirades against bohemianism, a host of male anxieties were expressed: envy of men who did not seem to accept a full, manly responsibility for proper breadwinning; concern that one's sons, in an age when paternal authority seemed to count for less, might slip away toward essentially feminine roles; a concern that manhood itself might be eroded if beauty or sensuality replaced tough realism. In its relaxation of community controls, the nineteenth century provided more outlets in fact for diverse male behavior than had been possible for the general run of men in preindustrial society. But this only increased the rigor with which most men, in working class and middle class alike, held to basic notions of what a real man should be.[30]

For a time at least the option of being a gentle man, always a subordinate theme in Western culture, lost much of its viability. Romanticism gave some currency to the tearful, aesthetic man, but the consumers of this kind of romanticism turned out to be disproportionately women (supplemented by some of the dreaded bohemians). Moreover, the importance of Christianity to males declined, in two senses. Exposed to a competitive, acquisitive economic world and, often, to a secular education, many men lost an active religious sense. Male recruitment to the clergy declined. In many villages (France is a classic if extreme case), and even more in working-class communities, regular church attendance was left to women.[31] And as the practice of religion fell more into women's hands—part of a new family division of labor, in one sense—so it could become more feminized and still less relevant to men's definitions of manliness. The image of God the father lost ground. Female saints won a new vogue in many Catholic countries, and the worship of Mary increased even more. Protestantism softened. Its churches became filled with songs and with flowers, the latter arranged by the women. The view of death itself softened, as women gained or were forced to take new responsibility for mortality.[32] Much of this was all to the good. Death, beginning with infant death, became less a matter of God's stern will to be endured than something to be lamented, wept over, ultimately combatted. More than men, women proved ready to submit human frailty to medical treatment, and from 1850 onward hospitals and doctors gained a disproportionate number of patients from the female population and those in female charge.[33] Ultimately, men themselves might be softened by a religion defined in more emotional terms or a new sympathy for illness and death. Through most of the nineteenth century, however, the image of manhood did not keep pace with these developments and may even have been rigidified by them, for gentleness—a sense of yielding to emotion and a sensitivity to the emotions of others—was defined more completely as a female specialty than ever before.

There were some unashamed weepers and esthetes among nineteenth-century men. But the "soft" men were not those who found favor among the general society. The male heroes were the unflinching captains of industry, the warriors, the frontiersmen, or even the two-fisted missionaries. These were the subjects of boys' books and the stuff of many men's dreams. For men, the nineteenth century, effectively launched and ended by major wars, was a militant, indeed military century. A greater percentage of men served in the military, even in peacetime, than ever before. To be sure, many a middle-class boy, as conscription spread after 1870, escaped his service, but this was a matter of common sense, not a defiance of military virtues in theory. The middle class could, in fact, wax rhapsodic about wars that other people fought, from the Crimea to 1914, and middle-class schools evolved elaborate military drills for the boys.[34] As for workers, their fondest memories might be of that period of military service that took them out of their rut and gave them a rigidly masculine society. Such was the opinion of many a German socialist, despite the party's hostility to the army.[35] Military virtues, precisely because they were not tested too often by actual combat, found little challenge. Scouting, disciplined education, and finally sports would serve to teach boys the aggressive instincts in a world that could too easily go soft.[36] The gentle man might easily wonder if something was wrong with him, if he did not fit the mold, and so seek to toughen himself or just abandon the pretense of being a real man among men.[37]

What tended to happen, in the first response to the new industrial society, was a polarization between male and female virtues corresponding to the increasing division of men's and women's work and family life. This was not a "battle of the sexes," nor a formation of two really separate cultures, which would have constituted a major departure from the ambiguous Western tradition of gender. But there was a sense that men and women were different, if only because they both faced new circumstances in which each sought to define gender rather rigorously lest all the criteria for self be lost. The image of the American frontier, spread so widely in popular literature, was an extreme but pervasive case in point, and we know it because we celebrate it still.

Many of the early stories issuing from the West described the latter as a man's place, full of danger, in which a woman would be at worst a nuisance, at best (as in the tales of the thrice-married Davy Crockett) an outlet for crude sexual vitality.[38] Other literature, including that of the women's magazines, stressed the maleness as well, but by the same token the need for the special virtues of women, to sooth and to civilize. (And to do the housework: one pioneer woman wrote of the impatience of men on the trail with household tasks. "It was really amusing to see the men stand in the river and wash their clothes—they all acted awkward, especially when wringing.") The tales of Daniel Boone emphasized the taming qualities of women, as Boone turned from a crude wilderness fighter into a model husband gingerly acquainted with the virtues of civilization. Southern stories offered a more chivalric motif of men ennobled by saving women from the savages. More simply, a woman's magazine lamented for a greedy gold-seeker who, abandoning his home, had "no fond arms wherein to rest his weary, aching head."

In the actual West, women might rough it along with the men, and even in imagery the Calamity Jane motif, the woman who could outman men, had some popularity. Real men and women might view their Western venture as almost a partnership. A Colorado pioneer noted that "there is not an enterprise that I have ever gone into that I have not talked the details over with my wife beforehand." But to many pioneers and to the larger number who merely read of the West, in Europe as well as the United States, the frontier seemed to write large the differences that seemed apparent even in more normal life between men and women. Although the industrial revolution was to bring a new level of civilization to North America and Europe, the qualities urged on men, perhaps indeed because of the novelty involved, harked back to the warriors and the hunters. In times of change, people found some comfort in invoking the most primitive qualities of the race.

The social reality of men and women was different, of course. But one of the ways to understand the legacy of the nineteenth century, the legacy of the first reactions to industrial society, is to realize that for a time men and women really did become more different than they had been in Western agricultural society (or were still, on the farms). Except in the family-run shops and crafts of the cities—and there were many of these—urban men and women spent an unprecedented amount of time apart from each other. Until the late nineteenth century, few business and professional offices had women working even in subordinate positions. Large branches of manufacturing involved no women at all, while in an industry like textiles men and women usually labored in different rooms. Sex separation in many schools reduced contact among the young. Recreation alone commonly provided the chance to unite men and women, but there was little time for it in early industrialization, and men often chose to take some of their leisure apart as well, developing their central definition of leisure in terms of maleness.

The simple fact was that, while both genders underwent some very common pressures—the cities, a commercial economy—their experiences differed substantially, and their perspectives diverged as well. Much more than women, men had to develop a new sense of time. This is a familiar theme in labor history, but its gender implications have not been assessed. In the factories and offices men were subjected to the clock, responsible for integrating small units of time into their daily lives. The worker had at most fifteen minutes' leeway from the first factory bell, or he would be locked out for half a day and fined as well as losing pay.[39] Most women's work followed older rhythms, punctuated only by brief contacts with man's time: getting the man up and off, and later getting children away to school. Women's time was the day, not the hour or minute and, in pregnancy, women had more contact than men with even a more basic flow of time.[40] The nineteenth century echoed traditional claims that women were closer to nature than men, a claim initially rooted in women's multitude of natural functions—from menstruation to childbirth—and men's greater exposure to their fellows outside the home, to a literally manmade world. Women's naturalness was not always held to be a vice, but inevitably the characterization had a rather patronizing air to it. Yet in the nineteenth century (not, it must be stressed, inevitably or forever), there was actually some truth to it. For better or worse, with varying degrees of success, men were plunged into a new level of social organization faster than women. Along with mother-in-law jokes, the early industrial revolution saw the basis for the long and only semi-humorous dispute between the sexes about punctuality. Men and women operated on different clocks.

They also operated according to different notions of work. Men gradually learned, many with great reluctance, that work was something to be done with considerable intensity. Middle-class businessmen set goals for themselves; factory workers had quotas set for them. In compensation, by the later nineteenth century, work was increasingly finite: do your job fast and you will have some nonwork time left over. Family work, in contrast, stretched endlessly through the day, but it could be accomplished with more self-determined breaks for rest or socializing. Men did not necessarily work harder than women, but they thought they did, for they could not see women putting in the intensity that they associated with work. Women did not necessarily work harder than men, but they thought they did, as they saw men's work terminate when theirs never seemed to.

The industrial revolution created or exacerbated other differences. Although the origins stretched into the eighteenth century, it was in the nineteenth century that women began to outlive men in the Western world. Their standard of living was typically lower, particularly insofar as men ate better, getting more protein (but also fat). But their less stressful and physically dangerous work, lower levels of drinking (and, some male doctors claimed, their slight ambition, their absence of passions other than love, or their tendency to talk more which preserved their interest in the little things of life; doctors found it more than a bit perplexing that the weaker sex lived longer)[41] gave them longevity gains that men could not match. Women's suicide rate was lower (not new, this, but a difference that increased in the nineteenth and twentieth centuries as the female rate increased only slowly).[42] Their willingness to admit illness and, gradually, to seek care for it was probably greater. After 1850 or so, the reduction in birth rate was also a vital female health gain. Men perceived the difference, although it is not clear that they resented it; by the 1890s workers argued directly that their wives would live longer than they as they sought support for widows.

Not all the new differences between men and women created tension, but they did reinforce the sense of gender distinction. Men's increasing size (their feet, particularly, grew faster than women's) may also have served to emphasize the distinction between the sexes. The early industrial revolution, in sum, calling men and women to rather different functions, created gender distinctions more noticeable than those that had prevailed in Western agricultural society.

Some of these differences roused acrimony. All tended to solidify men's definitions of themselves. In theory, they need not have had this effect. Women's greater longevity, for example, might logically have caused men to pause, to seek to imitate women's greater adaptability to industrial life. But in the nineteenth century this argument, never even put forward, would have made no sense. (It is being advanced today, but still with uncertain result.) For a man had to do what he had to do. The need to accept stress and danger for economic survival was at the base of this attitude, but from it flowed the need not to fail in the role of provider. A woman's gentle urgings to slow up, often modified by admiration for male energy and dependence on male earnings, stood little chance against a man's fear of being embarrassed before other men, indeed before himself. Men in the mass were not work- or risk-crazed. They sought to humanize their pace of work, and only a few actively sought the perils of the raw frontier or outright military combat. Nevertheless, underlying manhood in the nineteenth century was a perception that had some contact with reality, that men were a different breed; and, it was easy to add, different by nature (and it was tempting to add, nobler).

As some real differences increased, men's need of women if anything increased also. There was a strange anomaly in nineteenth-century maleness that must be mentioned even if its implications are not fully clear. As rarely before in agricultural society, men were raised by women. This was one of the inter-gender contacts that did increase. Few observers perceived mothering as a threat to manliness during most of the nineteenth century. Fathers were confident that their role, although infrequently presented, would shine through. At most the characteristic fear of a sissified boy, which remains to this day more active than concern about a female tomboy, might have been enhanced among men whose contacts with their young sons were limited. Mothering need not, in fact, have damaged masculinity. The manhood image of the nineteenth century could serve a useful model for mothers faced with unusual responsibility for raising male children. Contemporary studies suggest that mothers early seek some distance from male children, and raising them as proper little men constituted a good strategy for this, as well as one designed to win paternal approval.[43] But the boys raised by women to be men might have had unusual difficulty in internalizing their role. Not only their contacts but their emotional ties with their mothers grew increasingly intense. Working-class autobiographies in Britain, for example, typically mention the father as a harsh figure, rarely but fearfully glimpsed; the mother, patient and kind, is clearly the beloved parent. The male role is always a somewhat fragile one, the product of a painful separation from mother and imitation of father. Is it brash to speculate that this normal difficulty was somewhat augmented in the first century of industrialization? Did some men insist on, even exaggerate, traditional virtues of manhood because they were unsure that they could otherwise identify themselves as proper men? Certainly the disparity between what men were telling boys to be, and the images available in actual infancy, increased.

The new patterns of mothering played a role in the newly-ardent quest of adult men for female companionship. Despite the fact that women were in important ways differentiating themselves from men—indeed, because of the attraction of a differentiated mate and the need for her special skills—the desire for union with a woman became more widespread than ever before in Western history. There were still good economic and status reasons to marry, now that the possibility itself was greater than before. Women had their own reasons for participating in the expanding marriage market. But men also found in marriage a return to the softness of mother, to the lulling dependence which almost unalloyed motherhood could produce. Or they hoped to find this return. Men's image of women stressed the quiet purity of the maternal woman. (Women, in contrast, were more likely to sense marriage as a vital psychic independence from the mother figure, which may account for their prolonged apparent satisfaction with the role thrust upon them.) The new need for the care of a loving woman was an important addition to the arsenal of nineteenth-century manhood. Men were quick to admit that only this support made the burdens of more traditional manhood, carried on in the strange world outside the home, endurable. As Horace Bushnell, the Congregational minister, put it: Americans need "a place of quiet, and some quiet minds, which the din of our public war never embroils . . . Let a little of the sweetness and purity . . . of life remain." "God made the woman to be a help for man."[44] This was no matter of mere rhetoric. By the mid-nineteenth century, a new pattern of male mortality had developed, in close relationship to marital status, which persists to the present day and which contrasted increasingly with female patterns. The married man lived longer than the widower or bachelor. (Married women lived longest also, but their advantage over spinsters and particularly widows decreased steadily.) Longevity differentials are no clear measure of happiness, but men's fate was increasingly tied to dependence on union with women.

To what extent did the nineteenth-century version of manhood depend not just on explicit differentiation from women but on putting women down? To what extent did the new emotional contact follow from a desire to use women as sounding boards for male superiority? In the nineteenth century, fearful doctors, particularly Americans, urged ovariotomies on women to rob them of their sexuality.[45] Male politicians long resisted the female drive for the vote. Union leaders and working men resisted female entry into the manufacturing labor force, while male professionals derided women's intellectual capacity. Some men, unsure of their own masculinity, undoubtedly tried to prove themselves against women. But the surgery-happy gynecologists were small in number. Few ovariotomies were actually performed, and most of them were intended to remove cysts that would otherwise have been fatal. Men were more notable for resistance to new female gains—the vote, new kinds of jobs—than for trying to squelch women's "normal" roles. In fact, the nineteenth-century image of femininity was in some ways (admittedly, not from the contemporary feminist viewpoint) a step up for women.[46] And some men—not all men, but not just superstars like John Stuart Mill—sponsored and/or tolerated legislation granting new rights to women, notably in the areas of marriage and property. The nineteenth century, in fact, was a period of considerable legal emancipation of women, and while we may see this emancipation as too slow, at least it cautions against any simple judgments about efforts to assert masculinity by attacking femininity.[47]

Yet there are some indications that most men preferred dependent women. A Hamburg businessman, visiting London in 1851, wrote with some satisfaction that his wife cried and then fainted when she lost sight of him in a crowd. It was nice to be needed. Most men probably would have found a swooning wife more burden than ornament, but it might still be pleasant to believe that women in general were subject to peculiar frailties, and certainly there was abundant popular literature around this theme.

But the image of the weak woman should not be pressed too far. Changes in the marriage patterns of the two genders raised some fascinating possibilities about the type of woman a man sought. Along with higher rates of marriage came an increasing gap between male and female ages at marriage. In preindustrial society men and women were usually about the same age at marriage, the man only slightly older. Only in the aristocracy was there any widespread incidence of a substantial age gap at first marriage (in all classes widowers might of course seek a younger wife for her strength and fecundity, a pattern that continued in the modern period). With industrialization there was less economic reason for age equality at marriage. Fewer marriages, though still a goodly number, involved the kind of dowry that a family needed extra years to amass, while a man still needed time to establish himself in work or business. In the middle class a young woman may have been something of a nuisance in the parental home, relatively functionless, so that there was a positive desire to marry her off quickly. Possibly young women developed a new interest in slightly older men beyond the purely economic. Granting that marriage age disparity was now socially acceptable, why did it develop in fact? Lower female marriage age (particularly noticeable in the working class) increased fecundity. In a period when children were valued for their work, a younger woman might be sought to maximize the number of children born. And from this the habit of seeking a younger wife took hold, to last into the present despite the decline in the family size. Possibly it is somehow natural, economic conditions permitting, to seek a young woman as representing unsullied beauty. But perhaps men consciously wanted a woman not too mature, not too formed as a character, so that to their male superiority would be added the superiority of age and experience. Certainly this could facilitate the role of patriarch, particularly in middle-class families where the new husband was frequently thirty or older.[48]

There are scattered signs of increased father-daughter affection in the nineteenth century as well, which could be related to the more important change in marital patterns. At the end of the century when women won new rights in divorce and over child custody, men fought (rarely, to be sure) only when daughters were involved.[49] This might reflect a healthy expansion of the circle of male affection, combined with the new tensions with sons. But just possibly it might suggest that, on the average, men liked to be able to associate femaleness with childlike qualities.

Was it harder to be a man in the nineteenth century than it had been before? Surrounded increasingly by relative strangers, deprived of the comfort of many community structures and customs, people needed to seek new identity. Heavy emphasis on gender traits was a key result. The same tendency fit the needs of growing institutions—the factories, the schools—which needed simple formulae to characterize people who were essentially strangers. Men could do this sort of work, boys should take this kind of curriculum. But there was little thorough or explicit rethinking of what it meant to be a man, for the whole point of manhood was to provide an anchor amid change. Yet it was unquestionably more difficult for men to fit anything like the traditional image. Many men adjusted with relative ease, but there was a self-conscious assertiveness about nineteenth-century masculinity that deserves notice. A good bit of masculinity was vicarious now, the male bosom swelled with pride in reading about a frontier hero or a distant victory over some dusky tribe.

Yet nineteenth-century masculinity was logical and in many ways serviceable. Our contemporary, twentieth-century assessment is taking place in an altered setting which it would have been impossible for masses of men or women in the nineteenth century to anticipate. And we have been dealing in this chapter extensively with images that formed part of the reality of manhood in industrial society but not the whole of it. Behavior patterns need to be examined more precisely. They will reflect, not surprisingly, considerable diversity and also efforts, particularly in the later nineteenth century, to modify the criteria of manhood in practice.

The nineteenth-century middle class moved somewhat erratically toward a redefinition of masculinity itself, in part because men and women had not formed different cultures. The ambiguous Western tradition that posited some ultimate if incomplete moral equality retained a hold. But it was harder, in 1900, for the genders to understand each other than it had been a century or so before. Convenient images of differentiation had too great a sway, and women, including women who struggled for new rights against male opposition, held them just as firmly as men did. The first round of feminism, which was rather narrow in its demands compared to the contemporary wave, challenged positions over which many men thought they had but a tenuous hold. The second round risks asking for things that most men do not think they have at all, most obviously in terms of power positions and work satisfactions. None of this refutes the justice of feminist goals, but it does emphasize the difficulty of dialogue between the sexes. This, the partial but definite separation of male and female values and lifestyles, is what has fueled the controversy over contemporary manhood. Indeed, if men had not found it so difficult to convince themselves that they were measuring up to those prowesses that really distinguished the masculine from the feminine, they might not be subject to questioning at all.

4. The Emergence of the Working-Class Man

John Henry he could hammer
He could whistle, he could sing.
Every morning, went up on the mountain
Just to hear his hammer ring, lord, lord,
Just to hear his hammer ring.

John Henry said to the captain,
"Well a man ain't nothing but a man.
And before I'd let that steam drill beat me down,
I'd die with my hammer in my hand, lord lord,
I'd die with my hammer in my hand."

John Henry was hammerin' on the mountain,
An' his hammer was strikin' fire,
He drove so hard till he broke his pore heart
An' he laid down his hammer an' he died, lord lord,
He laid down his hammer an' he died.

Working-class manhood involved substantial contact with masculine traditions of physical prowess and grouping. It is hard to resist the notion that it was a more fundamental form of manhood than that of the office-working middle class. Though the middle class might lament and exaggerate the excesses of working men, a certain envy and understanding often accompanied their scorn. If males in the working class had no easier time than the rest of male society in living up to the criteria of manhood, they had perhaps a clearer, more elementary notion of what that manhood was. The working-class definition of manhood has proved extremely persistent; it has met real needs. The world of the working man remains distinct from that of working-class women and middle-class people of both genders, and the basic framework for this was set in the first generations of industrialization.

With the disruption of traditional agriculture and artisan manufacturing, stemming from population growth and incipient industrialization as early as the late eighteenth century throughout much of Western Europe and North America, the working class emerged as the first group with a perceived need to adapt masculinity to a new style of life. The class was by definition propertyless or nearly so. As its numbers soared, so also did the need to find male identity by means other than even the modest patriarchal style of a peasant smallholder or artisan master. Propertylessness also meant subjection to the direction of others; working men were trying to preserve a gender identity while being bossed by other men. There was also the threat from machines which reduced skill and raw strength as badges of manhood; John Henry died rather than surrender his masculinity. Workers also faced acute problems in controlling their sons and shaping a male identity across generations without property as a link and with rapid changes in skill requirements. But while the conventional canons of the gender were disrupted for the working class, the idea of gender most definitely was not. The disruption itself helped prompt workers to assert masculinity in the strongest possible terms in the areas that remained open to them. While the challenge of industrialization was the most obvious spur, there were new opportunities to gain a definite sense of manhood, as in the area of sexuality. Essential divisions of labor within the family muted any possibility that the working class would respond to the challenges to male canons by reducing the importance of proving one was a man.

Elements of working-class manhood thus developed early in the nineteenth century, and they have proved extremely persistent. They were invoked anew amid the second great wave of technological change, and accompanying disruption of skill, in the late nineteenth century. Important aspects indeed persist to the present day, though the style of working men as fathers and husbands, laborers and drinkers, has been modified since the end of World War II. We trace, then, more than a century of the evolution and reassertion of a major type of the modern man, that reached full flower in the last third of the nineteenth century. We are, furthermore, dealing with a male type that, in broad outline, arose in response to industrialization throughout the Western world. This type was a bit more prone to fighting in America or England than in France, sports-minded somewhat later in Germany than in England, and in all regions attached to different specific customs, particularly in use of leisure time. But this Western working man was identifiable across national lines because he was shaped by broadly common pressures.

There are three dangers in attempting a characterization of the working class male. These men had their own individual styles, and we cannot pretend to convey this variety. Some were tender, some brutal. Some loved their wives and children, others beat them (sometimes, perhaps, while loving them but simply feeling the need to vent frustration somehow). Some dreamed wild artistic visions at work; some became poets. More, perhaps, thought about sex and football and a beer after work. In trying to capture a style of working-class manhood we inevitably do injustice to individuality. But the style was important in suggesting main lines of behavior and values that even very diverse individuals would be aware of. Working-class manhood had a rigid quality about it, and those who did not live up to the image would usually feel alienated from their peers.

One must also avoid the temptation to patronize. I find the working-class style of manhood understandable and admirably direct, but ever since adolescence I have always been a bit frightened by its physicalness, and I find the main lines of workers' manhood a bit dull and depressing. Hence a judgmental tone is here that I find best to state frankly rather than to gloss over. As noted, working-class masculinity is both comprehensible and durable. I find it possible to hope, nevertheless, that it will change, if only as manual labor itself is rendered increasingly obsolete.[1]

The final danger involves what is in a way a patronizing approach of another sort. Some historians and sociologists so want the working class to be the fount of virtue that they resent any criticism of it. The working-class male a sexist? Nonsense. Look at occasion X, when working men and women banded together in harmony. See how the socialists defended the rights of women and defend them still. But working-class masculinity, in fact, depended, and still depends quite heavily, on what we now term sexism. This is entirely explainable. One can argue that capitalism itself imposes gender distinctions (or, better, since the distinctions were not new, elaborates them). I rather think that the nature of industrial labor, regardless of precise economic system, is at the root of worker maleness, but the geographical scope of this essay does not allow full assessment of this point. Working men did try to use their gender not only to defend their jobs but to form their basic definition of self. Sometimes they were so pleased at being men that they neglected opportunities to protest industrial life in the name of class interest. Certainly they helped create a distinctive and, again, not entirely attractive life-style for women, although they were pushed to this by forces over which they had no control.

Working-class males lacked a definitive rite of passage to manhood. A good many of the efforts of young men—which set the tone for manhood in general—can be seen as an attempt to create one. There was every desire to become a man quickly. Manhood meant authority. Men were people who bossed children at work and sometimes beat them; they were schoolteachers and policemen who also occasionally beat them; they were, above all, fathers who at times physically disciplined their children. And yet men, particularly in the years of their offspring's infancy, were not around very much. Except among craftsmen in traditional centers, the working-class father was normally absent.[2] It was difficult to figure out what he—which is to say one's future self—was like. But there was no question that the boy was to become a man. Working-class culture was intolerant of the sissy, the dreamer, and especially the homosexual, not merely because they lacked the toughness necessary for survival but also because they challenged the values essential to male identity in a class regularly subjected to the authority of others. If some families encouraged bright boys to think of rising to nonmanual work, more typically the attitude—not unkindly but quite realistic as well as customary—was: What's good enough for dad is good enough for the boy.[3] The father, though frequently absent from home, was a vivid authority figure. He might use violence against his children, particularly his sons, to substitute for other patriarchal controls that were beyond his reach. More commonly, he simply came home tired and, without intending to, lashed out against an unruly boy with words or fists.[4] Sons resented this, but most of them hoped for little more than the chance to become authoritarian in their turn.

Working-class boys could, of course, strike out on their own in adolescence. They were not nearly so closely bound to home as their preindustrial counterparts had been.[5] In good times a youth in his late teens could earn more than enough to support himself. But after the first disruptive decades of migration to the cities relatively few working-class boys took such a lonely path; in this sense working-class culture stabilized considerably after 1870 or so. Now the working boys delayed full economic independence by living at home until marriage. Or, married rather young and without enough savings to set up a proper household, they substituted one dependence for another and went to live with the wife's parents. Typically they went into the same kind of work as their fathers, often the same company, unless prevented by a declining economy. In some working-class communities there were few job alternatives. Mining villages were a case in point, where boys, terrified yet fascinated by the mines, had no other work choice without the more difficult decision to leave home and community.

A father's influence helped assure a good start in work. Trade unions in both factories and the crafts fought vigorously to assure preference for hiring sons of the members, and usually employers were quite willing to agree in the interests of labor force stability. By 1900 up to 95 percent of all miners' sons followed their fathers. The same was true of up to 70 percent of all weavers, an occupation that was losing its vitality. Among German workers able to explain why they took the work they did, parental guidance, which undoubtedly meant paternal prompting in most cases, was the leading response.[6] Frequently a boy was hired by his father in the first place. Because they were home so little but eager to assume patriarchal responsibilities (and of course to add to family income), factory workers directly hired and trained their own sons more often than traditional artisans had done; economic benefit and confirmation of the father's manhood here went hand in hand. But this system merely increased the impatient dependence of boys themselves. Worker fathers could be notoriously tough on their son/aides. Whole trade-union movements, as among British metallurgical workers, were bent on keeping the sons in line, sometimes preventing independent protest or organization of any sort.[7]

Economically dependent, young workers cast about for ways to assert their manhood. The ultimate dilemma was that they never really could. They might leave home, set up their own household and boss it in turn, have their own sons to order around, but they could rarely aspire to property or to the power to make independent decisions. They were always someone else's creature. The final fruit of manhood would always escape them. Young workers probably sensed this. They must have been stirred by the anomaly of their tough father taking orders in his turn, often forced to drag back to a job that he did not like. There had to be something else in manhood, something else to prove that one had made it.

A vigorous subculture developed among working-class male youth, designed to prove masculinity through fighting, wenching, and sometimes drinking. ("When I was eighteen I knew it took four things to be a man; fight, work, screw and booze.") When the son first went with his father to the neighborhood bar or first got drunk with his pals, was he then considered a man? Or was it when he had his first woman? Fighting, which was less conclusive, was common in the schoolyards or even at work. Young workers were not all brawlers, just as many did not drink, but the successful fighter, like the wild drunk, was respected. As laws about juvenile behavior became more rigorous in the later nineteenth century (a product of middle-class uneasiness about youth in general and the working class in particular), the rituals of young working-class men often brought them up against the authority of the law. By the twentieth century, as many as half of them might be arrested, as in Britain, for minor acts of violence or theft.[8]

The lower classes had always given young men some leeway. Villages offered adolescents chances to fight, even to commit certain kinds of vandalism. Young journeymen took a few years to wander from city to city, free from adult responsibility, not infrequently engaging in one of the otherwise senseless gang brawls that still marked the life of construction workers or dockers into the nineteenth century.[9] Outside the controls of village or guild, there was a potentially unrestrained quality to the strivings of young men. Youthful hooliganism could become serious crime; bouts of drinking might lead to lifelong alcoholism.

Youthful sexuality was the clearest addition to the roster of manly attributes. There is no question that heterosexual activity among young working-class men increased from the late eighteenth century, in the countryside but even more in the cities. Rates of illegitimate births rose from about 1780 until 1870; this phenomenon was almost entirely restricted to the propertyless classes. So did rates of conceptions before marriage (prebridal pregnancies) and so, as we have noted, did the rate of youthful marriages.[10]

Young people were freer from parental and community control when they worked away from home. Living in a large city, even dealing with strangers in a village market economy, they had contact with more potential sexual partners. This, along with improved diets, pressed the age of puberty down among men and women alike. Eighteenth-century boys' choir directors noted despairingly that their charges' voices were beginning to change by age sixteen or earlier, the first step in a long process that still continues. The sense, however inaccurate, that children were now an economic asset, part of working-class culture until the later nineteenth century, removed a traditional barrier to early and frequent sexual activity. There was a vague belief that sexual pleasure had won new public acceptance; some governments, interested in encouraging population growth, did remove laws against fornication. Around 1810, a Bavarian girl explained why she had a number of bastards by simply saying: "It's OK to make babies, the king has OK'd it."[11] For many men and women, making babies was fun, and surely sexual pleasure seemed necessary, as well as socially acceptable, to compensate for some of the uncertainties and hardships of growing up in the new industrial society.

Some historians have argued that the new sexuality of young people in the lower classes reflected a change primarily in the behavior and values of women. They see young men rather as ever lustful, ready to pounce at a moment's notice. What was novel, in this view, was the fact that women began to define themselves in terms of sensual pleasure. Popular sex began to shift away not only from the purely procreative but from the unimaginative, animal-like approach. Sexual emancipation, a key to women's emancipation that permitted a new individuality in pleasure-seeking, began first with the workers.[12]

There are several problems with this interpretation, apart from a lack of much evidence. Male sexuality has not been a constant. It undoubtedly increased in the eighteenth and nineteenth centuries, as the drop in the age of puberty suggests. And, as we begin to know more about working-class sexuality in the twentieth century, we find that it is not often very imaginative, and that many women do not derive much physical pleasure from it. It is more likely that while female consent to early sexual activity increased in the working class, for good female reasons, young males saw it mainly as a means of quick satisfaction and demonstration of prowess. Certainly the pervasive image was of a good stud, conquering hosts of women and taking his pleasure quickly. Assuring the partner's satisfaction was not required, although if she were capable of a quick orgasm it would certainly be all right. The sexy girl was the available girl, possibly promiscuous, possibly ready to do interesting things for men that both gave them pleasure and enhanced their sense of dominance (unilateral oral sex). The fact that men usually took sexual partners the same age or younger than they were, when the male sexual appetite exceeded the female appetite, might promote a lack of concern for mutuality.

This observation, it must be noted, is to a considerable degree speculative.[13] It makes sense as it follows from the need to find new outlets to demonstrate masculinity. It does not preclude some pleasure-seeking and pleasure-finding working-class women. But at the other extreme it fits also the working-class girl who used sex to support herself, the occasional whore. Girls in the textile factories of Rheims, France, talked of sex for money as the fifth quarter of their working day.[14] Outright sexual assaults were not uncommon, though not of course confined to the working class.

The introduction of young men to sexual activity was often clumsy and embarrassing. Ten-year-old Moritz Bromme, in late nineteenth-century Germany, believed that the stork brought babies, but later learned "how people are made" from an apprentice who had watched his master and his wife in the bedroom he shared with them. Several of Moritz's friends, at age thirteen, smeared sap on their faces and pubic area to stimulate hair as a sign of "manliness," though Moritz himself hung back. Pornographic cards educated young workers. Others saw intercourse in the factories, or heard women taunted. (Women sometimes replied in kind: "Anna, can I take you out tonight?" "Yes, if you haven't messed your pants.")[15] One boy watched as older workers cheered while a man took a woman down in the factory yard and simulated intercourse, while the woman spit on him. A few were directly introduced to sex by older female workers or servant girls. Many masturbated but were ashamed or worried about the practice, which was as disapproved among workers as in the middle class; one worker decided to "become a Don Juan instead." Visits to prostitutes or sex resulting from dating initiated still others. A German farm hand, too poor to marry, began to spend his nights with his girlfriend, for "the bedroom window of my Dora was not obstructed by a nasty lattice."[16]

Impelled by their own budding sexuality and often by the urgings of their peers, young working-class men firmly integrated sexuality into the trappings of manhood. If shy, they were teased. If unsuccessful, they covered with boasting talk. For like most good examinations, the early sexual test of manhood was a delight to those who passed but mortification to others, complicating the very business of masculinity that it was supposed to ease. All the more reason to try to prove oneself against a woman whenever the chance arrived.

And it arrived most commonly in courtship. Young women participated in the new outburst of sexuality for a variety of reasons. Some were forced, some sought money, some gained direct physical pleasure or companionship and asked for no more, but most undoubtedly saw it as a way to achieve marriage. And here the working-class battle of the sexes began, increasingly ritualistically as the worst instability of urban life wore off in the later nineteenth century. The boy seeks sexual release, esteem among his peers, a sense of mastery. His joy is in the hunt. The girl might enjoy the hunt as well—working-class culture, exhibited for example in the British music halls around 1890, invariably touted courtship over the deceptions of marriage. But both parties recognized that the hunt had a trap. Some men escaped it by abandoning the pregnant woman; hence the rising illegitimacy rate until 1870. Others lived with woman and children for years before finally taking the plunge. Increasing numbers, however, married before the first baby was born. "If I hadn't got my 'bride' pregnant, I probably wouldn't have married for a long time."[18] In a British working-class novel, a couple dates for twenty-three months before the man, in "no hurry" to marry, found he could not honorably delay.[19] In some cases, particularly in the countryside or among workers of recent rural origin, there was a positive desire to make sure the woman was fertile, given the high valuation of children as economic assets and proofs of virility. New workers in the Daimler automobile plant talked of "not wanting to buy a pig in the poke."[20] More city-wise workers, knowing that children were a mixed blessing, yielded to necessity. They had to prove their maleness and they took the consequences.

With marriage, stereotypically, the most demanding tests of manhood ended. The dutiful worker-husband loosened his ties with the peer group, cut back his drinking, tamed his fighting. Real tension remained between the responsibilities of family and the tests of youth. In an English mining village, admittedly out of the mainstream in 1959, "where nothing compares to how well a man stands in the eyes of other men," fighting remained important among the married miners; a nonfighter might be liked, but he was a nobody. "Above all, the Dinlock collier regards himself as A Man, in every department of his life. The slightest traces of femininity, of softness . . . of sexual ambiguity, are ruthlessly rooted out, or suppressed." And when a good brawl was not available, the men lulled themselves in the bars with countless retellings of fist fights in the past. And their wives sat to the side, or stayed home.[21]

Drink remained, even more commonly, a solace for the adult male. In one poll, around 1900, a fifth of German miners said that drinking was indispensable to them, even though they came to work unhappily hung over on Monday. A German locksmith, earning good money and fond of his family, invariably took Monday off to get drunk.[22] A minority of older workers were alcoholics, their youthful enthusiasms taking them beyond the point of no return. This was however a sign of manly degradation, not manliness. In general older workers, though they might use drink, had neither the money nor the zest for frequent, competitive drinking. Sex remained an outlet. Almost certainly workers had sexual intercourse more frequently within marriage than their preindustrial peasant antecedents had done; some dallied outside marriage as well. But fatigue, fear of too many children (particularly before the late nineteenth-century development of artificial birth control devices), and possibly a wifely coldness resulting from a continued lack of mutuality could limit any continued sense of manliness through sexual prowess. The worker was increasingly thrown upon work and the broader features of family life to show that he was a man. In both, workers stuck as closely to tradition as their new economic situation, including propertylessness, allowed. They wanted to be men as their fathers had been (or as they thought they had been). The task was not easy.

Domineering fathers could sense the difficulties of controlling their children, though they could claim enough success to keep trying. More caring fathers, the kind that liked nothing better than to bring home a surprise gift for their daughters, had their own problems. If they aspired to see their children rise in society, they could easily be disappointed. Many a worker father planned to win his son an artisan's position, where a man could more easily control his destiny, only to find that the apprenticeship was too costly or the trade shrinking.[23] Success had its own threats, as when a son rose above his parents only to tolerate them uneasily. Even humbler aspirations were risky.

At the end of the nineteenth century, workers in many skilled occupations, fearful of new machine competition, saw their sons go into more prosperous factory jobs. Some complained of the boys' ingratitude, their heedless desire for a quick dollar. Others, granting the correctness of the choice, had to wonder about a world that would not grant their own work dignity and permanence, that would not allow it to be transmitted. Fathering was difficult for all social classes amid change, but workers suffered keenly because their goals, shaped by tradition, so easily outstripped their means.[24]

Siring children brought some satisfaction to most working males. Workers were slow to adopt artificial birth control, though most in the later years of female fertility undoubtedly reduced their rate of sexual intercourse. A twenty-nine-year-old German farm laborer stated in 1917 that he and his wife did not practice birth control. "My wife is far too stupid for that. She doesn't understand it, and wouldn't want it at all. I also don't want it. It's not the fashion by us. They do that in the city."[25] A few decades earlier other workers professed their ignorance of birth control devices. Condoms long seemed so strange to German workers that they called them "Parisian articles." A group of English workers around 1900 condemned birth control as "wicked and unnatural."[26] More positively, certain kinds of workers long seemed bent on associating large families with successful masculinity. The very poor in the cities sired many children, but here ignorance and habit supplemented any vigorous notions of masculinity. Among miners and construction workers—relatively well-paid men in highly physical occupations—birth rates also stayed high.[27]

The idea of children as an economic asset died hard. Some men doubtless enjoyed the emotional pleasures of conscientious fathering. But for many, the act of siring, the proof of potency, may have been the main thing. Yet birth control was, finally, a necessity; it developed widely in the working class in the final decades of the nineteenth century. Countless numbers of working women and workers' wives obtained abortions. As men cooperated, pressed by the expenses of a growing family—it is not clear which gender in the working class most commonly decided on birth control—they normally relied on withdrawal (*coitus interruptus*) or on the condom, for women were unwilling or unable to use the devices available to them. Was there psychic cost in this conversion? Did men feel unmanned as they gave up a proof of virility and economic success, particularly given the practices most commonly involved? Certainly, in contrast to the middle class, few worker-fathers produced any rationale for smaller families other than necessity.

If children were an uncertain resource for the family man, so in many respects were wives. A good bit has been written about romance replacing economics as the basis for the working-class marriage in the nineteenth century. The contrast is largely spurious. Economics declined as a criterion for mate selection, to be sure, and men and women both had greater freedom of choice. But that they married for love is uncertain. The male culture of the workers was not easily compatible with love in any event. Sexual attraction, yes; desire for a companion-partner, without question. But love as basis or result of marriage was probably as accidental as it had been in preindustrial society.[28]

Relationships between working men and their wives can be traced in three other areas: violence, budget, and division of labor. We have noted that the society-wide resistance to married women working outside the home had functional utility as well as traditional roots. Nevertheless, the intensity of working-class insistence, often amid great resulting poverty, was striking. For workers lacked the new middle-class ideology of unsullied woman and all-encompassing mother that could justify and grace woman in the home. Working-class wives may have put additional time into mothering in the nineteenth century, but this is not clear. Nor is it clear that men saw any merit in such a venture.

Many women did find compensatory labor at home, doing manufacturing chores and particularly taking in boarders (who, being male, could cause a great deal of domestic disruption on their own). Women spent much of their time serving as the family's consumer agent, seeking decent bargains for a meager budget. They, as well as their men, insisted that a woman's place was at home. Yet the definition was vitally important to the men. Pulling the wife out of the labor force was literally the first material goal beyond sheer subsistence for many laborers. Unskilled German workers in the 1890s, for example, insisted that their wives stop working when their income reached a bare one thousand marks a year.[29] Quite generally, only widows and wives of the drunk and disabled went out to work. A working wife was a disgrace to her husband, an admission of basic failure as a man. The horizons of working-class wives were limited far more than those of men; equal interests were not part of the normal marriage arrangement. Fundamental power and distinctiveness rested with the man alone, an unchallenged family breadwinner.

Studies of the poorest worker families in the nineteenth century suggested that men turned their earnings over to their wives for spending. In some cases rituals developed whereby the pay was transferred outdoors so the neighbors could see that the men were keeping nothing back.[30] Here was an important power for women, if slightly secondary, a real basis for independent decision-making. Here, too, was an important responsibility, for in turning over the pay the male felt that he had discharged his obligations. The wife was now expected to arrange for food, rent, clothing, even insurance money; when things did not go well, women were open to severe criticism. "I never interfere about anything, because I think it's your part to attend to the house, but it seems to me you don't manage things properly."[31] Acrimony of this sort, increasing after 1900 as inflation began a longterm rise, could be both unfair and unfortunate. But more important was typical male behavior when their earnings climbed above the subsistence level. Now men began to hold things back, keeping their wives on a fixed budget (even, on occasion, after inflation was underway) and leaving them ignorant of their real earnings. One English worker gave his wife about half his earnings; the rest was for his own spending. Another, earning fifty to sixty-eight shillings per week, gave his wife twenty-eight. Doubtless many men used part of their share to buy things for the family, but this would be at their discretion. Many were motivated by a desire to avoid pressure from their wives when earnings fluctuated, the source of many a quarrel and many an aspersion on their manhood. Nor did wives necessarily express resentment that they did not know what their husbands made. But they were kept in economic inferiority, failing to share fully in gains in working-class prosperity, and their economic role in the family declined. All of which made it more advantageous to be a man and easier to fulfill one's role of family breadwinner, insofar as expectations were kept down. As we will see, the margin, fragile as it usually was, typically went for other manly things.[32]

Working-class marital relations could easily be punctuated by violence. Wives did not always live up to their functions; some bought new clothes for themselves instead of paying the rent. Many wives were shrewish. German workers complained that they came home exhausted and then were expected to spend the evening listening to a rehash of their wives' daily battles with the neighbors. One wife regularly berated her husband for having "given" her too many babies.[33] Many insulted and taunted their husbands for inadequacies real or imagined. Male workers frequently saw violence as a proper retort; a beating was the wife's fault, not theirs, for insubordination was not to be tolerated. "I found my wife was out when I returned home after closing hours, so when she did come in, I knocked her down; surely a man can do a thing like that to his wife."[34] Besides expressing the frustrations of the male role, violence suggested the insecurity of men in claiming dominance over their women. Working-class wives, aided by female kin, had carved out something of their own sphere of activity within the limits of the home, and husbands needed to see women's inferiority as a support for their own fragile manhood. Wife-beating was not necessarily frequent—we have no way of documenting its incidence—but it was usually accepted in working-class culture. It seems to have declined, in London at least, in the later nineteenth century. Workers, more accustomed to industrial life, may have become less actively frustrated. Higher earnings, even if not fairly distributed, helped wives meet their own housekeeping expectations and so reduced their complaints. Possibly women themselves became more passive, adjusting to the claims of working-class masculinity.

It is of course easy to moralize about husband-wife relations in the nineteenth-century working class. Middle-class observers were aghast at reports of wife-beating; this was not their idea of masculinity. Wife beating was "unmanly," violating "every instinct of human nature."[35] But there are various ways of putting women down; the working-class approach, by no means universal within the class itself, was simply quite direct. It is understandable that men sought to use their physical and economic superiority to claim power in the home that they lacked on the job.

The results of the attempt to dominate women are somewhat ambiguous. If

English wives courted beatings less often by 1900, they may have become sloppier housekeepers, expressing resentments in this way.[36] Gradually, too, from 1890 or 1900 onward, the percentage of married women working outside the home began to inch upwards. New inflationary pressures played a role here. So did compelling changes in working-class consumption expectations. At some point a desire for a bit more living space could conquer the need to keep women in the home. Some married women actively sought work as an antidote to boredom. Some men were doubtless sufficiently secure to assimilate the shift in roles, even to approve. But many must have wondered where they had gone wrong, and as the trend continued in the 1920s and 1930s, relationships within the family began to shift.

Until that point, however, men could feel somewhat satisfied with their domestic power. But men were claiming to rule a roost which they had little time for. Workers polled about what they thought about on the job rarely mentioned either family joys or family concerns.[37] Unhappy family life might drag a worker down, but unhappiness at work would be more likely to do so. While families might feel the impact of fatigue and frustration at work, when the man came home, they rarely provided the kind of solace that would keep a man feeling manly in a degrading work situation. There was, until well into the twentieth century, too little time left over for the family for it to serve as the principal, ongoing support to the male ego. Many a wife, dutifully deferential at the dinner table, really ran the show. She knew it, and so did her children, including the boys whose confusion about the claims and powers of manhood would carry over into their own adult relationships. So quite possibly, without admitting it, did the old man himself. Patriarchy, sometimes almost completely hollow, was too limited to assure the working man of his masculinity.

As a man's waking hours were filled mainly by work, so was his conception of his manhood after the courting and brawling days were over. Workers struggled to believe that they had a trade, and to assure the stability of this trade, for psychic as well as economic reasons. The crutch was insecure. Industrialization never destroyed skill, else the whole castle of worker masculinity would have crumbled. A large minority of urban workers could rightly claim mastery of an important skill in 1900, on the eve of the assembly line, and many unskilled workers were winning a slight upgrading into semiskilled ranks.[38] Long before this, however, workers had learned that the principles of industrialization were hostile to any stable skill. Artisans, with the advance of direct machine competition, realized that the idea of labor-intensive production was jeopardized and they struck out, though without fundamental success. The newer factory skills seemed more durable, but workers by the late nineteenth century faced erosion of these in turn as more automatic equipment reduced the need for highly trained personnel.

The question of what value workers, whether male or female, can find in modern industrial labor is a thorny one. We should be careful not to overemphasize a picture of degradation and despair. Printers, with a hoary tradition of skill and among the most articulate workers, were pressed around 1900 to convert to mechanical composing machines. They worried about the impact of the new technology on employment and pay, but they also feared that a reduction in skill would make their jobs less interesting, their training and so their self-indentification less distinctive. Yet convert they did, and reported no basic diminution in their job satisfaction. To be sure, they used only one hand rather than two, but because they were handling more material they were able to read more. The majority of workers worried more about the future erosion of skills than about present job alienation. Many were able to identify with new machines. Locomotive engineers, to use an extreme case, noted their sense of power as they rode their monsters through the countryside. In some cases, particularly when employment levels were high, workers even seemed unconcerned about a reduction in hours of work, so complete was their personal identification with their jobs. It proved difficult, for example, to convince metallurgical workers that a twelve-hour shift was inappropriate; these were big men, proud of their strength and ability to withstand heat, proud of their skill, bossing a host of younger male aides, and secure in their jobs. Even in the twentieth century, the age of assembly lines, the association of work with a sense of skill and mastery does not cease.[39]

Yet apart from worries about the future, identification of self with work became increasingly risky. The increasing size of companies brought not only more impersonal direction but also a new kind of direction, aimed at reducing the autonomy of skilled workers on the job. Supervisors, trained in the time and motion studies dubbed "scientific management," sought to make their human charges as machine-like as possible. Henry Ford's engineers specifically attempted to eliminate thought, for thought meant delay; workers should become creatures of endless, repeated motion. But industrial workers had to knuckle under, for many could see no alternative livelihood. They had to accept the fact that it was their bosses, not they, who determined what their work was, who in some instances tried to dictate every movement. How could a man believe himself a man in this setting?

The trends of industrial work raised specific difficulties for manhood. Particularly before seniority systems were established, skill levels decreased with age. Older workers, in the factories and in many crafts, found themselves downgraded, often by thirty-five or forty years of age, often pushed into the ranks of the unskilled at a time of life when the assertion of sheer physical masculinity was rapidly losing its joy. When this decline was associated with the disappearance of the pleasures of male youth, it was hard to avoid the conclusion that old age and even later middle age were basically emasculated stages of life.

Physical danger declined on the job with the introduction of more sophisticated equipment and safety devices. There were still appalling accidents, and problems of occupational health hazards often increased with the rise of chemical production. But increasingly, complaints centered on nervousness, not risk. The rapid pace of work, under unfeeling supervision, left many workers jangled at the end of a day, sometimes unable to sleep at night. Many workers attributed their snappishness in the family not to sheer fatigue but to tension. This was not of course a specifically male problem, but men who could accept physical risk could see nothing acceptably masculine about meeting nervousness and conquering it. Real men were not supposed to be nervous, yet now they were. It all added up to a feeling among many workers that job quality was deteriorating and that it was becoming less masculine.

Workers sensibly sought shorter hours, and increasingly they won them. But for men this involved the serious question of what a man was supposed to do when he was not working, given the interruption of any regular habit of leisure. More generally, workers began to adopt an instrumentalist attitude toward work, which involved a basic dismissal of any intrinsic work satisfaction, an acceptance of any changes in organization or technique that might be imposed, in favor of non-work rewards, notably pay and benefits.[40] A certain amount of instrumentalism is basic to any work; we support ourselves, and instrumentalism obviously appealed to a male desire to justify his life in breadwinner terms. But unquestionably instrumentalism was on the rise in the working class from the mid-nineteenth century onward. This meant that more and more men labored at jobs that at most indirectly, by their rewards, proved they were men. The jobs themselves might be actually degrading; many workers wanted women banned from jobsites because of this, like the miner who "did not want my wife to see me in the muck."[41] Or they might be neutral, even acceptable as a routine, but involving nothing positive toward a sense of self or a sense of manhood.

The breadwinner role was a safer bet than the skill role, and it was the only one available for the unskilled male. But it too was difficult. Economic slumps, illness, a host of personal or collective disasters called it into question; so might old age, with decreasing earnings; so might a working wife. Men were, of course, supposed to be the creatures who surmounted obstacles. Economic fluctuation was no novelty for manual laborers. As peasants, their forefathers had known crop failures with results more devastating than those that industrialization usually produced. Yet the urban worker pinned so much on his breadwinning and was so lacking in supplementary resources that failure in the breadwinning role became harder to accept than ever before. Unwillingness to accept sickness lest it interrupt work, a perverse pride in working under conditions of great physical and nervous difficulty, the total collapse of morale which could come when the breadwinning capacity broke down—all related to the intense association of the male self-image with the ability to support a family.[42] We know that workers were not, in the main, work addicts in the middle-class sense. They did not work to maximum intensity or try constantly to rise on some job mobility ladder (in part because they feared to jeopardize their breadwinning by overproducing or taking personal risks). And, of course, their clinging to work was an economic necessity, particularly as the family division of labor left no one else capable of providing prime support. Which is also why male workers found it so difficult to accept retirement, seeing it as a deprivation of economic manhood along with other, less reversible indignities of old age.[43]

Many workers protested. Working-class unrest rose in two waves in the nineteenth century. The first, culminating in western Europe in 1848, broadly attacked propertylessness and the increasing proletarianization and mechanization of artisanal labor. The second, more subtle, spanned the period 1890–1940. Along with the growing association of collective protest with the working class came an increasing link between protest and manhood.

By 1900 female participation in the manufacturing labor force was beginning slowly to increase. Still concentrated primarily in industries such as textiles and clothing and shoe manufacture, where it was in the main accepted if, even there, confined to the less skilled work, quite small numbers of women workers caused consternation in metalwork, printing and machine building, where more automatic equipment encouraged a search for cheap semi-skilled labor. Here was a convenient focus for grievances about threats to masculinity in work. "Another thing is women . . . there's thousands of 'em nowadays doin' work wot oughter be done by men."[44] Craft unions in many countries attempted to ignore women workers.[45] The neglect of women by organized labor added to the workingman's belief in female inferiority: women were too docile, too easily deceived, and the proof was that they resisted the unions.[46] Seizing on different judgments of work, male workers undoubtedly used women as scapegoats for broader problems in defending manhood at work. And male hostility was not uniform: socialist-inspired unions saw both ideological and practical sense in recruiting female members, though ideologists like August Bebel, in Germany, believed that in a proper society women's place was in the home.[47] Still, there was widespread resistance to women on the job that reinforced the association of maleness and work, except in the few branches of production where the influx of women was overwhelming. It also reinforced the male quality of working-class protest. Gender tensions at work reached a peak during and right after World War I, and the males statistically won out. Large numbers of women hired for manufacturing jobs during the labor-short war years, even then often kept away from the most favored male positions in a given industry, were dismissed. Yet could males really win, could they help but feel beleaguered when women could even consider, and be considered for, work that had once been the epitome of masculinity?[48]

The main point about masculinity and working-class protest, however, goes beyond male dominance of the leading protest form (quite disproportionate on a per capita basis of potential strikers by gender), or reluctance to organize women, or the outright attacks on women. Manhood was occasionally invoked by strikers directly, not against women but against basic features of industrial work. A German miner spoke of needing "conditions worthy of men." More revealingly, a group of British workers, agreeing not to return to work until some blackleg laborers were fired, explained that "this would be contrary to our manhood." A bookbinder on strike tells an employer trying to lure him back, "I am a man, sir."[49]

Many strikes were in fact intense expressions of male bonding. They derived often from men's camaraderie at work. Many small strikes embraced only those men who worked together in a single unit, often bursting forth when one of their number had been offended. The atmosphere of some strikes reinforced a pride in the grouping of men: the brave marching, the chanting, the fights with nonstrikers, the women watching (whether with pride or annoyance, watching). Even strike rates could reflect something of the masculine tone, for they were usually highest in industries like construction or mining that demonstrated other signs of intense manhood: an entirely male labor force, significant skill levels tied to physical strength, and a birth rate higher than the working-class average.[50]

Of course, neither bravery nor bonding was a male monopoly. If women played a supportive role in many of the big miners' strikes, where clear gender roles did not prevent and may indeed have enhanced a family unity in protest, in other cases women lashed out, by themselves or with their men, against huge odds. Particularly in the United States, the labor movement soon had its equivalents of the Calamity Janes of the West, who could march and fight and even dynamite with the best of men, as well as more sedate and ordinary women. Men's conditions could be defended only if women's conditions were not allowed to sink too low, and so attacks on women workers or a willingness to allow developments in the female occupations (the rapid technological change in spinning, for example, compared to male weaving) that would have been resisted in the male, gradually waned. If sometimes attempts to win equality for women barely masked a desire to overprice them, to eliminate their comparative advantage and return them to their homes, at least the masculine front had been breached. French strike leaders early in the twentieth century regarded the wife as the worst enemy of protest. Her interest, so they thought, was to see the husband return to work and provide the family budget once again. Hence strikes most commonly faltered on Mondays, after wives had been with their husbands during the customary family day. The remedy? Involve the wives. Hence male marches gave way to family picnics, particularly on Sundays. As in work itself, the masculine prerogatives in protest steadily diluted.[51]

The tide of protest from the late nineteenth century onward proved incapable of defending manhood at work. The grievances that were hardest to win were those involving efforts to win a greater decision-making role or, more commonly, simply to attack an abusive supervisor or to defend traditional skill levels or reduce nervous tension at work. The labor movement itself in practice, regardless of professed ideology, turned increasingly to instrumental demands that united larger numbers of workers and that were easier to win. So strikers fought for shorter hours, which actually tended to increase the intensity of work itself, and above all for higher pay. The labor movement inevitably became more formally organized, which raised additional problems for the worker who was a real man. For "real men" were those who worked with their hands, who sweated, not the pencil-pushers who began taking over the unions and the labor parties. The labor movement had to damp down the spontaneity of protest and to go beyond small-group bonding of men if real advances were to be made, but in the process they could add to the uncertainty of working-class manhood.[52]

Here was an increasing dilemma for workers around 1900. Work was not satisfactory in terms of male criteria, not hopeless usually but a declining resource. The logical reaction, a new degree of instrumentalism, required the development of male criteria off the job. The family was important but it raised its own problems. Male authority, strong in theory, might prove hollow if exercised too often. Tensions with sons and sometimes with wives played a role, but more important was the fact that, during the first century of industrialization, the family had come so heavily under female influence. The worker went home to a crowded apartment filled, not uncommonly, with his in-laws. And so he went out again, and sought to establish his manhood somewhere else.

The working class steadily elaborated a male-based recreational pattern. The chief reason for the growing budget manipulation by working-class husbands was to provide differential resources for leisure. Male workers called heavily upon tradition as a basis for their use of leisure time, for the village and guild past had precedents for male games. Nonaggressive physical contact among males was, to be sure, largely avoided now. The all-male dances, like the English morris dance, usually died as the villages died and as purely traditional recreational patterns were rooted out during the early industrial revolution. Only a high level of ethnic consciousness, as among Greek-Americans, has preserved even a trace of what was once a common male expression. The increased importance of heterosexual prowess as a criterion for manhood was undoubtedly the prime factor in converting the dance almost entirely to courtship purposes for men.[53]

Working men drank together. So had village men, though, being poorer and less pressed, they drank less often and usually with beverages lower in alcoholic content. A few of the bars that spread so widely with industrialization allowed wives and husbands to drink together. Textile families in Lille were known in the 1830s for their habit of doping the children with laudanum, a working-class babysitter, so that the parents could go off to the neighborhood bar.[54] Later in the nineteenth century, young men were drawn to some of the fancy bars that sprang up in imitation of middle-class spots, where they could take a woman on a date. Generally, however, working men focused on a neighborhood tavern that was rigorously masculine, where men could drink, talk, and play cards or darts without distraction.[55]

Working men played ball together. Soccer, rugby, and football spread like wildfire among workers in the later nineteenth century, derived from traditional English games and spread to North America and the European continent. Miners in Wales by 1900 were organizing their week around soccer matches, and at the factories the young men even played during breaks from work. In ball playing, men could take pride in their physical prowess and skill, the very things that now seemed rather useless at the workplace, and they could do it in groups. Individual sports found less favor among workers, not only because of the greater cost involved. Bicycle riding, as it spread downward from the middle class, attracted bands of young working men when it served as a vehicle for recreation. Working-class sport obviously evoked basic features of the hunting tradition, usually with overtones of violence, as in the brutal working-class version of rugby in England, or in American football.[56]

Older men, accepting a spectator role, eagerly went off to the weekend football match or the races (including pigeon-racing) and enjoyed vicarious prowess and the company of the spectator group. Betting on the local club offered its own form of risk and competitiveness. (Working-class women often gambled as well, but separately and from the home, usually on numbers.) The maleness of spectatorship—even now so visible despite the efforts of the media, like labor unions before them, to bring the women in—was a vital product of the growth of working-class leisure. In sports, fathers and sons might develop shared interests—even the role model/apprenticeship link—that were being jeopardized in what work-oriented critics are still pleased to call the "real world." In fact, sports, enjoyed as either participant or spectator, increasingly became if not the real world, at least the best world, because they so clearly confirmed the male identity.

Not all leisure was male-centered, of course. The best forms of male leisure involved exertion and some expense and so, for one or both reasons, were less available to older workers than to younger. (Here too working-class culture failed to solve the problem of preserving manhood with age, although informed spectatorship was a partial solace.) Workers in Germany around 1900 listed gardening, family walks, and sleep as their favorite pastimes, though if candid they would have added drinking. Workers clearly did not shun women after courtship, and their leisure patterns reflected the need for family time and individual repose. There developed an attempt to balance personal and family leisure with male leisure. Belgian miners arguing for a five-day work week around 1908 insisted that they needed one day for sports and drinking and a second day with the family, to recover. Some admitted that they had long taken Monday off, to drink, after a day with the family but they preferred to reverse the order. Others noted that family demands had gone up, now that cheap railway excursions to the countryside were possible; they needed the extra time with their own kind. Legislation itself, increasingly setting all or part of Saturday aside, reflected the workers' battle for maleness.[57]

Working-class masculinity, by 1900 an elaborate if somewhat insecure entity, followed from tradition and from an initially sensible family division of labor. It was associated primarily with physical strength, which meant that satisfaction in manhood inevitably waned with age. It was pinned to economic attributes—skill, secure breadwinning—that were unreliable in the industrial economy, resulting in sources of anxiety as well. Perhaps most important, they were pinned to certain half-fictions about the male position in the family. Committed to maintaining distinctive gender roles, the working class need not be criticized unduly. It was hard to be a worker, and so it was hard to be a man. Male workers took up the most direct challenges of industrialization. Their lives were not necessarily harder than women's—they were usually better off materially, and could find greater interest in life—but their manhood was open to more challenge than was the womanhood of the working-class female. Women formed something of their own world, operating with effectiveness for themselves and for the class as a whole, but they were closer to their traditions and psychically more secure. Indeed it was precisely because men, too, tried to preserve customary gender values but in a much more novel setting, that their enterprise was riskier.

In the new conditions of industrialization, in fact, the working class came close to forming two gender cultures, a strategy which, as most non-Western experience suggests, can be quite successful. Certainly, the approach has been durable, if only because it tends to be self-perpetuating with sons, however angry with their fathers, imitating them; hence even contemporary working-class gender patterns reveal huge chunks of the past. The middle class evolved a different style during the nineteenth century. Its development is more important because the class is culturally dominant, and so capable of influencing workers in the long run, and because by the mid-twentieth century it was simply more numerous. Yet the middle-class male has moved in some of the same directions as the working man, and for similar reasons. He cannot in fact fail to recognize most of the working-class attributes as validly masculine, which produces interesting modifications of class stratification. (Workers, however, with their stress on physical labor, cannot necessarily identify the male qualities of brain work.) Middle-class man may be taught to deplore some traits of working-class manliness, but he can relate to their masculinity. (Only briefly in the nineteenth century did middle-class culture look on drinking prowess with unambiguous condemnation; blasts at, and exaggerations of, worker promiscuity were leavened with some frank envy at sexual expression unencumbered by responsibility.[58]) Middle-class man may indeed wonder if his own masculinity, insofar as it is somewhat different, is not also wanting. The public school experience, when not completely class-stratified, here can provide a vital test, for the more physical proofs of manhood seem much more compelling, and readier to hand, than masculine prowess at science and mathematics. The kinds who fight, play sports, work well with their hands, and then lead the class (or claim to) in sexual experience and drinking easily leave the middle-class boy uncertain. Even in later years, as a bar-hopper or a football-watcher or a father, middle-class and working-class males may share important features of self-definition. Gender prowess can easily cut across class boundaries.

But for all this, the middle-class boy and man were supposed to be different. The working-class legacy to manhood involved not only characteristics and values of workers themselves but also a standard, half-real, half-mythic, from which middle-class men in the nineteenth century tried to distance themselves. Recognizing worker maleness, more than a bit envious, middle-class men thought they had to carve out an equally masculine but admittedly more artificial image.

5. The Emergence of
the Middle-Class Man

As industrial society began to take shape in the early nineteenth century, across Western Europe and the United States, business and professional men sought to adapt their gender image and behavior to rapidly changing conditions. They controlled property, or expected to control it, and could use its real and symbolic authority to prove their manhood. Early industrial society saw the elaboration of a paternalist style that sought to ensconce a family-type authority in the larger society. Employers found it easiest to understand the workers in their charge as children, and insofar as they succeeded in acting accordingly reinforced their own traditional sense of manhood while damaging that of the workers. Yet even the middle class was not able to import traditional modes of manhood into the new society without change. An early sign of this was a vital switch in gender definitions of sexuality. The need to redefine maleness would extend to relations between father and child—reexamined during the first half of the nineteenth century and considerably restated in the second half—and even to work. By the final third of the nineteenth century, indeed, the world of the middle-class man was severely disrupted. As ties to property weakened, the paternalist social stance lost some of its validity, and schooling modified the socialization of sons. But we begin earlier, when the public manifestations of manhood seemed relatively serene; for changes in gender definitions in the first half of the nineteenth century, and in the actual roles of men and women, had their own impact on the growing confusions of the century's end. We deal with a two-stage process, with the characteristics of middle-class men in the last third of the nineteenth century increasingly recognizable in contemporary terms. By then, as with the working class, a class definition of the problems of manhood was emerging that informs the definitions that prevail in our own society. But even the reactions of men in the first phase of industrialization, in the apparent heyday of the Victorian paterfamilias, have had an enduring legacy, as they altered the terms of debate about male/female relations and about parenthood alike.

The Uncertain Hunter:
The First Version of the Middle-Class Man

Even on the surface of gender imagery, middle-class men during the first two-thirds of the nineteenth century were not content to rely on ownership to define masculinity; rather, they supplemented this by reviving rhetoric of war and the hunt. Like the working class, they reacted to a new society by identification, at least in discourse, with the more physical traits of manhood; the tone runs through descriptions of business life long before it was enhanced by social Darwinism, and in countries like France, where the ethic of competition has long been seen as somewhat muted. All of this constitutes a first indication that gender was being called upon to take on new symbolic importance. The imagery of struggle constitutes a thread that informs middle-class male identity even in the present day, for it easily outlived the early forms of industrial capitalism. But a more profound clue to the uncertainties that underlay men's existence in the new middle-class world comes in the attention to sexuality; a specific culture was formed that would wane by the century's end, for Victorian sexuality in its strictest sense was a period piece, but one whose broader implications for male/female and family relations continue to affect middle-class life.

During the late eighteenth and early nineteenth centuries, in North America as in Western Europe, the definition of male as well as female sexuality shifted substantially, becoming almost a mirror image of the conventions of previous Western culture. Women, earlier characterized as instinctively sensual, now became passive partners with little sexual appetite. This was a basic ingredient of the pedestal image, a commonplace of Victorian culture in the United States perhaps even more than in England and continental Europe.[1] Man was now the boss, born to be aggressive in sex as in other aspects of life. Images, of course, are not reality. Historians now recognize that a number of authorities were urging women toward sexual enjoyment, particularly during the later decades of the century. We know that many women displayed considerable sexual appetite.[2] But these important modifications of the pedestal image verify the image in one important respect. Doctors and the writers of marriage manuals who encouraged female sexuality knew that they were arguing against a commonplace. Women who noted their own sexual enjoyment reflected an expectation that the sexual initiative would come from their husbands, that their pleasure depended on their husbands' skill and care; they were far from asserting clear rights to pleasure. Man had become the prime agent in sexuality, and partisans of the female side of things argued in the main only that the gender differences need not be as great as generally believed. Man was not now the embodiment of rational control and restraint against the eternal Circe.[3]

This transformation was particularly interesting in that both the specifics of sexual advice and the image of man's nature in other respects embodied a vast amount of purely traditional wisdom. Hostility to masturbation and a belief that too much sex would damage health were not new notions. The idea that orgasm was equivalent to the loss of forty ounces of blood had a hoary past. The sexual warnings received unprecedented prominence in the nineteenth century because of the need to adapt them to new concepts of man and woman. The idea that could be harmed received new stimulus when it was believed that man harbored natural lusts that he had to restrain against his own impulses. The nineteenth century publicized this and many other pieces of relevant advice on a far larger scale than before.[4] Man in the nineteenth century was still rational *in general*, woman emotional. His presumed sexual aggressiveness fit into a larger pattern of competitive behavior that harked back to another kind of tradition, the virtues of the hunt.

How can we explain the shifting sexual imagery? More was at stake than simply making it clear that men were different from women; the traditional view of the sensual woman and the vulnerable man was quite adequate for this. Tradition was certainly more flattering to men, or at least less flattering to women, than the nineteenth century transmutation was. Women's historians have seen the Victorian pedestal as a snare for women, elevating them to a graceful uselessness while their men grabbed the rewards of industrial society. But aspects of the image were at least initially an improvement over the child-of-nature view of women in the past.[5] Woman now symbolized purity. She alone was fit to rule the home, and Victorians considered the home the true center of life. Ultimately the new view of womanhood might prove a trap, but it was not so conceived at first, which is why women accepted elements of it so readily (and why many still do). So the question remains why men did not do better for themselves when they, and the growing number of women authors undoubtedly deferential to a male view, were painting gender pictures. Part of the answer, of course, lies in the fact that the middle class was divided. Leading spokesmen on sexuality—ministers and even many doctors—felt bypassed by the raucous world of business, and in attacking the male sexual impulse they were attacking the aggressiveness of the new businessman. But businessmen came to accept the resultant imagery, which means that it is legitimate to seek reasons for some gender uncertainty in the class as a whole.

Middle-class men had several points to account for during the first half of the nineteenth century, when the revised image of manhood was taking shape. They had the problem of demonstrating that men who shunned demonstrations of physical strength and physical risk were sufficiently masculine. This had in turn two facets. Businessmen had to be justified in masculine terms, for although not a new breed they were far more numerous and important than ever before. Never in fact had a notion of mercantile activity been integrated fully into an acceptable definition of manhood, although there were hints, from the glory days of merchant adventurers and from the association between manhood and property, that could now be picked up once more. Professional men had to be justified also. This involved claims that were less novel about men's greater rationality and did not require any modification of a traditional estimation of male/female differentials. Early nineteenth-century intellectuals who vaunted men over women were not in fact talking distinctively as Victorians at all. They were simply saying, very loudly, what Western culture had long contended: When it comes to thought, leave it to us. Hence for Hegel, women were educable only in the lower arts, not at all in science and philosophy, for they were not rational but rather prey to every intuition. "The status of manhood, on the other hand, is attained only by the stress of thought and much technical exertion." Michelet, Keats, Comte, and Balzac echoed similar sentiments. Comte reckoned that women were not different from children; Schopenhauer, sadder but wiser, placed them between children and men, incapable of telling the truth, interested only in love, dresses, and dances. Similar views persist today. This attempt to maintain an association of manhood with distinctive rationality has been crucial to middle-class gender relationships.[6]

It was, however, business opinion and the impact of business activity on nonbusiness observers that were more novel and more important in shaping Victorianism. Commentators on men might mix metaphors, agreeing with the intellectuals on man's rationality in one breath and portraying him as a seething, powerful jungle beast in the next. Similarly, a woman might be at once a vain simpleton and the essence of purity. But businessmen did not see themselves primarily as rationalists; they were by nature profoundly distrustful of theorizers, and some of the same intellectuals who criticized empty-headed women had to turn against philistine businessmen as well. The theme of man-the-reasoner gained importance only as the world of business began to turn into the world of professions in the later nineteenth century.

Why did businessmen need a specific image of gender at all, much less a rather new one to respond to conditions in early industry? There was scant competitive threat from women (in contrast to the situation in the working class). Early industrialists and related merchants often worked closely with their wives, leaving to them vital tasks in accounting and inventory (brain-work, in fact). But women as independent actors did not penetrate the big companies. Doubtless men would have invented a host of good reasons why women were unsuited to business had there been a real competitive challenge. But in fact it was men, old-fashioned men to be sure, who were wondering around 1860 why business wives were staying home, instead of pitching in as their foremothers had done.[7] Clearly, the image of man in business, and the corresponding image of the woman he needed, developed before it was used as an exclusionary device, explaining to men and women alike what qualities men lacked that women had to make up for. This image in turn, with the duties it entailed in practice, quickly separated most married women from business. The whole image was used explicitly to exclude women from the upper reaches of business only later, when women were in a position to reenter in large numbers. An assumption that gender image was adapted to protect men's domain is thus correct in terms of long-run effect, but not initial intent.

Initial redefinition of gender stemmed rather from the fact that early industrial businessmen had to justify themselves—to themselves, to their families, and to a world of government officials, lawyers, aristocrats (the old middle and upper sectors of society) who had been taught that concentration on money-making was dirty and who saw nothing in the stench of the early factories to convince them otherwise. There was tension within the business community itself. Old merchants scorned new factory owners, and the latter were insecure even among themselves. An industrialist in Lille set up a giant spinning plant around 1840, using his parents' money, only to find that his parents, smalltime manufacturers themselves, would not set foot in his creation because such a grandiose venture was immoral. Businessmen used a variety of images for what was an implicit and very necessary public relations campaign. They talked about benevolence. They invoked the new doctrines of liberalism. And they pointed to their manhood.[8]

War and the Darwinian jungle were the moral analogues of modern business.[9] Not a few of the early industrial businessmen had military experience in the wars that spanned the 1770s to 1815. Still more thought of business organization in terms of military chains of command, with themselves as generals.[10] Business was hailed as the modern substitute for war, with none of the bloodshed and devastation (only rising prosperity) but with all of the male virtues. "Henceforward there will be business centuries, as in the past there have been military centuries."[11] To a middle-class world tired of war, this was appealing. Certainly it made the businessman no whit less a man.

Business as battle, the business world as the jungle, corresponded to what men thought they saw around them, what they themselves were creating. It was a world of combat, individual and soon corporate, with the effects of overworked adrenalin in oversedentary bodies the cost instead of wounds. Predatory behavior there was in fact. A man had to be aggressive to stay afloat. The business mentality produced campaigns, fights, victories, and bitter defeats.

There were men who relished this from the first, and as business ideology spread still more men were raised to anticipate their entry into the fray. The world of industrial capitalism was not a natural, at least not an inevitable, product of manhood. Even as it recalled the hunting virtues, it violated them. Middle-class men, trained to be suspicious individualists, found it difficult to bond together. Clubs and fraternal organizations might be exclusively male, but there was among capitalists a certain limitation to group behavior and so a real loss of a traditional male support.[12] Furthermore, though the image of man the hunter had been preserved more fully in Western society than in most other advanced civilizations, doubtless one of the reasons that industrial capitalism was possible, it had not been a primary definer of most men in agricultural society.

The early industrialists were not uniformly comfortable with their role. Many took risks with great misgivings, often arguing that they lacked free choice amid the pressure of competition. Many were doubtful about the ethics of increasing urban misery, hence the industrialists who contributed to utopian socialist efforts to ban machinery and return to the countryside. Many were not sure that a man was supposed to live the way they were living. This is the ambiguity that runs through the evolution of modern business and among businessmen themselves; a love-hate relationship with the competitive life that prompts few men to stop running the race lest they be unmanned, but one which encourages many to want to believe in an alternative. The image of business as war, the world as a jungle, was a statement of fact as well as a commendation. In one mood, it is good that men *are*, when manly, cutthroat competitors; in another, it is a shame that men *have* to be cutthroat competitors.

And in that latter mood, of course: isn't it good that we have a home to go home to. We can begin to move closer to an explanation of the early nineteenth century conundrum about gender sexuality by noting what men thought they needed of women, and what women thought they needed of themselves, amid the new imagery and reality of the business world. The Reverend Samuel Osgood stated what became a commonplace: "To the one sex (God) . . . has given, in the largest measure, strength,—to the other, beauty; to the one, aggressive force,—to the other, winning affections; to the one, the palm in the empire of thought,—to the other, the palm in the empire of feeling." Here is the essence of Victorian public culture, with a bit of a dig at women's intellect but massive respect for the role which women had to play, and in this different from the more traditional views of formal philosophers.

Part of the revised definition of gender came from churchmen and their wives, who saw no profit in attacking capitalism directly but who deplored many of its consequences and who invented the female principle as a possible modification. Essentially traditionalist in social outlook, they nevertheless saw no way to harness the new man of business to older values of economic restraint. So they commended to him the love of a good woman. And to women they gave a truly attractive moralizing role. But moralizing and sexuality don't mix, at least for traditionalist Christian ministers who had additional reasons for urging sexual restraint in the visible sexual "immorality" of young people in the lower classes.[13]

The wives and daughters of businessmen might share a sense of discomfort in the urban, industrial world around them. (So might many sons, some of whom abandoned business; but it was probably harder for a middle-class male to criticize business behavior because of its association with manliness.) Hence women developed and advertised their nurturing spirit, increasingly taking over key charitable functions. They followed here a sensible division of middle-class labor, just as they were to represent their families on the boards of cultural institutions. But without confronting the male world head-on, charitable women promoted the idea that men are naturally harsh—had they not created conditions of appalling poverty?—and the corollary: that women are naturally soothing, beneficent. Women writers, more commonly the daughters or wives of ministers than in the business world themselves, painted vivid pictures of the industrial life that men made—because as men they could not help themselves—and the bounty that a charitable woman could bestow. There were also to be sure grasping, shallow women in the popular novels of women like Mrs. Gaskell, and men of subtle goodness (though usually rather one-dimensional men; the interesting characters of nineteenth-century novels are disproportionately female). Overall, the picture of stern, if just, men (God the Father) balanced precariously by feminine compassion won considerable currency.[14]

Businessmen themselves largely accepted the new gender definition; certainly they constructed no alternative view. Many men vaguely perceived their wives' charitable efforts as appropriate if token modifications of their own capitalist strivings. A French public works director described the process by which businessmen had to toughen themselves. Often they began with considerable social conscience and were genuinely saddened by the miserable condition of their workers, but their sense of competitive pressure was still greater, so they became ever more adroit in avoiding too much contact with poverty. "Their hearts harden by habit, often by necessity, so that all charity is soon extinguished."[15] Yet a certain discomfort might linger. A number of French industrialists confided to the socialist Flora Tristan that they found social problems increasing with the progress of industry, but that they were powerless to intercede. The noninvolvement of businessmen's wives and daughters in the messy world of business might, in these moods, provide a bit of comfort. At least one could have some contact with purity after the long working day was done. In protecting the women in the best chivalric style, men were doing something to prevent the money-grubbing contamination from affecting the whole of society.[16]

Most businessmen felt regret about social injustice only rarely. A host of complementary value systems sprang up, such as the economic version of man the hunter, to give money-making more prestige than it had ever won in Western (or any other) civilization. Yet it was hard to shake off an occasional feeling that there should be higher goals in life as well. If one was creating a situation where women could express these goals through their charitable endeavors and cultural activities, there was some hedge against the pangs of conscience.

The middle class was building its own new division between the values of men and those of women. Men were the individualists in the world of competition and struggle. Women, kept at home, retained a sense of collective interest, expressing themselves through devotion to the family. When they moved onto a wider stage, as in the reform and charity movements in which they figured so prominently, they projected the values of an older society, in which individual self-interest required modification. Since the men themselves long retained some feel for these same values, though little ability to act upon them, it was easy to see women as representing not only a different but a higher social principle.

The same gender division followed from a more personal tension. The new businessman might in fact be caught up in the excitement of building his ventures. Yet even to himself, and certainly to the outside world, he phrased his personal goals in terms of his family. Why was expansion necessary? To provide patrimony for one's sons, dowries for the daughters. Business and family were inextricably intertwined during the first decades of the industrial revolution, as merchants and manufacturers sought to solidify their companies as the basis for an enduring family fortune. Typically, the early industrialists talked in terms of their "house," and many of them long attempted to keep outsiders away from any shared control, preferring to rely on relatives for any staff assistance they might require. Businessmen were preserving the motives of a family economy, adding an aggressive, expansionist quality. They were acting as individual agents, not as part of a family decision-making apparatus, which is why their social outlook and that of their women typically diverged. But they really thought they had the family constantly in mind, that their individual interest and the family interest were one. But while the establishment of the family could have an abstract quality to it, in imitation of the aristocratic "house" and its lineage, it had reality as well. It was the place men repaired to after a long, sometimes confusing working day. As a place of repose, it was not to have the same qualities as those of the outside world; it was not to be a place of struggle and competition. The businessman was bifurcating his values, seeing one set as appropriate for business but irrelevant to domestic life. A patriarchal approach to the family was one key to keep it separate from the competitive quality of the business world. Yet because the economic struggle was so demanding, businessmen lacked the time to extend patriarchal control over every aspect of the family operation. They needed their wives not just as submissive agents but as capable family managers. It was not a question of time alone. Many businessmen recognized that they were consumed by a market mentality which, while fully justified, was not appropriate as the moral basis of the family. Here was the domestic translation of their uneasiness about their competitive values. The wife and mother was necessary not just as subordinate, but as a counterweight to provide the family with a sweetness and tenderness that the man felt necessary but beyond his powers to provide. Certainly the women involved saw every reason to keep the taint of commerce at the doorstep. It was no mean role to be civilizing agent in the new commercial wilderness.

This gender division, formed because of the time constraints on men in the early industrial revolution and because of their hesitations over the ultimate validity of the competitive values they trumpeted in public, naturally perpetuated itself. The businessman's son would typically be taught to imitate his father and prepare for the roughness of the new economy, but he would also learn that there are other values in life beyond profit and expansion. He should be ready to grant women's importance as bearers of these values, just as he readily granted the importance of his gentle mother. What started in male indecision and anxiety in an immensely difficult period of transition to the new economy was erected as a durable, gender-based duality in the middle-class world.[17]

The result was an ongoing ambiguity in the position of women reminiscent, not surprisingly, of the ambiguity launched by Christianity in Western civilization but with a distinct new twist. Women, the hearth-guarders, were not capable of the rough and tumble of a man's world. They were too frail, and the nineteenth century saw an unending elaboration of images of female frailty and a supporting medical apparatus to match (the fainting woman, the nervous woman plagued by almost unmentionable female disorders, etc.)[18] It was easy to scorn such creatures or to take them under one's gallantly protective wing. But women were also family partners, not in the sense of being economic co-workers but as moral agents, doing tasks that the man could not perform. As such they were obviously different, but fully as important as men in the social scheme of things, even deserving of significant new rights. The partnership involved some windowdressing, of course. As men became sole economic agents, they obtained new kinds of power over women, whose fate depended so heavily on their own: the idea of partnership could be rather hollow when a man brutally wielded his financial control. Yet the moral role of women was not merely an ideal; it had genuine purpose in men's eyes as well as women's. It was bolstered by the churches, which women increasingly dominated, and by reform institutions capable of tweaking the consciences of the businessmen, reminding them that while they had power, they might not have justice. The role was, finally, new: Women had never before been granted moral supremacy. Not surprisingly, religious imagery stressing the woman as latter-day Eve, properly subordinate for her sin, yielded to that of woman as redeemed and pure, to whom more worldly men were urged to look for their own spiritual guidance. Indeed, novel thought, women might even be better than men.[19]

This latter idea found expression in the growing belief that women were better parents than men. It suggested, particularly by the later nineteenth century, that men might do well to imitate women in important particulars.[20] It reverberated in aspects of feminism, even feminism that so bitterly attacked the Victorian trappings of womanhood, suggesting again a fundamental female moral superiority (give the world to us and we won't war, we won't cheat). But it had its first, admittedly limited and ambiguous, expression in the sexual relations between middle-class men and middle-class women.

For the image of special female purity depended heavily on the transmutation of gender sexuality. Christian culture had always esteemed sexual abstinence as a badge of closeness to God. Men who needed their women to be pure, women who saw role and value in purity, would naturally think of sexual modesty. Yet the new emphasis on woman as sexually passive and even more, on man as sexually agressive did not result from the need for female purity alone. The final cause of the redefinition of gender lay directly in a new set of sexual and reproductive problems that confronted the middle class in its literally formative decades at the end of the eighteenth and early in the nineteenth centuries. The result was also an ongoing confusion in the actual sexual relations between the genders, which has been altered greatly since the Victorian period but which still shows traces of its parenthood.

The problem was that the danger of having too many children increased while the temptation to sexual activity increased as well. Members of the middle class, unlike many workers, maintained traditional defenses against unwanted children, notably by long preserving a late female as well as male marriage age. Yet tradition no longer sufficed. Improved nutrition and some improvements in sanitary conditions in the middle-class home increased the chances of infant survival, part of the general demographic development in Western society from about 1750 onward which struck the middle and upper classes with particular vigor. The nineteenth-century middle class still had infant deaths to mourn, but only about half as many as its analogues a hundred years before. Yet the class was particularly sensitive to the problem of having too many children for its self-definition leaned heavily on the ability to "provide properly" for each child.[21]

Many a patriarch was impelled to greater business dynamism because of the burdens of having too many surviving children along with the traditional sense of what was fitting for them. Camille Schlumberger, a fairly ordinary master artisan living in the Swiss city of Mulhouse, which became French in 1797, found, to his astonishment, that he had twelve sons and daughters, all of whom showed every sign of living to maturity. So he gradually built on his prosperous craft, employed more workers, and ultimately set up a small factory. He was no risk-taking hero, no partisan of an expansionist economy; he was simply a man trying to do right by his brood. Yet the result was a family firm that pioneered in the industrialization of textile manufacture and that produced two sons who were among the most dynamic entrepreneurs in all of France.[22] Yet few families could match this kind of success story, and few would want, generation after generation, to try. Since a return to conditions of traditionally high infant mortality was out of the question, the birth rate had to be cut. The middle class was the first to see this. This perception and the behavior that resulted constitute a basic defining principle of the middle class.

Important segments of the middle class had already limited their birth rate before the 1830s, in most Western countries.[23] This was clearly true in both France and the United States, where general birth rate decline can be traced to that decade and where certain middle-class groups are known to have cut back earlier. The situation is complicated by lack of class-specific statistics in England,[26] but even when these emerged, by the mid-nineteenth century, it is clear that the middle-class family had long fallen short of producing the number of children biologically possible even after a marriage in the mid- to late twenties. Middle-class families would later reduce their birth rate still further, at least in part through artificial means and even with an increase in sexuality; to this phenomenon we must return. But they effected their later changes on the basis of a quite-early adjustment in traditional birth rates before artificial measures were widely or effectively utilized.[25]

Even a dynamic businessman, around the turn of the nineteenth century, might contemplate with horror the idea of having to marry off four daughters and place four sons (while two additional infants died). Quite apart from placement, children in this number would eat away at capital that was vitally needed to invest in a new business. So the need for birth control was obvious. It was enhanced by a redefinition of parental obligation that, while just beginning, can be traced to the eighteenth century among American Quakers and more generally among those people affected by the educational ideas of the later Enlightenment. As the infant mortality rate declined, it was possible to invest more in them emotionally. Yet emotional investment, which came particularly from the maternal side, meant a heightening of obligations that would be difficult to fulfill if spread over a too-numerous progeny. Here was a special reason to pull back from excessive childbirth and yet to accept this without a sense of diminishing parental value. For in treasuring each child, one was a parent as one's parents had not been, regardless of the fact that there were fewer children born. The middle class was not, at this point, trying to reduce the number of children surviving to maturity, but rather attempting to restore the traditional level so sorely tried by the improved infant survival rates.

How were these noble purposes to be accomplished? Mainly, by birth control. There were, in these pre-vulcanization days, no artificial devices of any reliability. Animal bladders, used as primitive condoms, were most common. The only recourse was abstinence or coitus interruptus, the practice of which is difficult to document.[26]

But without question the middle class early became a firm partisan of sexual restraint, as would follow from the methods available to them. The ministers and other defenders of traditional morality fulminated against the new license of the lower classes, attacking the illegitimacy rates in countryside and city alike. Businessmen, too, claimed to see the ill effects of unlimited sex. They commented acidly on degrading sexual practices of workers in their factories. They sought to punish workers responsible for illegitimate children. They held, as did the gloomier liberal economists in a more rigidly theoretical way, that sexual license was responsible for poverty by burdening a family with more children than it could care for and robbing the worker himself of vital energies. With poverty concentrated in the cities, more visible than ever before and associated with hordes of hungry children, the middle class gained yet additional reasons to curb its sexual appetites.

Why, though, put the burden on women, who had always before been judged the sexually more active gender? Coitus interruptus may be more successful when the woman is a passive partner. The new emphasis on female purity, including the incipient expansion of the functions of the mother, may have helped set the stage. But it is also possible that at this moment of history women *were* less sensual, that men found their sexual appetites increasing just as the social danger of unrestrained sex was growing, and that the redefinition of gender sexuality, particularly the new emphasis on man as the aggressor, had an initial empirical base.

Businessmen in the early industrial revolution had contact with a wide array of potential sexual partners, many of them social inferiors as well as female. The early nineteenth century witnessed a vast expansion of the numbers of female domestic servants in households that previously had had no servant at all beyond a neighbor girl, or a male servant only. Here was a temptation to which men yielded all too frequently, as dismissals for pregnancy suggest. Dalliance with a servant was a common form of sexual initiation for a "young master," and a number of family patriarchs doubtless unbent as well.[27] For textile manufacturers the factory setting, full of young girls economically dependent on their employer, often working in partial undress, provoked some abusive sexuality. Many men who did not yield must have felt new stirrings that had to be suppressed, and a sense of guilt toward wife and family that needed to be purged. Men were simply out in the world more than their wives and sisters, and what came to be seen as a natural difference in sexuality resulted in part from their social contacts.

Beyond this, the emphasis on personal aggression as a desirable competitive quality may have had some impact on men's sexual approach, differentiating them not only from women but also from their own more stolid male forebears. These were men unusually open to self-expression, to conquest. As they glorified economic lusts, it was easy to give vent to more fleshly lusts as well. Men found their own desires changing at a time when to express them, particularly within the family, was dangerous. Small wonder that both they and their women redefined gender sexuality. The woman was made the prime defender of sexual restraint because, for a time, she was most capable of playing that role. Once the role was created, both genders might see validity in its maintenance.

Middle-class women were not, of course, uniformly restrained. Pamphlets and marriage manuals in all Western countries urged female sexual pleasure. "Why should not the female state her passion to the male, as well as the male to the female?" wrote a male pamphleteer in 1825; many doctors conveyed the same message.[28] With time, the view of women as sexually passive yielded still further. And behavior often followed suit. A small sample of college-educated American women around 1900 revealed that the vast majority experienced orgasm with a high degree of regularity.[29] Clearly, the sexual differences between men and women in the nineteenth-century middle class must not be pressed too far.

But a great difference could exist, on more than a random basis. A French wife demanded divorce because of the excessive zeal and "unnatural caresses" of her husband, though the court sided with her husband who claimed he was only trying to please her and increase her affection for him.[30] Pervasive images discouraged many husbands from expecting their wives to be sexually warm, and their own subsequent clumsiness might create frigidity where it was otherwise unecessary. For although men and women were not, overall, locked in complete sexual misapprehension, the belief in female passivity, which even the more balanced manuals realized they had to combat explicitly, was combined with differential experience before marriage to create a good bit of divergence. Young middle-class women, with an ever-younger age of puberty and a stable age of marriage, were kept from sex with, apparently, rare exceptions. This was not new, although it required increasing rigor in an urban environment. Girls flirted, they dressed coquettishly—sexuality found tiny outlets—but, carefully chaperoned, they rarely came near to consummation. (A boy might in fact be excused for finding girls of his own kind not so much havens of purity as sterile teases, and seeking sexual pleasure elsewhere.)

Another new development in the nineteenth century was that men were less likely than before to postpone their sexuality until marriage. Here was where the increasing sexual drives and opportunities of middle-class males found clearest expression. The sexual double standard spread more widely than ever before and defined the behavior of men, particularly before marriage. Men were still urged not to begin sexual activity too early. They were warned of the myriad diseases that resulted from premature or excessive sex, and of the venereal diseases (a real danger) that might result from promiscuity. But, freed from chaperonage at work or school and not marrying until an unusually late twenty-eight or thirty, many men began their initiation early. "It is rare to find in the present state of our morals boys who are virgin after seventeen or eighteen," wrote a French doctor. On holidays and Thursday half-days, French brothels swarmed with secondary schoolboys. France may have been distinctive in this. Paris had over twice the number of prostitutes per capita than London in the 1850s. Even today, in marked contrast with England and the United States, about half of all French men say they were initiated to sexual activity by a prostitute.[31] But the use of prostitutes was common among American college students, a tradition that persisted among prep school graduates into the 1950s. Young men in both England and the United States were also avid patrons of the flourishing pornographic press.

As husband, the man—older and probably more experienced sexually—was supposed to instruct the wife in pleasure, for the age gap widened sexual diversity in the middle class more than in the working class. But many people find teaching a bore, and in this case numerous men had been conditioned to believe that proper women were not good pupils anyway. "I make love with my wife when I want a child. The rest of the time I make love with my mistresses. Wives are to produce heirs. For pleasure men seek other women."[32] Thus stated a fifty-year-old French industrialist. Few middle-class men could afford mistresses, a habit much more suitable to the small upper class. Occasional patronage of the growing number of classy brothels, not intended for workers or schoolboys, was more likely. Many men undoubtedly found their wives responsive, despite differential initial experience. Countless others lived within marriage most of the time even though their wives' upbringing and their own clumsiness and haste led to a life of rare sexual satisfaction. The double standard undoubtedly applied to the experience of adolescence far more than it characterized relations within marriage. Insofar as it did exist at any point, however, it tended to confirm the idea of a basic difference in sexuality between the genders.

Apart from the marital disappointments of both men and women, there is a final implication to the double standard and to the whole conversion of the sexual images of men and women that deserves comment. Unlike earlier aristocratic dalliance, men's rather common sexual behavior now met condemnation. Of course an important male subculture approved the double standard. As late as 1966, a French poll showed that while 60 percent of young girls disapproved of premarital sex and 74 percent thought that adultery damaged married life, the boys voted 66 percent for premarital sex and 50 percent for the compatibility of adultery and marriage.[33] The schoolboy too timid to visit the brothel could be subjected to manly derision, just as American male adolescents in the twentieth century checked on their fellows to find out who scored on a date. Married men might be more taciturn about their strayings, but some could count on a sympathetic male audience if they were discreet. Yet the fact was that man's sexual nature as it was now defined, and certainly any actual adultery, were held up not just against traditional Christian morality but against the inimitable purity of their own women. There was something unsavory about this aspect of maleness, and many a wife on her way to becoming a domestic matriarch took pains to point this out.

Women were warned against all sorts of sexual interests, but they were told that they probably did not want to pursue them anyway. This was a distortion, a cruel if understandable hoax, but it could be a comfort as well. Men were told that they did have active sexual interests but that, if they were really proper people, they should sublimate their desires. If they turned to the double standard, their sex lives might be better than women's but their moral lives suffered. Here was the first of several ways in which the gender definitions of the nineteenth century pulled men in contradictory directions. Raised increasingly by mothers who were at best rather reticent about sex, at worst bitterly disillusioned by it, boys were taught that they had stronger sex drives than girls, but that if they were real men, kind to their mothers and to the gentle natures of all ladies, they could conquer their animal qualities.

Victorian culture severely proscribed male masturbation.[34] Female masturbation was considered equally unhealthy, but it was believed to occur less frequently, given women's passionlessness. Male self-abuse was "an uncleanliness, a filthiness forbidden by GOD, an unmanliness despised by men," according to Queen Victoria's personal physician.[35] Social democrats in Germany, cereal manufacturers in the Midwest, and the whole medical establishment raged against the evil consequences of masturbation, which was said to cause diseases ranging from blindness to insanity to acne. The belief was sincere, indeed traditional, but it was more widely and intensely expressed than ever before. It merged the public desire for sexual quiescence among adolescents of both genders, in the interests of middle-class respectability and control over unruly youth. By means of parental bed-checks, school inspections, and preventive contraptions, and even institutionalization for insanity, the furor against masturbation expressed the new fear that the male sexual impulse was inherently unruly. No double standard or male subculture could protect boys from the fear that something in them was evil. The middle-class male could easily grow up wondering whether he best proved his manhood through sexual conquests or through dominance over his own sexual nature. If he chose prowess, he might be assailed by doubts about his own morality; he could wonder about his unfairness to his gentle wife or, if he took childhood lessons too seriously, about damage to his health. If he chose restraint, he might wonder if he was lacking among his peers.

The sexual quandary, the first of the modern moral dilemmas of manhood, did not, initially, loom too large. The early generations of middle-class men had little difficulty defining their manhood, and they tried hard to pass the lessons on to their sons. Sexual prowess was not a key part of the definition in any event, and before a schoolboy culture was formed, many businessmen may have found it logical to sublimate undue sexual desire, at most vaguely aware of troubling passions in their devotion to the clearer purposes of men. For the key fact of middle-class masculinity in the first half of the nineteenth century was an effort to adapt tradition into a new definition of self, in which relationships with women played a limited role. A middle-class patriarch-alism developed, based on the preindustrial variety but involving an adapta-tion to industrial competition and, from this, a new concern for the raising of sons. This latter-day patriarchalism raised certain difficulties even at the time, for it was not easy to maintain, and many men failed. It promised more difficulties later, for it assumed a paternal omnipresence that became in-creasingly impossible. At its best it produced men who were tough without violence, competent in a world which they bent to lean on their shoulders. In later years a man could look on these days with envy.

The key to patriarchalism remained property. The new middle class was conscious of the importance of property as it was of nothing else. Husbands used their legal dominance over property to control their wives. In a marriage, the middle-class wife moved to the husband, in an essentially traditional pattern. Fathers used property to control their sons, training them to take over their businesses and earnestly attempting to build up the stake they would leave to their future generations.

But property, while the base, was not the only weapon. A French observer noted that, in England, home was more a moral than a material entity, and that men prevailed by moral at least as much as economic ascendancy.[36] The key to this was an effort to redefine the individual will and to develop new ways to train it. A middle-class man was urged to restrain all excessive emotion, including, of course, undue sexual passion. There should be no wild spending. Businessmen eagerly improved their standard of living—they were, in the main, no Puritan ascetics—but they long trained their sons in the virtues of economy and savings. ("If you want to become rich, let your savings equal your expenses.")[37] Wasting time was even worse than wasting money. A life built on work, with no frivolous distraction, was the key to success. Leisure time was shunned and many a middle-class man, gladly sending wife and children off to a fashionable spa, rejoiced that he did not have to suffer the idleness of a vacation. Drink, gambling, excessive emotion of any sort, anything that would impair a strong will and the zeal for work, were shunned. It was in this atmosphere that the most rigorous businessmen proclaimed their responsibility for both success and failure. If an individual slipped, if he failed to advance, if he failed to save, all would be his fault. He could not blame chance or society, for a proper man was captain of his fate. Success was the reward for a properly directed will. "There is nothing more noble than to be the father of one's achievements and the author of one's fortunes." French industrialists publicly proclaimed that their own "talent, courage, perserverance" had enabled them to "command wealth and make it spring from nothing," and they saw themselves inspired by "the sacred fire which makes one surmount all obstacles."[38]

It was against other men that middle-class man tested himself. Workers, unless they managed to rise by their own effort, were not considered complete men. Their lack of success proved that they lacked the virtues of a proper man, a bit of reasoning that delighted the middle class. But many businessmen failed to make the grade as well. The manly code was just that; it was not a description of behavior. Many businessmen did drink, many did gamble and overspend, and a distressing number saw their firms fail.[39] But this did not at first dent the code; it merely proved the fitness of those who survived (for the business world was in fact Darwinian well before Darwin).

Latter-day patriarchalism found ample means of expression in both work and family. Employers, once they rose above the level of survival, were constantly tempted to play father to their company. Workers, though they had their faults, were best viewed as children. (Middle-class women, unable to stretch their maternal role into such an overarching image, may have had more trouble in day-to-day dealings with the lower-class elements in their charge, the new domestic servants, though their charitable efforts often stressed maternal care and training.) Businessmen readily dabbled in efforts to extend their moral authority over their workers, as they periodically tried to teach workers to better themselves, to save, to become sober, to achieve sexual morality. The larger employers developed a farther-reaching paternalistic policy, a much more precise, revised edition of older ideas of noblesse oblige. They provided some housing for their workers, and some medical care, and savings banks and insurance funds. Their efforts made economic sense, as a cheap means of recruiting a labor force and tying it to the firm. But paternalism also corresponded to the employer's view of himself as father of his enterprise and all who were involved with it. Like a good father, he tried to educate his charges (up to a point) and to help them in their troubles. All he demanded in return was loyal work and unaltered gratitude. Though paternalism was often hollow and inadequate as a system of benefits, though it might be challenged by worker protest or state regulation, it remained one of the most durable strategies of the new manufacturing class because it corresponded so closely to their visions of their own patriarchal manhood.[40]

Paternal authority over children was a far more pervasive feature of the middle class. Many fathers relied solely on a traditional combination of functions as provider and disciplinarian well into the nineteenth century. Francis Wayland, in Rhode Island, typified the approach of many evangelical parents: "The *Right* of the parent is to *command*; the *duty* of the child is to *obey*. Authority belongs to the one, submission to the other." Wayland, confronted with a fifteen-month-old son who cried violently and refused to eat when ordered, shut the boy in a room for over two days until the boy not only ate but opened his arms gladly to his father. A child's spirit had to be broken—again the traditional view—until he was gradually infused with a parental view of what a proper spirit was.[41]

Even in the early decades of the nineteenth century, the most direct forms of physical discipline waned in popularity in middle-class homes. Wayland himself was proud of the fact that he did not beat his children. It was vitally important for this version of the paternal style that obedience and docility were still treasured, beginning to yield clearly as an ideal only after 1850 despite the earlier preachings of child-oriented educators like Pestalozzi in Switzerland. But emphasis on a paternal function to guide the child's will by moral ascendancy, rather than breaking it, received increasing attention.[42] Possibly a new love for children entered into this vision, among fathers as well as mothers, though the early industrial father remained a rather formidable figure, only occasionally unbending to romp with his children, typically demanding formal address from them. The basic economic controls remained. Sons of early industrialists could expect to enter their father's firm at an early age, working their way up in a quick apprenticeship after primary school and perhaps a brief period of secondary training. Here was the clearest sign of the successful transfer of patriarchalism to the industrial setting. Many middle-class families, sustained by property ownership but without other legal privilege, could point to an enviable succession of generations, steadily defending and building the company, from the mid-eighteenth sometimes into the twentieth century.

The standards of the middle-class man must have seemed comfortably secure in 1850 or even in 1870. Again, many men fell by the wayside as personal or business failures. But standards were confirmed, not threatened, by those who could not measure up. It is no wonder that the world of the mid-nineteenth century middle-class male is evoked with nostalgia by observers who see a tragic lack of discipline—personal, familial, and societal—in contemporary life. There were many neurotic products of the paternal style, particularly among those on whom the newly emphasized sexual discipline weighed most heavily.[43] But men were raised to standards; a clear inter-generational link among men could be preserved. Even some workers seemed to accept the tutelage of businessmen, for a generation or two at least. The widest assertions of paternalism were not obvious or immediate failures.

We stress the formative period less for its reassertions of traditional male strength than for its ambiguities. The businessman, for all the evocation of competitive achievement, was rarely an untroubled hunter, totally confident in the justification of the kill. He allowed, even if he did not fully credit, a supplementary imagery that suggested the moral superiority of the female. The sexual development of young men almost automatically persuaded them of some disparity between their nature and propriety, even when self-discipline (or lack of opportunity) could resolve the dilemma.

Most basically, the paternal style itself was newly threatened. Moral guidance was harder than will-breaking in the best of circumstances; an old-fashioned authoritarian may have had a better hope of seeing his sons turn out in his image. (Francis Wayland's memory, for example, was cherished by the son he had disciplined, who dutifully followed his father into the ministry.) More important, middle-class men, working long days outside the home, had less contact with their younger children. Simultaneously, they had to yield much of their claim to moral authority to their women, whom they endowed with a superior nature and who, above all, had the time. Like their working-class counterparts middle-class men did not develop an alternate definition of fatherhood, and they often gave up effective authority although more slowly, armed as they were with more compelling weapons of property. But in important ways middle-class men conceded more in principle than the workers did, for they admitted a competing authority, the sternly moral or, increasingly after mid-century, the comfortingly moral mother. The innovations that had been introduced into the male image—man the business-man/jungle fighter—offered no real support to the paternal role, and indeed detracted from claims of moral guidance.

The first version of the middle-class man thus offered an ambiguous legacy. Redefinitions of gender images were suggested which continue to confront and confuse us. Contradictions were outlined between man's moral and sensual nature that affect us still. It was possible, in 1850, to believe in a complete man, with distinct roles and gender characteristics at home and at work. The key lay in toughness, in domination over family, workers, and above all over self. Yet men had already admitted that toughness was not enough, in granting a new moral role to their women. Soon they would have to wonder if even their toughness was secure as challenges arose to the conventional badges of authority at work and in the home. The second middle-class male response to industrial society, emerging in the last three to five decades of the nineteenth century, saw an elaboration of initial contradictions in the functions and traits assigned to each gender and a decided reduction in the ability to claim that any were inviolate.

The New World of Educated Men

The second half of the nineteenth century raised considerable complications in the masculine world of the middle class. Men's ability to play the economic warrior was reduced, even if the rhetoric soared to new heights with the social Darwinism of successful industrial magnates like Andrew Carnegie.[44] As more and more middle-class men worked in the bureaucracies of business and the state, the imagery of ownership and independence as badges of manhood declined in validity. The values might remain: British industrial managers in the late nineteenth century who came from business backgrounds typically felt that they had declined in status, even though they wielded great power, because they could no longer imitate their fathers in aspiring to outright control.[45] For managers, professional men, and the hordes of new clerks and salesmen of the lower middle class, the ownership of producing property no longer crowned one's economic efforts. This brought confusion in the criteria of measuring economic self-worth, as income had increasingly to replace ownership, and it reduced the generational continuity of the middle class, for what a man could pass on to his sons became far less tangible. Bureaucrats could maintain their sense of the competitive jungle, proud of their ability to support their family apart from the rough world of business. As ownership declined, the sense of participation in a hostile economy, armed only with one's own courage and wit, could increase. There was, however, a disjuncture between the independence sought for economic manhood, with its traditional property measurement, and what most men could attain, and this was not easily assimilated.

There were other tensions as well. The rise of feminism, particularly in the English-speaking countries, brought direct challenge to male privileges. Male response was by no means uniform, but some men were appalled at women's claims for new jobs and new political powers. Certain forms of feminism also extended earlier challenges to the moral basis of modern manhood, as when French feminists attacked the principles of the sexual double standard. In general, during the final decades of the nineteenth century, the strictures of Victorian sexuality eased somewhat, but men could still believe that they had to war with their nature.

Finally, patriarchal authority was increasingly modified in the home. The contradictions between paternal claims and available time, as suburban-ization rapidly increased the distance between home and work, became steadily more apparent. Education replaced apprenticeship, even for most businessmen. No longer was the teenage boy taken directly into his father's firm for guidance. Building on the earlier reduction in physical discipline, patterns of childrearing continued to be modified, with one result a clear increase in the valuation of motherhood.[46] Educational theories and chil-dren's literature alike began to de-emphasize ritualized discipline of any sort. Rote learning, for example, became less popular as an educational mode. Even self-control became somewhat less important, and certainly a sub-missive child was now a sign of parental failure. Childhood began to be seen in more sentimental terms, just as the figures of boys' literature changed from models of disciplined work to impulsive heroes who exemplified daring and courage. The child needed encouragement to individual impulse, and the loving atmosphere that a mother could best provide. The stern parent came in for increasing criticism. There were disciplinarians still, but as parents increasingly turned to child-rearing manuals for advice, they were taught that the things a child needed were not the things a father could best provide. Fatherhood had never been associated with emotional warmth, for fathers had always related best to children through some orderly system that would, among other things, permit cooperation and training in work. In theory, fathers could have shifted their tack, but this demanded time and attention that most no longer had for the details of childrearing. Businessmen working outside the home could not be primarily responsible for the cultivation of childish impulses and emotions. The importance of motherhood steadily increased, and with it the implicit downgrading of the paternal role. Many fathers began to serve essentially as disciplinarians of last resort, invoked when the more complicated maternal methods had broken down. ("Wait till your father comes home." "Don't hurt him.") Maternal authority itself would be challenged, with the rise of school-based peer groups, but this simply removed the father still further from effective control of his progeny. Male teachers lost ground, too, at the primary level. One of the reasons they accepted their decline—rather willingly—was the joint admission that young children had strong emotional needs and that only women had the necessary warmth to deal with these needs. Paternalism as a style became increasingly hollow, though it was not really replaced in the nineteenth century itself. Coincidentally, the paternal style in the larger society encountered challenge, notably from newly restive workers.[47]

Several of these developments require further comment. The decline of property in the middle class did more than modify the bases of patriarchalism. It raised basic questions about work satisfaction. Similarly, the reduced paternal role, itself influenced by birth rate decline, brought a need to define men's family satisfaction, and especially the relationships with one's wife. Before turning to these points, however, a final change in the position of middle-class man must be sketched: the need to associate economic manhood with claims to specialized knowledge.

This was a development that touched many facets of late nineteenth-century society, complicated as it was by contrast with earlier imagery of economic manhood; by the new activities of women; and by the integration of schools into the socialization of boys. Particularly in the growing professions, but also for businessmen directly, claims to training increasingly supplemented or even replaced claims to property. Formal professionalization—the professionals' answer to the rise of business—involved these claims directly. Old professions and new followed a similar pattern: formation of associations to spread information and identify qualifications for membership; development of tests to assess professional training, typically with state backing; and promotion of special training programs, from which of course emanated the great professional schools of the modern university. But as business bureaucracies themselves looked increasingly to academic criteria to guide their hiring, the world of business was touched by a similar association of success with expertise.

This process, in turn, required a claim that the new expertise fit the special mental qualities of men. The claim was not developed simply to exclude women, though it set the framework for a later, bitter battleground. Of the older professions in the nineteenth century, only doctors had to worry about female competition; among the newer professions, only teachers faced a female threat. The downgrading of women played a role in gender battles in these two fields, but it was more broadly necessary to bolster masculinity itself, even in all-male professions; for the professional had far more difficulty than the businessman in laying claim to a positive male image such as that of civilized hunter.

Most professionals, particularly doctors and lawyers, received classical training in the secondary schools, and they read the works of intellectuals who had even more classical training. The classics, of course, assumed the inferiority of women. In Western history as a whole, the key point about this classical tradition was that it was *not* taken up fully; on few subjects have the ancients been cited less often than on gender relations, for the Christian teachings substantially qualified their views. But for educated men in the nineteenth-century context it was hard not to cite the Greeks on women while citing them on other subjects. Certainly one of the reactions to growing anxiety about an economic definition of manhood in the middle class was a diverse array of attacks on women; they were intended to keep women in their place, to be sure, but also to bolster the claims of a special manly expertise. Thus, while hosts of doctors proved sympathetic to women's needs, as in the area of sexuality, the most vociferous ones undeniably sought to discover what really made women so weak and emotional.[48] They sought a basic female principle, most commonly in uterine disorders; they built on the classical belief that menopause rendered older women utterly useless, though they were somewhat embarrassed by the barely admitted knowledge that women did live longer than men. Their pronouncements undoubtedly encouraged the general tendency of educated men to point to women's special disabilities.

Women were claimed to be irrational, and thus unqualified to receive the new professional knowledge. The male who had attained a professional position was therefore suitably manly. What was new about this old claim for male intellectual leadership was the importance of rational activity and the deeply felt need for such rhetorical vigor in separating men from women. It would, in fact, have required an immense compensatory effort to bring significant numbers of women into male professional training in the nineteenth century—we still face today a female lag in mathematical ability after ages twelve or thirteen.[49] It was far more convenient to hold the gender line rigidly and insist that no woman could defy her exclusion from the new kingdom of the professional mind.

Professional training obviously tended to increase the differences between the socialization of boys and girls. Whether boys were naturally more rational or not, they had to be trained as if they were. And women were progressively pushed out of arithmetic fields such as accounting, which they had often handled in a family firm. The prophecy was neatly self-fullfilling, at least for a while.

As educational systems proliferated in the nineteenth century, women were excluded from classical curricula as well as scientific and mathematical training. American schools officials could argue that girls exposed to rigorous education would be "condemned to invalidism for life." The Cincinnati School Board in the mid-nineteenth century used this argument, claiming that women lacked the brain power for "severe" reasoning of the mathematical sort, and also invoked the more practical, and in the long run accurate, concern about the effect of equal education on the division of family labor: "good, sound substantial knowledge in women prevents their attending to their domesticities of wife, mother and friend."[50] So women were funneled into religious and moral training (in all social classes women were much more likely to receive religious instruction than men), domestic skills, and maybe a smattering of the arts and French. Piano playing, for example, was compatible with housework. Middle-class men, typically in different school systems or classrooms at least in the secondary grades, received not only the standard classical training but also the growing emphasis on the hard sciences. Even before their entry to school, they were given distinctive educational toys, stressing building and reasoning skills, in a century that greatly advanced the integration of playthings with education.[51] Girls received the dolls and cooking equipment that would prepare them for wife- and motherhood. Throughout childhood, middle-class girls and boys received parental rewards as they showed aptitude in the skills appropriate for their gender. This was quite explicable in terms of the middle-class economy; it would have been amazing had it been otherwise. Clear role differentiation was actually an aid to mothers, newly responsible for the bulk of the orientation of young children, in the absence of husbands at work, given the fact that boys were both different by nature and destined to different careers. A clear male route avoided confusion, and so the young boy was prepared to reason, the girl to emote, a distinction that, taken up at all levels of education, could be lifelong.

Women are still fighting their battles against the attitudes that shaped nineteenth-century educational policy. For men, there is an obvious link between the rhetoric of the nineteenth century on female inferiority, and more recent reactions to new female roles—the magazine stories, for example, particularly after the new incursion of women into the labor force following World War II, that fictionally returned women to an active home life which would presumably satisfy their simple mental requirements, or the references to a debilitating female biology that have greeted new feminist claims. (It was in 1942, for example, that a mayor of Galveston, Texas, commented on a group of women who began to monitor meetings of the all-male city council: "The trouble with these damn women is when they reach menopause they have nothing more to do."[52])

Yet, while most men probably harbor some comforting thoughts about female irrationality or emotionality, the key point about the nineteenth century for men is that it failed to satisfy the claims of male superiority in the educational sphere or of a special maleness in professional knowledge. Women were kept different, but they were not kept out, which was ultimately the most significant point. And middle-class men themselves, quite apart from women, began to diminish the stress on a specifically masculine rationality or on rational activity as a principal criterion for manhood. This also confused the relationship between manhood and professional training. From the mid-nineteenth century onward, the schools for the sons of the middle class were made to test values that related more to the hunting imagery of the business world than to male claims of professional expertise. This dual change in the later nineteenth century—the proportionately more rapid educational advance of women and the partial transformation of male schooling into an outlet for the expression of physical masculinity, combined to dilute the manhood/knowledge link, even as the educational criteria for economic success steadily increased. The rise of schooling added real complexity to the process of acquiring manhood, despite efforts to claim a peculiarly male hold on reason.

Many sons of professional fathers, exposed to the expanding secondary school systems that marked every industrializing country in the early nineteenth century, may have found educational prowess a logical expression of manhood, or even simply of self, having their fathers' image before them. But as the educational experience spread to the business sectors of the middle class, some tension inevitably developed. For the bookish boy was not a real boy in the general culture of the middle class. How could the quiet man of learning be reconciled with the latter-day jungle fighter? Though the jungle-fighter might scorn lessons, for example, he was uncomfortable with a son who did too badly in school—for competitive instincts could operate as well—and the annoying fact was that the knowledge was useful as industrialization became more complex. Obviously these values need not conflict. An aggressive, competitive instinct could work as well in school systems as in business systems. Yet there was a certain strain between the two vying images: man-of-learning dominated by his superior reason, and man-of-war, dominated by his aggressive capacity. It was not easy to pursue both models simultaneously, just as it was not easy to be told that one was sexually active by nature but required to moderate instinct with a cool head. The changing demands of the industrial economy, expressed in the extension of education, added considerably to the complexity of defining manhood for most middle-class boys.

By the middle of the nineteenth century, the secondary schools and universities began to take account of the gut-competitive as well as the rational (and spiritual) sides of male image and ideal by introducing active athletic programs. (They also maintained a military program, from the British public schools to the officer training programs on American campuses.) English and American schools led the way. Sports never became as important a part of the middle-class experience on the Continent, particularly in

France. But in Germany, hikes and gymnastics served some of the same purposes as did football or soccer in the Anglo-Saxon countries, though without such a pronounced competitive flavor. The trend was common, for essentially similar reasons. There was a desire to imitate the leisure skills of the old upper class, which had included some kinds of athletic ability, from fencing to horseback riding, while providing a more appropriate, possibly less military and less expensive range of middle-class alternatives. By the mid-nineteenth century, the middle class, led by England, was increasingly concerned with the problem of leisure time, now that the worst strain of launching the industrialization process was over. Families that had been content with some reading at home, church, and perhaps an occasional concert now had to broaden their range, for there were time and money that demanded special use. Athletics helped ease the transition to enjoyment of leisure because, as the early English recreational magazines stressed, they had such obvious applicability to work. It was no sin to play a game that would improve one's fitness and mental alertness, and sports obviously did this.[53]

Middle-class sports were not as purely male as those of the working class. A family recreational pattern persisted in the popularity of croquet, tennis, or bicycle riding (so useful for courting). But the school sports were aggressively male, and on the whole the rise of athletics brought the middle class to the same association of manhood with athletic prowess that the working class had developed. In a period when manhood needed new proofs, both classes headed back to the physical basics. Women did not need the same emphasis on fitness and alertness that justified training for men in the middle-class schools, because they were not the ones saddled with stressful work and the demands of ratonal thought. Athletic prowess was in fact a delightful contrast to their pallid games. Competitive sports for men provided a direct training ground for the aggressive instinct so necessary in later life. Schools now reproduced on playing fields many of the characteristics of the hunt: physical courage and skill, an uneasy team coordination balanced by an individual desire to excel. The athlete, as American football coaches have not tired of saying in over a century, was a man. No doubt about it.

The middle class imported into the schools some of its tensions about the proper criteria for manhood. No question about the athlete, but what about the intellectual? The ideal was dual: a boy good in schoolwork but not sissified, and hell on wheels on the playing field. Rhodes scholarship committees have sought and found such types for years. But for the boys not adept at sports, or simply not interested, the athletic criteria were troubling. Without question, physical activity and, to a lesser extent, discussion of sports, became the major vehicles of communication for boys. Yet academic achievement was needed as well, economically necessary and attractive in its own right in a rapidly professionalizing society. Only the very good athlete could get by without serious attention to its demands, though, particularly in

American universities, enthusiasm for sports and the male-bonding behavior of athletes and alumni, so useful for getting good business jobs, seemed on occasion to eliminate the academic side.[54] At best, the middle-class definition of manhood produced a reasonably well-rounded person, perhaps deficient in emotional expressiveness (a field still left to women), but trained in both mind and body. At worst, it furthered an almost schizophrenic polarization between the physically aggressive and the rational impulses—both seen as manly but easily at odds—within a class of boys or within the same individual.[55]

To this not unattractive but fragile brew the schools added another element: girls. Increasingly, brothers had sisters with whom they could compare school experiences. Tentatively, beginning in the United States in the early nineteenth century, boys and girls went to school together directly, even sharing the same classes; coeducation gradually spread upward from the primary schools. The patterns that resulted would ultimately affect male-female relationships in all social groups, but because of the particular definition of middle-class manhood, and the overall emphasis on education, the most enduring effects have been middle-class. On the whole, women's educational rise, and coeducation itself, have made the achievement of manhood more complex.

Why was the educational system not maintained as a male monopoly, as it had been save for private tutoring and some church-run elementary schools, in preindustrial Europe? What was important about nineteenth century education was not that it set separate tracks for men and women, but that it so lessened the gender gap. Middle-class girls were to be educated. They were taken out of the home for this, which gave them a valuable opportunity to find bonds among their fellows similar to the bonds long available to men. They might be shunted into arts and cooking classes, but they did learn to read, they were encouraged to think at least in some directions as no large group of women had ever been encouraged before. Educated women indeed took over a great deal of cultural patronage, which gave them a commanding, humanistic role and another claim to a distinctive superiority over the brute male even in an age when the humanities were declining.

Finally, women might follow some of the educational paths of males themselves. With a lot of hesitation about the damage it might do to the special constitutions of women, the men in charge of education allowed and even encouraged this development. The same Cincinnati school board that woried about the impact of "severe" reasoning let women into the high schools in 1848 and by the 1860s was arguing that women could perform the same mental labor as men.[56]

The Christian tradition, already ambiguous about women's equality, received a tremendous boost from the Enlightenment and subsequent liberalism, which could hold that women were men's equals in ways other than the sight of God. These doctrines spread particularly in the middle class, the same class that produced such hostile condemnations of women's capacities. The growing emphasis on the special purity of women and their real importance as homemakers and mothers raised women's status in fact and theory alike. How could purity be kept ignorant? How could men, in some ways the grosser gender, deny women the right to add to their charm and ethical sense? If liberal doctrines did not justify female education, the new, halting sense of moral inferiority would. The businessman could easily accept his wife's implicit arguments that he was essentially a money-making clod and that educated women were vital to take the edges off rough maleness. Not only their roles as mothers but also their special reform efforts brought women to a logical interest in education. The nineteenth century saw a host of reforms in women's position: new property rights, new rights in divorce and child custody, and ultimately, new voting rights. This reflected pressure from women, to be sure, but also the combined impact of liberalism and notions of moral inferiority on middle-class men. Men remained profoundly divided on the increase in power of women. The middle class produced articulate opposition to every new gain, particularly from professional people who sensed in women an economic threat (like many schoolteachers in Germany who began to oppose feminism even before it directly reached their country from England), but the educational door continued to open.[57]

For boys, the presence of girls in school made the complexity of their own gender identity more clear and precise. In the United States it was becoming evident by the 1890s that boys, in the early grades, did not perform as well as girls; their lower grades and snide comparisons by teachers vividly brought this home to them. A boy might avoid this losing competition and choose instead to emphasize his physical abilities, including his propensity to fight and his orientation toward sports. His roughness and aggressiveness, his difficulty in paying attention had helped put him behind the girls in school anyway. Working-class boys could commonly plump for this course, for they had little that would call them toward schoolroom success as a definer of masculinity, and girls' abilities would merely increase the sense of the difference between the sexes and the irrelevance of school to real worth. But the middle-class male could not make the choice so easily. His competitive training called him not only to physical excellence but also to excellence in the classroom.

The school experience, particularly when directly coeducational, thus brought a sense of the differences between male and female into a competitive approach on the part of males that would be carried into adulthood, into reactions to women's demands for entry into male professions or parity at work. It certainly colored reactions to the schools and to images of manhood. The fact was that women not only did well in school; they also threatened to outnumber men in schools at least in the Anglo-Saxon countries (if only because boys had more breadwinning responsibilities and earlier job opportunities). They increasingly taught in the schools. The whole impact of gender roles in education received considerable, and inconclusive, attention in the later nineteenth century. Some men warned that women teachers, who would naturally favor the docility of their own sex against the proper spirits of boys, would try to "quench all the natural pugnacity of our boys below the point of even chivalrous spunk." Some male authorities railed against the "increasing femininity of the schools" that tended to "overvalue the softer and more showy arts at the expense of the hard essentials."[58] More perceptive observers saw the larger problem. A Chicago high-school principal put it this way: "How many parents have been utterly discouraged because their boys behave so badly compared with the girls' standard, and how many boys have become as deeply discouraged by being made to believe that they were abnormal." Boys' higher dropout rates, though probably mostly for economic reasons, were seen as having some relationship to this gender problem, and a few classes set up just for boys were viewed as helpful.[59]

The schools did not, of course, cause the tensions of middle-class masculinity, but rather reflected them. The real problem remained an uncertainty about the masculinity of purely mental activity (and a no longer distinctively manly level of mental training). The issue of gender in the schools was therefore left untouched. Women were cheaper as teachers. They were, perhaps, morally superior as guides for young children anyway, which counterbalanced concern about sissification. Despite the advance of women, middle-class men could still dominate the professions that mattered; they could still believe in their ultimate rational superiority and act on that belief. If the boy, doing "all right" in school, could really throw or kick the ball, if he showed a proper sense that girls were weaker, surely there was nothing wrong? (He would presumably grow into greater academic achievement as well, in the higher schools.) In sum, changes in the demands of the middle-class economy complicated the definition of manhood and the values necessary for socialization to it. Boyhood and manhood were more distinct than before, which could make both experiences more difficult.

Schools certainly contributed to the widening gap between fathers and sons. Many men dismissed the whole business of preprofessional training as a maternal responsibility. For while men and ideas of manhood shaped important features of the education of boys, men's routine responsibility for boys in the middle class steadily eroded, and with it a key element of patriarchalism. Schooling brought familial as well as economic change to the socialization of boys. No more than the working-class male could the middle-class male ultimately maintain the patriarchal role at home while carrying out his responsibilities at work. Schools, cutting into apprenticeship training, may have reduced maternal functions in fact, but they reduced paternal responsibility as well and cut the father's functions, in some cases, down to nothing beyond procreation itself.

Middle-class patriarchalism had supports that were not available to the working class. If random physical violence was usually unacceptable, corporal discipline was not, and the hold of property and the ability to finance and direct the proper education remained valid in many cases. But father-son tensions could increase when the father maintained strict goals for the son, and diminishing means to enforce them, without a frequent physical presence or even a direct training role. The glorification of mother was not idle. Women took over the whole childrearing function. They might dutifully attempt to promote the male qualities of their sons, or they might try to raise their sons in their own image; fathers, correspondingly, might be more or less pleased with the results of the division of family labor. We have noted some changes in the ideal child, in the later nineteenth century, for which women were supposed to be particularly responsible. But while genuine partiarchs remained—authoritarian households survived into the present century— the sense of masculine fulfillment through being a father declined in the middle class as among the workers.[60]

This was heightened by the rapid reduction of family size, increasingly (from 1850 or so onward) through artificial methods of birth control. Men might urge birth control as a means of fulfilling their economic needs, because the middle-class budget could be sorely burdened by too many children. Birth control might be practiced by women on their own initiative; some of the new devices were advertised as usable without the husband's knowledge. But the decision usually was mutual. It involved strain for both parties. Women were in many ways most affected because their self-definition depended more exclusively on parenthood. But they could claim the endlessly growing responsibilities of motherhood as a partial compensation. The early twentieth century produced a new psychological needs for infants and children which were the mothers' responsibility. The father, with a shrinking role for each individual child, inevitably turned his attention elsewhere, a vicious circle in which each new job distraction further reduced the fathering function which in turn reduced the satisfactions from fathering.[61]

In this situation, domestic patriarchalism depended increasingly on husband-wife relations. If the woman, as childrearer, was the subordinate agent of the husband, a man could still claim some hold as family boss. This was what many men strove for, and some women accepted, aided by the earlier definitions of male and female in the middle class. Patterns varied widely from one family to the next. Areas of stronger religious, particularly Catholic, sentiment maintained patriarchal dominance more fully than else-where. Housing patterns were important, and remained so into the twentieth century. Countries like France, where most urban middle-class families lived in apartments, made patriarchalism easier, for men could still live relatively close to work, often coming home for lunch, while close quarters made greater family discipline necessary.

It was the solidity of earlier gender definitions that played the greatest role in bolstering the sagging patriarchs. Suburbanization, so rapid in England and the United States after 1850, fulfilled some shallow though appealingly primi-tive patriarchal goals: One had one's own castle and could express age-old impulses to defend territoriality by putting up fences or fighting with the neighbors and could indulge the newer imagery of the economic jungle fighter winning a livelihood for his sheltered brood. But suburbanism increased the physical separation of the man from his home, and left the woman in greater effective control.[62]

Inevitably, despite a strong conservative impulse, public definitions began to shift away from full patriarchalism in husband-wife relations. Male superiority remained, but it hovered over the home rather than being expressed in it directly. As a French doctor wrote in the 1870s: "Happiness in marriage is not possible unless each keeps perfectly within his role and confines himself to the virtues of his sex, without encroaching on the prerogatives of the opposite sex." The husband's function, based on his superior force and activities, was "to represent the family or to direct it in its relations with the external world and to ensure its preservation and its development. The wife, so well endowed with grace, intuition and a ready emotional sympathy, has as her mission to preside over the internal life of the house, whose well-being she ensures by her knowledge of domestic details."[63] The man might take great pride in providing for the home, but would there be anything distinctively manly about being in it, now that it was his wife's domain?

There were three basic patterns open to middle-class families from the later nineteenth century onward, though inevitably they overlap. The first was a patriarchalism successfully maintained, by whatever combination of personalities and circumstances, so that a man could judge himself ruler in his house when he was there.

The second was a patriarchalism manqué, asserted, believed in, but no longer functioning well. The father would feel his grasp slipping over daughters as well as sons. Many middle-class girls began to pick up some novel habits by the later nineteenth century, wearing shorter, looser skirts; bicycling off, unchaperoned, with their boyfriends; playing new games. It was daughters, after all, who became the "new girls" of the turn of the century or the flappers of the 1920s, with their short skirts and clinging dresses, their smoking and drinking, their wild dances. Daughters' loose behavior might stir some primitive emotions of paternal jealousy; they could certainly rouse disapproval, a sense of failure. (And indeed the new behavior, including aspects of feminism, probably did reflect a breakdown in the patriarchal role, a failure to provide, through a clear masculine model, a means of perpetuating the standards of one generation into the next.) Both parents might be shocked by their children's new behavior, and mothers might logically look to their own prime responsibility for childrearing. But this could be no comfort to an outraged father, whose authority seemed so blatantly defied, whose children were escaping him so completely. It has been suggested that many a mother was at most ambivalent about each successive generation of "new girls," not approving their behavior but envying it. For patriarchalism could break down in husband-wife relations too, as wives tired of their small domestic realm and began to press for new functions or, as feminists, to agitate for new rights. A man might, as a good liberal, approve of the goals that his wives and daughters were generating, but he would seldom understand the women's new values. While married middle-class women did not yet defy their roles to the extent of entering the labor force in large numbers, they did acquire increasing legal equality in domestic rights, a further blow to patriarchalism. They could own property independently, control earnings and divorce. A French law of 1938 even gave them a right to object to moving, should the husband decide this unilaterally. Laws and court interpretation steadily moved from giving women equal rights in child custody disputes to virtually exclusive rights, by the 1920s and 1930s, under "tender years" doctrines that held that any child under twelve naturally went to the mother—a complete reversal of gender privileges and responsibilities in less than a century! The patriarch, clearly, had to defend himself outside the law.[64]

The third large pattern, attracting increasing interest throughout the nineteenth century, was to abandon a patriarchal in favor of a mutual relationship with the wife. As the middle-class family lived in increasing isolation from other kin, with fewer and fewer children, husband and wife were inevitably thrown more together, if not in terms of time at least in terms of emotional alternatives. The decline of economic considerations in middle-class marriage (though they by no means disappeared) encouraged affection, even love as the basis for marriage, and popular literature touted the love match. Differences in gender function, between work and hearth, did not prevent a sharing of key decisions. The new prestige of women, as bearers of purity in a troubled world, could enhance mutuality. In practice many men had to respect women who successfully took over the huge tasks of running the home and raising the children.

Yet there were problems with mutuality. Huge remnants of patriarchalism had to be cut through, for both men and women. What of the woman who carried mutuality beyond the home, to bother her husband with complaints about her unfairly boring role in life? Sexual barriers might inhibit love even in a "love" match. If many women, by 1900, were reporting sexual compatibility with their husbands, most middle-class couples entered marriage with differential sexual experience and with rooted beliefs in male roughness, female passivity. It was easy to be clumsy, particularly for the man to be overhasty, and so set a pattern of tension for a whole marriage. New birth control devices, and unfamiliarity with them, didn't help matters.[65] In a real sense, men and women were not conditioned to love in the same way. Men were not supposed to be emotional; they might have difficulty handling the interdependence which shared love implied. If they did love, and many doubtless did, they added another conflict to the definition of manhood. For the man already told to overcome his natural sexual lusts was now told to be at once a tiger in the outside world and a gentle, compassionate person at home. This was a difficult balance to achieve, and it was not aided by the fact that all the new masculine traits seemed so clearly feminine. For the kind of mutuality that was being groped for was quite new, and not just in its implication of shared family power. Men had never before been urged to put such an emotional stake in a relationship with women, though many had obviously done so in fact. While their unusually extensive contacts with their own mothers prepared them in part, there was a perceived dependence involved in mutuality, a denial of self through return to a mother figure, which was naturally resented and which a woman, who separated herself from mother in heterosexual love, could not readily comprehend. Mutuality or some approach to it gained, but it was not easy and, as the rising divorce rate suggested, it was by no means uniformly successful.[66]

Many men, unable to fulfill a patriarchal role or unable to find in mutuality a clear masculine image, turned away from the family for their specifically masculine satisfactions. Work remained a male sphere. Laments of some secondary-school teachers about female competition showed a sensitivity to threat, as did bitter resistance to the entry of women into law or medicine, but the fact was that men were still unchallenged by women in most middle-class forms of work. Here was an advantage that had been less available to workers. Some middle-class men could see themselves as decision-makers, as owners, or simply as candidates for mobility, and so achieve or anticipate a masculine independence that few workers could even aspire to. There was satisfaction, too, in the conquest and mastery of knowledge in the professions and technical fields. The middle-class work ethic allowed some men to identify themselves completely with their work.

Yet this recourse was not open to the majority of middle-class men; the work ethic was no longer completely viable for most people in the class that had developed it.[67] In the later nineteenth century, producing property was concentrated in fewer and fewer hands. Companies became more and more impersonal; few men could look at them as their own creations. Management, the new directive principle, provided various gradations of power over people and things, but usually in a hierarchical setting in which there always seemed to be another layer on top. Even paternalism declined, although it did not disappear. The new labor unions sought to rob businessmen of any belief that they could be father figures to their workers. These developments were part of the ineluctable dynamic of industrialization, and some of them, like the modifications of paternalism, partially righted obvious inequities of the first industrial decades. Yet they created a certain element of dependency, a feeling of loss of control, in large sectors of the middle class and they directly challenged some of the earlier criteria of manliness. Furthermore, much of the work being done in the business bureaucracies was dull; it was hard to imagine oneself a bull male while pushing papers about a desk. The middle-class began a historic split between a minority who found their jobs gripping, who would easily define themselves by work, and a majority who, while not completely antagonized by labor, would have been foolish to identify with it too completely.[68]

Yet what else was there? Many white collar workers fell back on their own version of instrumentalism, wrapping their manhood in their earning level and in the material symbols this could acquire.[69] The jungle, the lair of the competitive hunting male, turned into the ratrace, where the war was for survival and self-justification as a good provider. The goal was to prove one could hang on in a bureaucratic slot, where men easily exaggerated their difficulties of survival, and to prove to other men, and to one's women, that one could hack out an improving standard of living. All of this could involve a good bit of otherwise unnecessary escalation of needs. It kept men slogging away at jobs that they could not even admit they did not like (for here the middle class lacked the obvious protest outlet of the otherwise disadvantaged working-class male). Job security was occasionally risky, for jobs might be lost. Technology, while not nearly so ominous as for the working male, threatened possible displacement from the 1880s onward; a combination of typewriters and female secretaries, for example, virtually did away with the male clerk in many offices. After 1900, particularly in the 1920s, inflation could erode the possibility of maintaining living standards; the depression of the 1930s cast the pall of unemployment even on many professional people, with literally suicidal effect. For if the work failed, the man had failed, and this in an economic system where only a handful of men could claim anything like personal control.

There was some effort and some success in developing male expression off the job. Although many middle-class men were poor consumers, leaving basic decisions to their wives, certain consumption items were tossed up that suggested special male qualities. The automobile, so long a largely male preserve, was the most obvious case in point, its speed and power endlessly fascinating, its characteristics an obvious conversational link with other men. An interest in drinking prowess could develop, although again not always separate from female activities. Even in the nineteenth century, particularly on the Continent, groups of business and professional people developed an interest in drink and pride in their capacity from their school days onward. Prohibition in the United States furthered the association of drink with middle-class social and business life. Athletic interests could be maintained, and the middle class provided hosts of spectators for the new professional sports which they could afford more readily than most workers. In the United States, professional baseball rose to prominence by its appeal to middle-class men after 1900; the sport conscientiously presented itself as a framework for individual prowess of the sort that had made male America great, and by drawing players from college ranks, into the 1930s, it offered ready social identification as well.

The middle-class male remained somewhat nervous about the very principle of leisure. Was leisure not frivolity, and a man destined rather to work? Middle-class people did in fact learn to play more, or at least to devote more time to non-work activities, but often with an air of apology. Emphasis on physical activity had some of the same limitations for older men as it did for workers, casting them prematurely into spectator roles, men-by-proxy. At the same time, middle-class men, after their school years, had more trouble than workers in finding pleasure in grouping. Their home-centeredness was marked from the early nineteenth century onward. Of course there were all-male clubs and organizations associated with business or community; veterans' activities, so huge and militant between the world wars, provided a reminiscent maleness for middle-class men particularly; politics itself was often a male preserve for the class. In the United States conventions of one sort or another, fraternal or professional, provided periodic outlets for expressions of masculinity in drink and wenching. But male associations, sometimes even intense male friendships, were limited by the competitive principles of the middle class. Friends were often rivals at work or rivals in status display; it was dangerous to get too close.[70]

The middle class had long found home-focused leisure safer than male-associational leisure in any event, and more often than not the man with time on his hands went back to his family. Leisure outlets developed here too. The radio came to displace family reading as a gathering point. Many of the new consumption fads were based on family activities. Vacations became increasingly popular. Much of this was successful, much, indeed, immensely promising from the standpoint of future diversification of interest. But it was not too clearly male. And much of it returned men to questions about what their role in the family was, questions that so many had sought to avoid by concentrating on being good providers.

The dilemmas of middle-class masculinity should not be exaggerated. Contradictions in the values men were supposed to manifest—lover/boss, stud/monk, jock/scientist—also meant latitude in choosing a precise role. In this respect, middle-class men were definitely better off than workers. Many men successfully juggled slightly boring work, not fully adequate leisure, and a somewhat confusing family pattern into acceptable mix that gave them little need to raise basic questions. Yet the rough edges did show. The first major wave of feminism, around the turn of the century, challenged not only new political rights that men had earlier acquired, leaving women behind (though after the vote was granted the woman's movement largely fizzled as a statement of collective protest) but it raised questions about male job monopolies and about male sexual behavior that could easily be taken up later. Feminism followed in part from a new middle-class image of women, from new functions that men as well as women helped define, from a liberal approach that men could easily share. But it was a statement that, however favorable the reforms to date, they were insufficient for women and that gender roles required further change. Even without the spur of women, men harbored problems of their own that ultimatley had to find expression. They had to ask how industrial work and models of masculinity could be made to gibe; and how male needs and aspirations could be expressed off the job; and what kind of family a man needed to know he was a man. The fact was that manhood was losing some of its most obvious functional utility; it remained to discover how it could best be adapted as a means of personal identification in a world that offered all too few ways for a person to know who he/she was.

In this sense, the evolution of middle-class manhood in the nineteenth century presented many challenging questions. Economic manhood was at first bolstered by analogies between work and the hunt. Yet not only changes in ownership and bureaucratization but the rise of educational levels complicated the definition, and so complicated the way boys were socialized. Mutuality in husband-wife relations hinted at a realistic adjustment to the reduction of time spent at home and the new valuation of women's moral worth.[71] The association of manhood with physical prowess—in bed, in sports, in battle—warred with a general middle-class aversion to violence (and a pronounced ability to avoid the military draft, as in France after 1871), with the importance and attraction of intellectual skills, and with the injunction of moral self-discipline.

The difficulties of male self-definition went beyond relationships with women or concern about how one appeared in women's eyes, though these were important. They involved proof before other men and above all before oneself. There was no easy test, no single rite of passage, and the proof was a matter of lifelong endeavor.[72] Only in late age could a man give up the effort to meet tests, often with a loss of personal worth.[73] Small wonder that men (not only middle-class men, of course) manifested an increasing number of socially pathological symptoms, always disproportionately male but now even more so: crime, suicide, alcoholism, premature death. Small wonder that attractively simple male images won such popularity: the Westerns, the Tarzan stories of the 1920s. Small wonder that the denigration of women, though at odds with real social trends and with the new middle-class valuation of women, constantly recurs through the late nineteenth and early twentieth centuries. More fully than the working-class version, middle-class manhood in the nineteenth century was associated with too many achievements that were, in fact, beyond men's power to control. This is one reason why middle-class criteria proved less consistent and less durable than the working-class counterpart. The legacy of the nineteenth century, for middle-class men, was less a viable redefinition of manhood, though elements of this were present, than a set of questions that had to be answered.

6. Manhood and the Contemporary Era

The character of contemporary manhood in the Western world differs from that of the end of the nineteenth century. Traits of working-class and middle-class men persist, but some adaptations have been made. If it is true that propertylessness still characterizes modern society—in the sense of ownership of producing property—it is also true that the worst shock has passed. Men do not now claim this kind of ownership as a normally expected achievement. Still more significant, the last several decades have seen a substantial acceptance of the decline of patriarchalism. While manhood is still operating within the framework of the society spawned by industrialization, reactions have evolved. Some may not prove durable. We wait, for example, to judge the extent of the waning of militarism in the Western world, and particularly in the United States, as the shock to conventional manhood administered by revulsion to the Vietnam War begins to fade. Some changes may prove durable but unfortunate, and manhood has also faced new jolts of more recent vintage. We are not, at this stage, positing either goodness or stability in the contemporary situation of men.

Yet the idea of a change in tone retains validity. What caused the break, and when did the break occur? It is difficult to suggest a precise periodization in modern men's history, partly because we do not know enough yet, partly because phenomena such as gender roles and behavior do not change neatly, quickly, or completely. But a number of developments came together in the early twentieth century that suggest a major break in the history of both genders, most obviously among women, but among men as well.

We have already touched on a second generation of industrialization, which spread in the factories as well as in crafts and offices, progressively reducing the need for physical strength and for traditional, male-dominated productive skill.[1] A growing minority of men also began to shift from productive to service work, which prompted the development of traits more relevant to pleasing other people. Here was a direct challenge to some of the work criteria men had spelled out for themselves in both major classes during the nineteenth century. At the same time, educational levels of women approached those of men and it gradually became clear that a male monopoly of the summits of scientific learning was not ordained either by God or by nature. Human factors have delayed the full testing of the new technology.

Women still collectively lag in mathematics and engineering. There are diverse reports about their performance on the floor of the steel mills. They have yet to be tested in a major war. But, clearly, the range of gender difference at work has narrowed; quite possibly we can socialize out any differences that do remain.[2]

By the First World War increasing numbers of men and women glimpsed the implications of the new technology and educational levels. Both genders had reason to pull back from a quick probe of the full implications for the economy. The problem with using technology to define a new trend in men's history is that its effects proved so gradual. Notoriously, for example, women hired for jobs in World War I were quickly displaced upon the return of men.[3] But it was in the 1920s and 1930s that it became clear that, if job equality was still distant, women were being preferred for employment over two groups of men, the old and very young, a trend with which we are still grappling as we retire the old men and leave the young unskilled in often appalling levels of unemployment.

It was not, of course, totally unprecedented to have a technology that drew women close to men in economic performance. The twentieth century is witnessing a closing of the gap which the nineteenth century had opened up, against the greater parity of roles that had existed in agricultural society. The family has become again a multi-producer unit, although its members now work separately and outside the home.[4] But the technological change came on the heels of a Victorian culture that had unusually elevated the image, if not the power, of women, while tying men to fulfilment in a work role. Here, too, there are implications still to be worked out, as women naturally move forward economically while retaining many claims to their Victorian purity and motherhood, and men seek a supplement to an economic focus for manhood.

Complicating matters further were the results of birth control, which, in returning families to a more stable size, recalled societies of the past but which has no precedent in its impact on women.[5] Birth control, as it had developed by the 1920s and 1930s in North America and Western Europe, summed up previous gains in nutrition and health care in suggesting that families and whole societies could maintain themselves demographically without involving women in childbearing and immediately related maternity for more than a short period of their lives. It indeed involved a belief that women could not, in the mass, be allowed to do more than this, lest family and social prosperity be jeopardized. Here was a huge blow to hoary traditions of femininity. Of course it took time for the implications to be absorbed. Women, abetted by conservative men, were inventive in devising new things that mothers could do for each child, new responsibilities, just as they steadily increased standards of home care so that these took as long to achieve as they did before the advent of domestic technology. There was no huge leap into alternative activities for women, or a culture to support these, until 1940 or beyond. Yet the stark fact was there: mothering was not what it used to be. There was time to be filled, new self-justifications to be developed. And this, inevitably, had huge implications for men, just as birth control itself did in reducing the most obvious paternal function.

The development of a new technology and the extension of birth control suggest the possibility of a break in men's history around 1900 itself, which has the neatness of corresponding with a new century. We have suggested, particularly in discussing the middle-class male, a host of contradictions that were cresting around the same time, some of them related to technological and demographic change, though it is true that the existence of a host of questions about gender does not assure that society will turn to answer them. A number of developments simultaneously closed some doors on aspects of manhood that had been of at least ritualistic importance.[6] Feminism, peaking in the second decade of this century, was a direct product of the changes affecting women; it did reduce the differentials between men and women in legal rights and privileges and could seem symbolically ominous to manhood generally, the first massing of women for specifically women's purposes. In the United States the frontier was closed, producing a symbolic sense of cramp even among men who had no urge actually to go out to test their prowess in the raw. The more general bureaucratization of society, reducing the reality of any images of the pioneer industrialist carving out his own and his family's independent economic place, was a more subtle but more pervasive restraint. For workers, unionization tended to curb male protest spontaneity.

World War I was a further blow. Men in the nineteenth century had touted the martial arts. Imperialism, now itself closed off, had offered cheap, vicarious boosts to this aspect of manhood. It was not of course clear that middle-class youths, raised to be competitive but not violent, were really collectively suited to war, but this was a contradiction of modern maleness that had not been tested. More important, even for the fully martial man, the war—greeted with such enthusiasm by the eager troops of France and Germany and the women who waved them off from a safe distance—was not glorious at all. Only the work of a few flying aces could give any solace to latter-day knights errant. Quite apart from being dreadfully bloody, the war was dull, routinized, unheroic. The only usefully manly feature was the small-group loyalty that trenchmates could develop (a new or renewed form of male bonding that researchers were soon to find in the factories as well), along with some comparatively infrequent opportunities to abuse women in the time-honored manner of conquering males.[7] Male bonding, continued among veterans, could produce continued support for militarism. World War I did not end the association between war and maleness, but it was a tremendous shock to Western society in all aspects of life, including the male warrior image. Large numbers of men, along with many women, drew the sensible conclusion that modern war and modern maleness should not mix. But this of course, while admirable, simply added to the problem of how men were to know they were men, if they could no longer even look forward to war.

Amid all this uncertainty many men and women alike rushed to bolster existing gender roles. The United States Congress enacted Mother's Day in 1914. Like many apotheoses, it was a bit belated. Nazism and a host of other, less vicious, reactionary movements expressed a desire to turn back the gender clock. Women were to dress in simple peasant costumes, stay at home, breed, cook, and pray. (Many women, disproportionately supporting the Nazi movement, found some charm in this.) Men of course, would not only work but strut, parade, fight, kill, and contribute their own mite to breeding. But the Nazi regime actually encouraged the rise of women in the universities and the labor force, for it could not afford a total war against the trends of the twentieth century.[8] And even most German men did not greet renewed war with any enthusiasm. Men in the Western Europe and the United States, who could see war as a manly defense of home and purity, may have obtained more of a lift, and World War II did see more opportunities for heroism than its predecessor.

More generally, despite a steady though modest increase in the employment of women, and a serious jolt to the association between manhood and work caused by the Depression, it remained true that most married women did not take paid jobs (and that most men apparently found this appropriate) and that the domestic image of wife and mother remained intact. A barely modified authoritarianism continued to describe the family stance of many middle-class men, particularly on the European continent, and working-class men more generally. Changes there were, as in the loosening of the public culture of sexuality and a broadening of the female image to include provocativeness as well as the gentler virtues. But in a fundamental sense the basic outlines of the definition of manhood, and the behavior of men, followed from patterns visible in the nineteenth century. There was too much inertia in gender roles for the impact of basic technological and demographic change, even supplemented by key events such as World War I, to induce a redefinition of gender. In dealing with contemporary manhood we must dip back into the 1920s and 1930s for suggestions of new trends, for the fundamental causes were indeed in place. The change of tone in manhood and in relationships between men and women, however, is more recent.

This raises another important possibility, as we seek a more definite point of change and reason for change: the dynamic of men's history has been taken over by that of women's history, and men are changing because women—feminists—are forcing them to. This approach is largely incorrect and misleading, but it has often been forcefully stated, particularly the United States, by various feminists.[9]

Never before in the history of the species have groups of women attacked men with more verbal violence than during the past decade in the United States. Never before have the conventions of gender differentiation been so thoroughly challenged. The earlier round of feminism, itself unique in terms of historical precedent, elicited comparably wide support from middle-class women in a number of countries. It was more violent in a literal sense, but it did not represent such a thorough rethinking of the bases of gender relation-ships, or challenge the male world at so many points, as the admittedly diverse facets of the present movement.[10]

It would be easy to turn a discussion of men in recent decades into a portrait of manhood on the run, assailed by unassailable feminists, or, even worse, embroiled in vicious and petty counterattacks. Without question, many men remain guilty of immense unfairness to women. Some of the unfairness is new, as women have altered the definition of what fairness is, notably in the world of work. Some is traditional, such as wife beating and sexual assault. Many feminists argue that even the traditional abuse is on the rise, as men turn to the more primitive physical response. Wifebeaters may range up to 20 percent of all men in the contemporary United States.[11] As wives strive for more independence, the motivation for wifebeating may indeed have increased. But in absence of historical record we do not know, for the only trend that is clear is a greater willingness of women to report the crimes.[12] Undeniably, a real problem exists, whatever its historical assess-ment. Yet, although some articulate feminists and some distressingly inarticu-late men bid fair to lock in a battle of the sexes, this is not the real story of relationships between the sexes or of trends among men themselves in the present society.

The temptation nevertheless exists, particularly in academe or at its fringes, to take the feminist claims as the framework for discussion of gender relationships or even male activity directly, during the second half of the twentieth century. One could easily deal with men as they relate to feminist demands, as opponents or adapters, and the male world as it needs to be redefined to fit not only the sought-after rights for women but also the potential benefits to human beings in general from a revision of gender roles.[13] At their best feminists have not so much attacked men as pitied them, taking up themes of female moral superiority which echo from the otherwise-despised Victorian culture. Contemporary feminist analysis of men has become a comment on how men have wronged and still wrong women and themselves.

However, the feminist approach to men in contemporary society is unduly narrow for several reasons. Feminism does not describe all women or a complete behavior change in most women.[14] Men can, without too much trouble, find women who agree with whatever their definition of masculinity is. They sense moreover that even many putative feminists, women definitely pursuing new roles, have actually an ambiguous attitude to such male functions as that of prime provider. Many women may be asking men in general to give them career room while still assuming that paterfamilias will serve as the economic backstop, in case the career does not pan out. This is quite understandable in human terms and in terms of the difficult transitional situation of contemporary women, but it does not require a totally new set of standards for men themselves.

Geographical problems loom large as well. The contemporary American feminist movement has no exact parallels elsewhere, in terms of substance if not of rhetoric. Yet other behavior patterns of women related to feminism, notably massive entry into the labor force, characterize advanced industrial societies generally. It is analytically preferable to try to grasp general developments in the activities of men, including their relationships to women, in these societies, before turning to American peculiarities. The American family definitely raises more questions than its counterpart in Western Europe; vastly higher divorce rates are of course a major symptom of this, but specific patterns of child raising may be involved as well. Clearly, and contrary to so much analysis that assumes that America is *the* logical product of industrial capitalism, American husbands and fathers are not the only kind around; they are not even, demonstrably, the wave of the future. We will argue that a number of large trends can be discerned for men in industrial society generally, based on Western tradition and the changing demands of the industrial economy. The American variants can then, as necessary, be pursued with relative precision; but they do not define the most basic periodization in the history of Western man.

Feminism is a product of large social trends, not primarily, to date at least, a cause of them. It encourages some of these trends and it is an essential justification for role changes that women pursue with logic but also with great difficulty. Feminist rhetoric, particularly in the United States and most particularly among intellectuals, may complicate male reaction to these same trends. The American version of contemporary feminism is not a necessary product of the trend, though some articulate feminist expression has arisen throughout the Western world, but it is a logical one, not an autonomous or aberrant product. In the terms most relevant to our inquiry about contemporary men, we can assess feminism as a several-layered amplification of an inevitable change in gender relationships.

The inevitability hinges on the decline in women's reproductive role. After a few generations required to assimilate the fact that a whole life could no longer be based around childrearing, increasing numbers of women simply had to find additional outlets, and most sought them in work. The entry of married women into the labor force swelled rather slowly until 1940, then picked up momentum. In the United States, 5.6 percent of all married women in 1900 were formally employed, but 40 percent had jobs by 1970 and 50 percent just five years later.[15] Comparable patterns developed in Western Europe. This change in itself has had major impact on men's roles, particularly within the family, reducing their ability and their professed desire to play the patriarch. In general, for economic and personal reasons, men have been able to adapt to the new economic balance between the genders at least insofar as it means that women will have some economically productive role.

Feminism, however, building on this trend, raises two additional issues, and concerning men's response to these the jury is still out. The feminists ask not just for jobs, which women are getting, but for good jobs, jobs equivalent

Power and Responsibility: *Creation*, from an anonymous fourteenth-century French manuscript (courtesy Carnegie-Mellon University Library)

Suffering and Compassion: Detail of the *Ecce Homo* by Guido Reni (courtesy Carnegie-Mellon University Library)

From the Age of Patriarchialism: *Family Portrait* by Cornelis de Vos, Flemish seventeenth-century (courtesy Editions d'Art Albert Skira)

Men's Work: Mining bituminous coal around 1900 (courtesy Carnegie Library of Pittsburgh)

A Striker's Meeting: Reacting to scab labor around 1885 (courtesy Carnegie Library of Pittsburgh)

The Brutal Husband (from *Punch*, May 18, 1874)

The Intemperate Man (from Timothy Shay Arthur, *Grappling with the Monster, or the Curse and Cure of Strong Drink*, Philadelphia, 1854)

From a German fertilizer advertisement, 1910

Midwestern Farm Boy, circa 1910

From a United States World War I poster

THE PARLIAMENTARY FEMALE
Father of the Family. 'COME, DEAR; WE SO SELDOM GO OUT TOGETHER NOW—
CAN'T YOU TAKE US ALL TO THE PLAY TONIGHT?'
Mistress of the House, and M.P. 'HOW YOU TALK, CHARLES! DON'T YOU SEE
THAT I AM TOO BUSY. I HAVE A COMMITTEE TO-MORROW MORNING, AND I HAVE
MY SPEECH ON THE GREAT CROCHET QUESTION TO PREPARE FOR THE EVENING.'
Punch Almanack 1853

The First Round of Feminism (from *Punch*, 1853)

"I'm getting tired of you throwing your weight around."

A Period of Domesticity (Copr. © 1948 James Thurber. Copr. © Helen W. Thurber and Rosemary Thurber Sauers. From THE BEAST IN ME AND OTHER ANIMALS, published by Harcourt Brace Jovanovich, New York. Originally printed in *The New Yorker*)

The Depression: Unemployed men on a Pittsburgh wharf (courtesy Carnegie Library of Pittsburgh)

Sports in the 1940s (courtesy Carnegie Library of Pittsburgh)

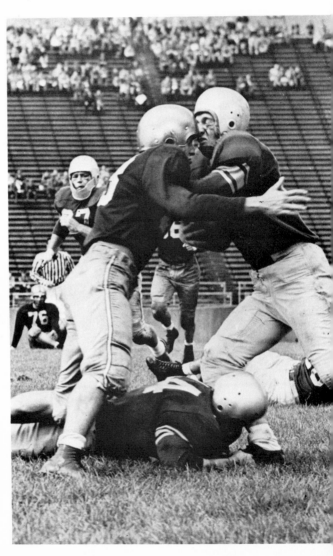

Grandfathering in the 1960s

to men's. And, facing difficulties in this quest, they amplify their demand with a host of comments about gender relationships overall and about men's own nature.

It is premature to generalize about men's reaction to these two aspects of feminism. Articulate women have been pressing men so far particularly at their most vulnerable point of professional self-definition, their claims to some special power to reason. Contemporary feminism, like its predecessor, is based heavily on the achievements women can boast in the schools, as feminists demand an equal share in the fruits of education, notably full access to the jobs deriving from professional training. Male professionals, particularly academics, have long been uncertain about the specifically masculine definition of their achievement in any event. For a heartening number of people, brains are brains. Unquestionably, women have faced huge difficulties even so. Beleaguered male professionals use attempts at humor to mask an angry attempt to keep women in their place, maintaining a definable tradition of rhetorical separation between women and rational power. "We might as well hire the one with boobs," says the history department chairman faced with unsurmountable pressure to add a woman to his group, and he gets at least an appreciative titter in response. Direct sexual abuse still confronts the woman professional. The female intern, ready for her first round of duty in the operating room, meets the male resident who asks, "Do you screw?" and persists as the woman fears to complain, worried lest a largely male review board label her a troublemaker or complaining woman in a profession in which being a good fellow is enforced as a basic feature of training. Legal suits have already been required to open professions and professional training to more than a token number of women—the European lack of a civil-rights mechanism to force these issues is one of the explanations of the milder tone of the European movement. In a real sense male professionals are still dealing only with token numbers of female colleagues and competitors. If a few academic departments have substantial numbers of women, mainly in the less important humanistic fields that men long since conceded as particularly feminine, most do not, and the key American universities have been recalcitrant even at the token level. Professions such as law or medicine can expect a new wave of women, based on current enrollments in the schools, but their basic reaction has at least been delayed. It is, again, too soon to forecast outcome.

But the concessions so far can be viewed as fundamental, and the lack of concerted, collective male response, as opposed to a great deal of degrading, individual rearguard action, really rather surprising. (Even the American military reports scattered individual grumbling, not focused hostility, over women's limited entry into male ranks, particularly technical jobs.) For contemporary society sees a steady expansion in the economic and bureaucratic power that is based on access to knowledge, and there is no sign that men are going to raise traditional gender differentiations as a means to block women's basic right to acquire the same knowledge that men can acquire. A significant number of men actually support women's advance with a reasonably whole heart, and it is certainly from many men in or around the professions that the greatest male sympathy for feminism has stemmed, and the greatest modification of male styles of life.[16] For women's gains in this area relate to the ambiguities about manhood that had developed with industrialization itself, the willingness of many men to see in education and professional life a satisfactory personal definition not tied to the image of the hunting male, or the physical prowess associated with this image. If some professionals long sought to mark their turf off against women precisely because it was less obviously masculine in itself, others could carry the modifications of work-based masculinity even further. If some of the real tests are yet to come, there is no inevitability to a pattern of increasing male defensiveness, in which maleness will be based on exclusion of women or at attempts to exclude.

The situation in other male worlds is less clear. Most men are not professionals (and many rejoice in this fact), and most women cannot aspire to be. The male games of businessmen have not yet been seriously challenged by female intrusion. A variety of hazing devices, intended initially to prove men among men, will certainly long retard women's advance beyond the subordinate ranks already conceded to them. Drinking and social associations that are rigorously male, a freedom to travel and clock-based work day that vitually preclude those women who attempt to combine any traditional home functions with their work, still keep much of the corporate bureaucracy a male preserve. Lower on the social scale, the male world of the working class, though not unchanged, has been largely immune to the onslaught of a feminism that is mainly middle-class. (Feminists, in attacking wife abuse for example, are actually following a path set first by nineteenth-century female reformers, who began to try to reshape the working-class male, and it is not clear that their efforts will achieve any more complete success.) Specifically male recreation areas, notably athletics, maintain a clear gender differentiation, though one could argue a somewhat less rigorous one than before; male athletes, certainly, can remain secure in the belief that they can beat comparable women in any direct competition and in the knowledge that women are uninterested in the sports most directly associated with men in any event.[17]

As women press effectively for further and more equal entry into the male world, at work and in other activities, the results are simply incalculable. Without question some men, remote from direct female competition for their job, are already worried. If we do not know the trend of wife beating, it does seem probable that rates of sexual assault are up, as men confused about their own identity among changing women prove themselves to themselves in the most brutal fashion. Remote from this extreme, hosts of men simply do not understand what articulate feminists are driving at, or even "their own" women who pick up some version of the feminist strivings. A young garbage collector is bewildered at his social worker-fiancée's job strivings; after all, a man should support a family and sire children and all this is so demanding that at least he should get a clear role in return. A psychiatrist says, with a good grace though overgeneralizing, that she knows of no successful marriage in which the woman's professional attainments surpass the man's. A magazine article describing and, on the whole, lauding those men who adapted (at least in part) to women's career goals prompts the following letter: "Real men aren't changing. They don't have to; they've never had the ridiculous hangups your article describes. So-called men who are changing aren't changing so much as they are allowing themselves to be cowed and browbeaten by a minority of lesbians, feminists and other female impersonators."[18]

Yet, without pretending to forecast, without denying many conflicts to come, it remains interesting that organized, articulate resistance to feminist goals has not developed. There are no men's groups designed to battle feminism head on; even established agents of reaction, such as the Ku Klux Klan, still prefer obvious racial, rather than gender, targets.[19] I think that a careful comparative study would reveal that the male reaction to the current round of feminism is milder than the one that greeted feminism at the turn of the century. Possibly we have become warier of overt, collective resistance to articulate trends that fall under a liberal banner, in this area as in others; it seems among other things to be rather futile. Yet it is not clear that men have disproportionately joined those women who battle feminist advocacy of abortion or who seek to associate feminism with lesbianism. Men could, in principle, resist more fiercely than they are, using their own power positions and the divisions among women themselves as levers. And perhaps someday they will. But for the moment men are clearly not united in gender defense; many of them, I think in fact most, are not haunted by the spectre of feminism; and some of course positively welcome aspects of feminism without being clearly labeled gender traitors.

The mildness of the overall reaction, I would argue, is unsurprising. It is in this sense that feminism, the product of major changes in the technological and reproductive basis of gender relationships, relates in part at least to trends among men themselves; which takes us back to the question of periodization in the history of manhood. In the first place, the ironically traditional features of feminism can strike a familiar chord with men, a sort of "yes, dear" response that can annoy the movement's proponents but is not entirely dismissive. For feminist comments on men recall the Victorian definition of gender in two respects. First, they preserve the women's claim to be family health expert, in the recurrent implication that many of the things men do are senseless and physically damaging.[20] And second, while vigorously removing women from the pedestal in most respects, many feminists keep a tentative leg up in stressing a moral inferiority of men, through emphasis on male violence, sexual abuse, unrestrained aggression and materialism. In calling

for men to purify themselves, either to control their nature or, more commonly now, somehow to find its androgynous quality amid the layers of accultura-
tion to a false maleness, feminists can evoke a well-established ambiguity, if
not guilt, among many men, particularly in the middle class. We were being
told a century ago that we were lustful and money-grubbing, and we are still
being told this, albeit by women who seek very new roles for themselves.
Feminism and related male liberationist comments really are carrying a step
further the kind of contrapuntal qualities of maleness that had clearly
developed a century ago. They are playing on currents of a loving, gentle
masculinity that indeed are older still in Western civilization. In effect, many
men can listen to feminist criticisms of the macho man because they have
long been trained to harbor doubts in themselves.

To be sure, feminism as a competitor for jobs and power and feminism as a
new civilizing agent beget their own contradictions. It is not always clear
whether articulate women want to beat men, or at least equal men, at their
own game or whether they want to soften the game for the sake of men as well
as women.[21] Correspondingly, a man may react well to one aspect of
feminism (respecting achievement-oriented women who can give him a run
for the money but not the preachments toward a gentler life), and not to the
other (disliking assertive women while also resenting aggressive men). But
even taken with its contradictions, as a plea for fuller realization of the
equality of women and men, feminism obviously strikes a chord for which
some men were being readied even in Victorian society. The desirability of
reconsidering conventional modes of treatment for women in light of a new
love for individual women or a new respect for the moral force of women in
general is by no means new.

Feminists have caused change. They may cause immense change in the
future if their activities prod men into direct resistance or if they somehow
produce the real upheavals in gender personality that some desire. But to
date, even in the United States, feminism has largely built upon and high-
lighted trends that followed from the technological and demographic changes
already sketched. This is not to dismiss feminism as a force, but to downplay
it as a fundamental force, thus far, in men's affairs. For men were changing
even before feminism, which is a final reason for the reception that aspects of
the movement have obtained.

The tone of men's self-definition has changed not just because of alterations in what women are doing or because of feminism as a subset of this,
though both factors are important. Men themselves have been altering their
patterns of behavior since the 1940s, a strand of causation that requires
careful attention. The new productive technology, reducing traditional skills
and heightening the importance of the middle class; the rise of the service
sector, with its stress on getting along with others; specific events, such as
the jolt of major war and of the Depression; and simple experience itself,
given the incompleteness of the nineteenth-century definitions of manhood in
practice and the contradictions of some key criteria, combined to produce

some rather new forms of male behavior, roughly from the end of World War II. It was at about this point, for example, that men began to spill over into service jobs previously monopolized by women, such as primary-school teaching, which tended to upgrade the jobs but also to emphasize a friendlier, gentler male personality.[22] Spurred without question by women's new work patterns as well, men seemed to ask some basic questions about their family role and the nature of their work commitment, the two areas where redefinition has been most active. On some key issues, sons simply decided that their fathers had been wrong, a rather interesting process that of course begs some questions about why: the best single answer may be the renewed separation of fathers and sons during World War II, but a cumulative effect of a number of longer-range trends comes into play as well. Men changed themselves, to some extent, in lagged response to a new technological and demographic structure. The changes among other things partially altered their relationships with women; they have conditioned male reactions to feminism, though feminists and many of the men's liberationists in their wake have ignored important autonomous trends in male behavior prior to and to an extent apart from their movement. One result is that the male roles attacked are sometimes slightly dated, and the goals held out to the adaptive male are less attractive than they might be if men were told to encourage ongoing trends, as within the family, instead of being urged to attack existing manhood directly.[23] Men's gropings to supplement the nineteenth-century reactions to industrialization, in some areas to go back to more traditional roles but bearing new characteristics as men, complete a sketch of the most recent break in men's history, and bring us to the task of defining what this break consisted of.

What we must trace in the following section is a substantial modification in practice of aspects of the nineteenth-century definition of masculinity, toward a reduction of the job-competitive stress and still more clearly, a groping toward a new familial role for men. The redefinition is in many ways inadequate. In saying that men have been responding not only to outside pressures we are not arguing that they have necessarily acted well, or even better than before. This redefinition has been occurring along with the changes in women's behavior that have culminated in feminism. Men as well as women have worked to tone down some of the excessive gender reactions to the first onslaught of industrialization. They too tacitly recognized one of the main facts of the twentieth century, that gender was decreasing in importance, not only economically but as a means of personal identification. If the nineteenth century revealed new gender attributes in the growing distinctiveness of the costumes of young men, so obviously the mid-twentieth century began to reverse the trend by homogenizing male and female dress not only in childhood but in youth. Similarly, a host of male groupings, from school fraternities to the corner bar—designed for separate gender identification and hazing rituals to prove manhood—began to fade by the 1950s.[24] These developments often antedated any formal feminist pressure, for they flowed from changes among men themselves. Indeed feminism in moments of rhetorical overkill threatens needlessly to divert the attention of men, by attacking a dated model of manhood or seizing on extremes of male behavior. Attention to men outside a strictly feminist framework can give a clearer picture of what men are and therefore what prospects there are for relationships between both genders.

The initiative in the rhetoric of gender relationships is clearly now in women's hands. Men can seem badly on the defensive. Some feminists enjoy amazonian games, attacking men as unnecessary and masculinity even as dangerous.[25] Men, for their part, have always been a bit awed by female assertiveness, wondering perhaps if women can in fact run the whole of life by themselves. Women's eagerness to explore the scientific and societal implications of gender is not matched by many men. Silence, not counterattack or acquiescence, is men's most characteristic gender stance at present. This is not, needless to say, a traditional posture; no one has argued that men are by nature more passive than women. And it is not a healthy one, even for feminism in the long run.

Obviously, no short survey of contemporary manhood can do justice to the host of possible criticisms of male activities by feminists and others. Some of them are contradictory.[26] It is possible to argue, nevertheless, putting bits of various recent social commentary together, that men are doing almost nothing right in any facet of the human trilogy of work, love, and play. They aren't even protesting their lot very well. Twentieth-century protest has definitely declined as a largely male province, as women joined unions and political agitation, even apart from formal feminism. The last great round of protest in Western society, that of the 1960s, although in fact largely led by men, was not clearly masculine, as it attacked not only war but the whole world of the fathers.[27] A decade later, as the tides have receded, more conventional social critics, feasting on the aimlessness of the counterculture, add protest to the list of things that men are no longer doing right. A crisis of male values here spills over into a crisis of values in general, unless we assume that somehow the feminists can save the day.

That we have a confusion of values relating to masculinity is I think undeniable. The feminist-inspired spate of manuals on how to be a man, the most tangible product of men's liberation to date, is a fascinating symptom of this uncertainty; but insofar as they urge men mainly to unlearn what they used to know about being a male, one may question their efficacy. Yet, though in transition and undeniably somewhat beleaguered, the man's world is not in total disarray. Men have been speaking, though more with actions than words, and what they are saying corresponds only in part to the laments of the contemporary Cassandras. While men's trends, which involve the adaptation more than the abandonment of the male past, do allow for some coexistence with feminist strivings they are not primarily caused by these strivings and indeed clash with them in some important respects. The clash is more subtle than a battle-of-the-sexes imagery can convey. I will argue that it can be made into a fruitful principle of new gender relationships, a new statement of a tension built into the gender links of Western society that is inherently messy, sometimes nasty, but fundamentally creative.

Gender relationships in the later twentieth century have, probably of necessity, reflected a lag between imagery and reality. Just as gender differentiation is decreasing in fact, new rhetorical heights have been scaled. This reflects the nasty trick that industrialization played on us, allowing an exaggeration of gender images before the possibility of convergent behavior. Men have too long played the strong silent type, a role that does not describe actual male behavior as fully as some culture critics maintain. It is time not so much to take a new course as to articulate the course that men have been on, to draw out its implications, indeed to figure out on its base what we want, and can legitimately ask for, that we do not have.

7. Themes in Contemporary Manhood

During the last thirty to fifty years, men have been trying to gain a fuller balance in their lives, seeking new activities that would allow them to express manly values, notably in the field of leisure, and new approaches that would allow them to regain functions effectively lost during the nineteenth century, notably in the area of family. Their use of time has certainly shifted, but so, more subtly, has their definition of what a man should be. Social class continues to describe a vital framework for manhood, and recognizable working- and middle-class styles persist, but certain impulses have been more general, and certain groupings, notably in the area of work, depart from conventional class lines. So we focus on areas of activity—the job, leisure, the family—that entail a significant reshuffling, though not a revolution, in what men are doing and what they think they are. Some of the changes have been forced on men by outside factors. Other changes result from a more explicit attempt to come to terms with the juxtaposition of manhood and modernity.

Work and Leisure: Is Jack a Dull Boy?

The issue of defining contemporary manhood begins with work. For most men, the outward, primarily economic, attributes of manhood, already challenged in the nineteenth century, became progressively more difficult to acquire as the twentieth century advanced.[1] The Depression was a severe blow to man-as-breadwinner. Those men who were unemployed for long periods could lose all initiative, yielding authority in the home as in the broader society. As one working wife noted, her ascendancy in the family growing as she earned its support, "I still love him, but he doesn't seem as big a man." A vicious circle began, where the family's scorn fed the man's own humiliation, reducing his participation in the family still further; sexual relations between man and wife often declined in frequency. Children became less respectful; no man could fully adapt to the new balance of authority. Idle men rebelled against doing housework for their employed wives, heightening a belief in the emasculating quality of household chores that continues still. Obviously, the minority of long-term unemployed was most seriously affected, but countless other men, unemployed briefly or simply realistically concerned about their job security, had cause to worry about their function as provider. For the men affected, the damage could be permanent. "Before the Depression, I wore the pants in this family and rightly so. During the Depression I lost something."[2]

World War II redressed the balance for some men by giving them a new focus and purpose,[3] but some scars could not entirely heal. More generally, burgeoning welfare systems, the logical response to the horrific unemployment of the 1930s, eased the impact of economic fluctuations on family maintenance, but diminished the male's role as provider. As working-class and middle-class women entered the labor force, largely as supplementary earners, the sense of a special male role was further reduced.[4] For the problem of the contemporary economy has become not so much providing, but providing well, amid mounting prices and rising personal expectations; and the aid that wives can offer, to ease the car payments or allow the purchase of the color television, was simply too obvious to be denied.[5] Men can still legitimately regard themselves as prime breadwinners; job identification remains a leading element of manhood, even if the most obviously male feature of work have declined. Middle-class families, particularly, locked in the escalating costs of maintaining one's place in suburbia, long continued to allow men almost a physical sense of bringing home the bacon, from the workplace to the carefully sheltered family. The 1950s saw a possible apogee of the male-provider role in the middle classes, with men slashing their way slowly up the bureaucratic ladder and wives and children waiting to receive them (graciously?) at home.[6]

The dream of controlling one's own property, making one's own manhood, faded even more dramatically. Small ownership, and individual ownership of productive property at any level, declined rapidly, continuing the obvious trend of industrial society since its early decades. Shopkeepers and farmers steadily, if reluctantly, gave way.[7] Even the small shops and producing operations that did survive increasingly took their orders from larger outlets. Most men, sensibly enough, stopped aspiring to economic mastery in the most traditional manner. Whether workers or clerks or managers, their futures were bound up in organizations that they did not control, that indeed often seemed beyond the control of any man.

There was some solace to propertyless manhood. Ownership of consumer property became ever more widespread, and this corresponded to the increasing shift of male attention from the job to controlling the rewards of the job and fighting for increasing rewards. The car. One's own machine, power beneath the fingertips, made men masters of their destiny if not at work itself, at least on the way to work. Automobiles most obviously fed masculinity when men remained the only drivers in the family, a relatively brief stage in the history of the machine, passing between the wars in the United States and in the 1950s and 1960s in Europe. But automobilized manhood does not depend on monopoly, and most women left the basic enthusiasm for the automobile, and the endless discussions of its annual intricacies, to men.[8]

The home. Here was a certain sign of property, particularly in the middle class and particularly in the United States. Here, if not at work, a man might be master of what he surveyed, and the impulse of territoriality was at least as basic as the impulse of keep up with the Joneses, this latter shared equally by women, in the careful effort to mark off one's own lawn, one's own garden or garage, from those of the common herd. It is terribly easy to poke fun at the suburban home-owning impulse. Lack of sufficient affluence and more stringent (and sensible) urban regulation denied this satisfaction to most European men in the bigger cities altogether, and they seemed to weather the blow. But the sense of pride in ownership, the joy in having a half-acre to rule supreme should not be ridiculed unduly. It helped to retain the association of work with property, if now at a substantial remove.

Propertyless men were not necessarily economically impotent men. The corporate man, even the worker in a seniority system, was ascending a ladder of modest power, in which success brought some control over other people and things. If few men could claim mastery over their destiny or independence from other peoples' orders, large numbers could aspire to the ability to dominate the work lives of underlings, and a variety of paternal mechanisms might be quite useful in this process. Men could feel that some portion of their company's operation fell on their shoulders, that they were more than cogs in a mindless wheel. They might fail. The ladder had downs as well as ups, and a new kind of job alienation arose among middle-class men, adequate providers, who simply did not rise as they expected. But economic manhood has always been risky in industrial society. One of its attractive features was that the risks remained, that one's own success could be measured against someone else's lack.[9]

An important skill component persisted as well. Unskilled male labor in fact teetered on disappearance—it is argued that it takes five years for a man unskilled in the traditional, agricultural sense to learn enough to fill an unskilled job in a contemporary industrial society. Machines increasingly took over the most menial physical chores and some of the most mindless office work, upgrading the skill levels of the men involved. To be sure, the skills were rarely conventional. Few men could claim a hold on a traditional craft, in which a product was carried from start to finish through one worker's hands. But the sense of a self-defining ability could easily inhere to a mason, or a machine rigger, or a computer programmer.[10]

Most of the key skills were less distinctively male than had been true even a half-century before. And many men were shut off even from these, locked in semi-skilled jobs that involved repetitious motions conveying scant job satisfaction or a sense that one's own identity was established by the work as opposed to the products of the work. Instrumentalism undoubtedly spread, in both the middle and the working classes, a belief that the job was defined by the pay, the rewards, not by any expectation of intrinsic interest.[11]

But skilled workers could maintain more than a fiction that they could intrude themselves, their personalities, into the skill process. An English survey revealed skilled factory workers more likely to express positive pleasure with their work, and the sense that they chose their work for reasons other than wages alone, than the semi-skilled operatives.[12] These same workers were simultaneously more likely to be critical of supervisors, believing that they themselves knew more about the production process than their superiors did. There remained a colorful tension, not a monochromatic resignation, to the work situation for many men. Men had to struggle, and often delude themselves, to sustain the belief that work expressed their individual ability. But the effort remained possible, and often worth the risk.[13]

Among middle-class men, many could believe that their work was associated with a specialized knowledge, either a management skill in manipulating people or a technical ability to manipulate things. Groups like engineers indeed preserved their sphere, where the physical environment was arranged at the most abstract level, free from significant female competition. For workers of various sorts, the job remained surrounded by various male rituals, from hazing tests for a new member of a construction crew, or a new member of an engineering or medical fraternity, to the half-tense, half-welcome social jostling of men off the job, where work relationships could be re-expressed on a golf course or in conversational rivalries at a cocktail party, when men drew off to talk among themselves about matters over which they alone had command.

Work, particularly middle-class work, easily fed and still feeds the association of manhood with competition and a quest for power. The jungle is still there, though its tensions may have become more subtle as a result of the friendlier, personal style that has infused bureaucratic contacts and service jobs. There are always hurdles to jump, new tests of one's real ability. A great deal of criticism can be directed against the continued competitive atmosphere, the male rituals, associated with many kinds of work. Women rightly note the artificiality of some of the competitive hurdles, which demand needless strain, needless time and which of course add to the difficulties women have in penetrating the male work world. They and others note the toll which the concept of work-as-struggle takes on men themselves, even the fittest survivors. But all of this is saying that an aura of maleness still surrounds many forms of work, against another common idea that work has lost all meaning for men.[14]

As men have been more explicitly trained for the industrial jobs they hold, as generations have passed on the job, and as bureaucracies have defined job criteria with increasing elaborateness, the job has become again an opportunity to demonstrate personal competence. A man knows his work. This can shade off into the boredom of routine. It can be challenged by unwanted innovation. But most men, working-class and middle-class alike, have a sense of some mastery in the workplace; for some, work is indeed the principal refuge in life, the area where there are the fewest questions about what a man should do.

Yet, with all this, gender identity through work has probably declined, in the twentieth century, just as the amount of time devoted to work has decreased. There are several pervasive, partially contradictory images about contemporary work, none of which is entirely correct but several of which, in proper combination, reinforce the sense of partial dissociation.

1. Workers are alienated from their work, seeing it only as something to be endured for extrinsic reward, expecting and finding no satisfaction in it.[15]
2. Men are work-drugged, giving themselves to the artificial games of the work world, ignoring their families, but, tragically, identifying with false gods, failing to find a sustaining life substance in their devotion. Hence, among other things, an incapacity to relax or to retire from the job.[16]
3. Workers are profoundly divided in their work reactions, with manual laborers disconsolate, white collar workers able, somewhat artificially, to pretend that they still find personal pleasure in their job.[17]

There are profoundly alienated male workers in contemporary society, angry over tense but routinized jobs which offer no voice in setting work conditions, no sense of purpose in the tasks they perform. Surveys in the United States, Britain, France, and Germany suggest that workers of this sort constitute between 25 and 35 percent of the blue-collar labor force. This figure may actually be smaller than its counterpart around 1900, though there can be no precision about this. Certainly, at present articulated alienation is a minority phenomenon.[18]

Most blue-collar workers say they find some satisfaction in their jobs. They may be trying to please a pollster, but without question they are trying to make sense of their lives, and it is difficult to admit complete failure in such an important area. Their pay, more than intrinsic satisfaction, may color their responses. The fact remains that men still find it possible to claim some pleasure in work, as providers, as people proud of strength or skill. But job pride is limited. Decreasing numbers of workers can associate work with exuberant demonstrations of physical prowess. Few, even if interested in a skill, can claim satisfaction in traditional mastery, in demonstrating that one can equal one's father at his own game. Hence, along with some indication of satisfaction, the factory worker typically adds that he hopes his children will do better, or that his job is all right but only "for the likes of me."[19]

This leads to a desire to find some external purpose for work and to limit the work experience itself; a man cannot be a worker alone. "It's a very mixed bag; sometimes you enjoy it, sometimes tolerate it and sometimes endure it." The most typical larger justification invokes the provider role, supplemented perhaps by a new domestic affection: "Everything I do is for my wife and children." "Family is the finest thing; something to work for, to look to and to look after." A minority of manual workers remain who define their lives, or at least their time, in terms of the job alone, preoccupied by the routine if nothing else; these are the workers who eat up their days with overtime, when it is available. But this is not the typical stance. The worker seeks a more balanced life and gropes for a fuller definition of manhood. His attitude to work itself is not necessarily new, for the working class was never intoxicated with the joy of unrestrained labor. But his perception of the need for a fuller identity has grown. So, without much question, has his desire to have defined periods of non-work. Workers report a new insistence on having work a confined experience, not to disrupt or even seriously to affect life off the job. A British worker suggests the new priorities: "While I cannot help bringing my troubles from home to work, I don't take my work troubles home. You can't switch your mind completely from your home because it is so much deeper than the work."[20]

None of this adds up to a new crisis of masculinity and work. It does suggest that the definition of manhood has become more complicated than workers were prone to believe in the past, when work more clearly defined life. The ambiguous attitude toward work suggests that while work remained an essential attribute of manhood ("A man, to be a man, has to work and earn his living")[21] there was no longer anything distinctively manly in it. Yet while there was a certain tension in this, there was some relaxation as well. It was no coincidence that complaints about immense nervous strain on the job declined except directly in the assembly line; no coincidence, either, that these same men could tolerate, even welcome the entry of their wives into the labor force, now that work and masculinity were partially dissociated. The open question was, of course, the extent to which workers needed a new area for the expression of maleness to compensate for the incomplete satisfaction of the job, the extent to which they could find masculine or simply human fulfillment at home or elsewhere that would spice the empty hours.

Most middle-class jobs are no more intrinsically interesting than those of the working class.[22] The great twentieth-century expansion of jobs in the services, in sales, and in the handling of information has made middle-class employment the predominant single form. But the elevation of many former workers into the white collar ranks had contradictory implications for manhood. On the one hand there was an improvement in status; the white-collar employee could judge that he had crossed a divide that separated the bosses from the bossed. And there was, on average, greater security of earnings, which facilitated the breadwinning task. White-collar workers could feel themselves drawn into that modern jungle where men used their brains and their aggressive instinct to survive. Yet the jungle was more often boring than enthralling, more prosaic than challenging. White-collar workers may have preserved a slightly greater sense of job satisfaction than their blue-collar counterparts, but the difference is not great. And many white-collar types had the disadvantage of facing more direct female competition, even the possibility of female supervisors. Their work, relatedly, involved none of the sheer physical challenge that manual labor could still suggest. Their skills, though real, had little sanction in tradition, the products really of a coeducational schooling in which even special male aptitudes, real or presumptive, had little advantage. White-collar workers might thus be more dependent than factory labor on a contrived putting-down of women on the job for their own sense of worth. But the main point is that they, too, saw work as only a part of life, not in most cases the essence of their identities.

The world of contemporary work thus creates a minority of profoundly alienated men, mainly in the factories, and a large mass of half-contented, half-discontented who assume a primary male responsibility for work but who seek basic satisfaction elsewhere. Rather than the quality of their work shaping that of their life, the predominant situation just fifty years ago, when problems and characteristics of the job dominated the man's attention at home and at play, the quality of life now determines performance at work. At an extreme, figures in the 1970s suggest that the percentage of males within the normal employment ages seeking work at all is beginning to dip; only 86 percent of the employable male labor force in the United States is listed as working. Many men are simply finding other things to do or not to do, for periods of their mature adulthood before old age.

The characteristic work situation is mirrored in retirement, which from the 1930s, for the first time in human history, became a normal experience for older men. There is a conventional wisdom that holds that men do not know how to retire, having meshed their identities with the pressures and routines of work.[23] Some men do find retirement difficult, even if they insisted on it as an end to a boring job. Retirement does entail a loss of male power, just as lack or loss of property did in agricultural society. Few retired men become directly dependent on their offspring. But they do, typically, become increasingly dependent on their wives, often taking a subordinate position to women whose functions have not declined so dramatically and whose health, on average, is superior (both because of greater female longevity and because women marry younger than men). For some observers, this change in the gender balance in later age is a sign of tragic emasculation, the special sorrow which aging brings to men.

A common analysis goes even farther, to associate retirement with heightened male death rates: deprived of work, his life's meaning, the man withers and dies. Again, no doubt true in some cases. Retirement does bring a difficult change in routine, and many men would prefer a more gradual withdrawal from the work world. It is also an economic shock, particularly in the working class, bringing a pronounced decline in revenue. But that retirement is a large-scale killer is increasingly doubtful. Death rates rise around retirement age because they rise around that age, not because retirement adds directly to the mortality process. Men have proved increasingly able to adjust to retirement, assuming a satisfactory income, and their ability actually seems to correspond most closely to their previous capacity to enjoy their jobs. The alienated worker, likely to be badly off, often in poor health, may be particularly dependent on the sheer routine of work. The moderately contented worker, be he blue- or white-collar, is also moderately contented to stop. Most men profess not only to look forward to retirement, but to enjoy it when encountered. Their family power may indeed decline, for the association of male work with male power remains real, but even this can be endured.

Manhood, once again, is not enmeshed with work, and possibly not with power either.[24]

At the top of society, and into the upper ranks of the middle class, men stand in a dramatically different relationship to work. Advanced industrialization produces a vast gulf, not neatly demarcated along conventional class lines, between the mass of men and the minority of work addicts, for whom the job remains all-consuming, its interest even increasing with time.[25] For the most part, men in this group also reap the greatest financial reward, and insist on it, but they come close to valuing work for its own sake. Their jobs consume them, and they have little other self-definition; instead of fitting work into their life, they fit life into their work. Recreation is normally a matter of better preparation for work, particularly toward the maintenance of physical health; it does not add new principles to life. Few women yet care to match the work addiction of this group; female doctors, for example, immensely high achievers in their own right, do not practice as long as men on a daily or yearly basis. Some men in this work group undoubtedly depend on hazing devices that help screen women out, and most have yet to face a substantial female influx. But, pending this, these men do not depend on an active image of women's inferiority to maintain their self-worth, despite some bows to the older rhetoric of female irrationality. Some lean heavily on their wives to take charge of those huge areas of life which they find pleasant to comtemplate but impossible to spend much time on.[26] But it is from this group also that men have emerged and are emerging who are most supportive of a wife's professional career, precisely because they do not necessarily depend on a female reflecting pool.

The work-addicted male may command property but his more general characteristic is mastery of a body of expert learning, whether in business or the professions. This is his joy and his source of power. Although the work compulsion describes only a minority of men, these are articulate and visible; modern society pushes an elite to a complete identification with work, in contrast to agricultural societies that distinguished elites by their devotion to leisure. For the clearest criteria of manhood, at least after a period of youth, remain those developed in the nineteenth century: achievement, successful competition, victory in the jungle. The minority of men who can meet these criteria, often patriarchal types, are accused of lack of balance in their lives[27] because they so readily rely on their one great compulsion: without ambiguity, they know who they are. Some feminists deplore the type, for few women have found it possible or desirable to focus their identification in the same way. It is tempting to decry the beast altogether, hoping to tame him into a moderation with which striving women can more readily identify.[28] Certainly, modern work steadily increases the difficulty of combining successful work compulsion with serious attention to the family. The patriarchal impulse may be there, but it depends on others for its execution.[29]

Yet it is easy to overdraw, just as it is too easy to exaggerate the family centeredness of the nineteenth-century patriarch. The work addict's prime identity does not preclude leisure or family time. He does not have to be the unbalanced monster that some recent characterizations suggest; we must still pay some attention to the other aspects of his life. The work addict's clearest fault is that he leaves scant room for any other personality type in the fields he dominates. He builds hierarchies in which the playful man, the low-key man cannot rise. Certainly one of the key criticisms of contemporary merito-cracy, the rule of a technical elite, concerns its insensitivity to other values; the society in which the work zealots are on top may prove ultimately no more successful that those variants of agricultural society that glorified the idlers. It is certainly not irrelevant to argue that the simplified male identity of the work addict, which concentrates masculine traits in the one endeavor—aggression, competitiveness, unemotional rationality—should be modified by a redifinition of manhood and by the addition of other personalities, including those of achievement-oriented women, to the ruling hierarchies of contem-porary society.[30]

More recently, criticism from another direction has emerged. Is the achieving male on the decline, and if so can society successfully adjust?[31] This is, it must be emphasized, a largely male comment. It tends to ignore the rise of achievement-oriented women, who could well balance any softening of a purely male ethic. It is not new for achievement-oriented males to worry about a softer new generation. Still, it is possible that the progressive withdrawal of the work-oriented male from the home has reduced the possi-bility of reproducing the type. Sons are only vaguely aware of the attributes of fathers they do not see, and follow the models set by peers instead, which press less wholeheartedly toward achievement. Hence a decline in career aspirations and a drop in scholarly competitiveness. A number of American observers have been pointing to a student generation that avoided challenge in the 1970s, while the protest of the 1960s can be seen not as a constructive alternative to the existing system but as a massive drop-out, which left only a shallow hedonism in its wake.[32] Hence while the student generation of the 1970s seems "straighter" than its counterpart of the previous decade, con-cerned about grades and moneymaking and other familiar landmarks, it enjoys the sensual remnants of the dreamy culture and, while interested in rewards, may care less about performance. These are only tentative reac-tions, of course, not only subjective but based on evidence too brief to serve as a basis for predicating trends. If work addiction does show some signs of faltering, with its most direct beneficiaries joining other men in seeking a wider array of expression, it may not be due to the sons alone. Work addicts themselves, brought under a steady barrage of criticism (from feminists; wives concerned about their husbands' health and about the amount of attention their husbands give them; psychologists and doctors advocating a balance in life), and drawn by the lures of the growing leisure industry developed some doubts about their own identification. If they did not relax their own compulsion to work, they might hope for a different pattern in their sons. Realizing how difficult it was for them to learn to play, the compulsive worker showed signs of reducing his pressure on his offspring. Certainly the school systems most likely to be involved with a work-addict population picked up some new signals, as early as the 1950s. In the United States, grading pressures relaxed, leading to a host of supplementary marking systems and a pronounced inflation of average grades. While this trend initially had some basis in an improvement in student abilities, it continued even after objective student abilities began to fall.[33] More tentatively, similar trends in countries like France involve a reduction of student categorization by tested ability level. The result is that teachers who had themselves been through a rather rigorous screening, which easily converted their own student days into a period of enforced work addiction, implicitly have been seeking a different fate for their student charges. This, too, might reflect a broader uneasiness about work as life identification in society as a whole.

Evidence about and judgments of male work addiction thus vary considerably. The power the minority of work zealots wield and the interest they claim to derive from life tempt feminists to compete, but the narrowness of their self-definition, plus the competitiveness and male ritual that surround them, also rouse a desire to condemn, to urge a moderation of this male ethic in the interest, at least in principle, of the men themselves, who have chosen a too-facile definition of manhood.[34] From this vantage point a relaxation of the work compulsion, which is now being suggested, would be desirable. Certainly the scattered reports of young men modifying career goals to mesh with their wives' interests and to allow more family time—an unwillingness to move, for example, when a corporation dictates, even with a promotion as bait—could be a symptom, and from the standpoint of the critique of the male ethic a fruitful symptom, of a change in the pattern of male identification. Doubts persist, because of the uncertain measurement of actual trends and because of a new worry, from unreconstructed achievement advocates, that society will suffer from undue diversion of the work compulsion. Yet to the extent that the socialization of males in the home and in school has itself broadened from an identification of work achievement with life success, trends within the work-compulsive minority echo those of the larger mass of men, without of course merging the two groups. The partial dissociation of manhood from work would here become an even larger statement about contemporary masculinity.

One further fact is certain. Work-based protest itself has declined as an instrument of masculine expression. As men find decreasing satisfaction in work, they can look to protest for only partial relief. The work addicts, of course, rarely engage in protest; their sense of uneasiness is conveyed in individual actions, including their socialization of children. Few of the larger category of middle-class men, the white-collar workers who win only moderate intrinsic rewards from their jobs, have been able to mount protest action that will express a distinctive sense of manhood, because of the admixture of women in their labor force. Protest in this group has risen massively in the last three decades, expressing a new sense of constraint in the ranks of teachers, bank clerks and the like, but it has obviously not been a male protest either in composition or in nature. Both white-collar and working-class protests have continued the older pattern of responding to unsatisfactory work by demands for better pay and benefits and, possibly, a further reduction of the time spent on the job.[35] Labor unrest in the later 1960s did suggest some effort to apply protest more directly to the work situation. Strikes by young American automobile workers, agitation in Germany and Scandinavia for a greater voice on the job and greater variety of tasks to lighten the monotony of work, suggested a welcome turning point, in which workers could demand that jobs repay them with intrinsic work satisfaction. But, although factory routines were altered to provide greater diversity, particularly on the European continent, the focus of protest did not really shift. Too many workers were largely if superficially content with their jobs. In the United States, older workers who had made their peace with the system and its extrinsic rewards resisted the efforts of the young malcontents who looked at the job with fresh eyes and whose pattern of extrinsic rewards, the life outside the job, was not yet set. Individual workers modified their boredom by absenteeism and periodic unemployment which reflected their dissociation from work but dissociated them from remedial action as well. More important, pervasive inflationary pressure helped return protest to a largely instrumental path. The goal had to be to mesh wages and benefits with rising prices. Twentieth-century protest remains relevant to the work situation, particularly in reducing individual abuses on the job and providing channels for complaint. This is one reason that some workers can end the job in their mind when it ends with their hands, clearing the decks for other interests. But this largely encourages the diversion of personal identification away from work and further relieves the association of protest with a work-based masculinity.

Important traces of distinctively male protest remain in the working class, of course. Great strike movements still engage a male mass in mining, construction work, and the like. The goals may indeed be largely instrumental, but protest itself can still convey a sense of male power and comradeship. This too has been partially diluted. Labor protest becomes steadily more organized and routinized, further dampening the opportunity to express male anger (though wildcat strikes in male-dominated industries recurrently seek the more direct outlet). There is no clear alternative to the bureaucratization of protest, given the power of employer combatants, for strong organization is essential for success; and it may follow from a reduced dissatisfaction with work in any event. But the opportunities for groups of men to march off in mutual loyalty are steadily reduced by the careful collective bargaining agreements between labor and business giants.[36] The growing admixture of women affected working-class protest as well, as female participation in some unions and in labor-based politics rose after World

War II. Thus, the female component of the French Communist party has steadily expanded its influence, creating considerable tension among male members. Protest variously declines as a vehicle of masculinity.[37]

There is quiet misfortune in a situation where a human being can describe what he or she does with a full third of his waking life with "it's not too bad" or "it's all right." There is misfortune in a system that gives countless middle-aged men, factory workers, or white-collar employees, schooled to think that manhood could be associated with high aspirations and achievement, the sinking but realistic sense that they have not made it and never will.[38] There is misfortune indeed in a society that gives no clear alternate or supplementary definitions of manhood to men who are barred from working. This includes forcibly retired men who may make their own adjustments to their new state as individuals, and who may even welcome the cessation of the old routine but who cannot but perceive that their position in their own families has eroded. It includes, still more strikingly, the young men (38 percent of young black Americans, at the present writing) who cannot get jobs, and that larger number who fear the unemployment or, more commonly, the dullness that awaits them after they make peace with their occupational lot. Here in fact there are signs of inchoate protest, in the crime and the unrest in the school on the part of young men who see no chance of tying into a satisfactory job definition of manhood, who chafe at the restraints of an educational system that holds them in bondage with a false promise of future reward.

For the mass of men, job satisfaction has not necessarily declined. We need not picture our farmer-ancestors joyfully enthralled with their work, save insofar as they had pride in property. The difficulty of young men delayed or prevented from acquiring economic manhood is distinctly familiar; so is that of older men who see economic manhood slip from them. Work and its rewards remain for most men just satisfying enough, still fulfilling the functions of man-the-provider, even of man-the-skilled or man-the-knowledg-able, to mute complaint. An enlightened economist writes of adding a good job, not just a job, to the list of desirable human rights in a modern society, which sounds fine. But his definition of a good job remains largely instru-mental (good pay and benefits, security, along with pleasant physical sur-roundings), leaving aside the issue of intrinsic pleasure in the work. Yet to suggest anything more seems utopian.[39]

The massive entry of women into the labor force since 1940 contributes to the erosion of the gender distinctiveness of work. For some men, having women as competitors and colleagues, even as co-protesters, made an en-durable work situation into a degrading one. For others, benefits accrued. In principle, men can use women's entry to reduce the burdensome aspects of their work commitment, modifying their responsibility as prime provider, taking the time to shop for appropriate work while depending on the wife's resources. To some extent this is occurring, which is one reason why there is, in fact, no raging battle of the sexes in the workplace. The reduction in the time and personal investment most contemporary men have in work already suggest an accommodation. Women are not attacking the entire citadel of male pride.[40]

Contemporary women at work however raise a more subtle complication for men. Their work ethic, on average, remains different from that of men.[41] The difference has narrowed since the nineteenth century; we are no longer talking about something so dramatic as distinctive senses of time. Most women remain apparently content with a supplementary, if important, earning role, a vital contribution to the family income but over and above that of the main provider.[42] They can be seen as less committed to their job. They remain disproportionately attracted to fields that allow extensive socializing at work, away from those involving the manipulation of things. Here may be a basis for a sensibly revised gender specialization, but it is confusing to male workers who perceive the different approach yet are simultaneously asked to accept female co-workers as equals and who suffer women's criticisms of their own work ethic.

Despite the increasing numbers of women who are high achievers and/or prime breadwinners, the overall standards of reference each gender applies to work inevitably differ. As men have experienced a hollowness in industrial labor, and have sought to diversify their interests, women—not just the articulate feminists—seem to be rushing to work with a new enthusiasm. Job frustrations are more likely to be directed against lingering discrimination than against intrinsic aspects of the work itself. Quite probably these differences will narrow with time, as women enter successive generations of employment outside the home. Possibly women will succeed in increasing the humanization of work, through an insistence on social contacts on the job and a downgrading of competitive achievement standards, and so benefit men as well; but it would be premature to pin too much hope here, for as men were acclimated to industrial work a century ago, they tried the same thing and failed. In the meantime men must beware lest women's new-found satisfactions divert them from an effort to define the satisfactions that they can legitimately demand, whether as men or as men-and-women, from their jobs. Men have every reason to examine their own ambiguous reactions to work, not because of female competition, but to recall traditions of male protest that have demanded an improved quality of work in the past and can continue to do so.

Most men will continue to seek to diversify their interests and involvements, to find personal meaning off the job. Here we must note a further irony, though perhaps also a promise, in the contemporary plight of the genders. In a real sense, men—even some in the work-compulsive group— have been trying to come back home in the twentieth century, just as women decided to leave. The most obvious non-work satisfaction for men, a reasserted family role, was thus potentially opened, as many women sought to reduce their domestic confinement. To this we must return in considering the family itself. For now, it is enough to note that, although a first logical recourse off the job, the family is unlikely to provide a sufficient alternate role for men and that, though with many hesitations, men on the whole have perceived this.

There is, happily, yet a third area, that of leisure. Here we face an immediate dilemma: men have used leisure not only to fill their time but also to provide a personal identity in the late twentieth century. But leisure has not been propelled into a clear mark of worth, save for leisure professionals whose activities in entertaining others can be called work.[43] Contemporary society at once engages in leisure activities ever more massively and shuns a formalization of a leisure ethic. This in part reflects the dominance of a work-oriented elite, including many articulate intellectuals, but the dilemma applies more widely. We are still not sure, as men or as women, that we are supposed to play. For many a contemporary radical, a person must be defined by work or by family. He may play in fact, but this is frivolity, not to be dignified by serious examination. Thus, Christopher Lasch, in his critique of the contemporary American personality, condemns the meaninglessness of work and the superficiality of the family, dismissing leisure as a commercialized trap in which no serious significance can be found.[44] Thus a host of European Marxists progressively dissect leisure interests as opiates, distracting the masses from examination of reality—meaning work and economic relationships.[45] Ordinary men clearly do not agree. They are playing, or think they are playing. They are, one might argue, creating a new reality, not denying that of work but adding to it. They have yet, however, to receive intellectual benediction.

Male leisure efforts may indeed be wanting, as other culture critics insist. Much leisure is a passive spectator activity; much is dictated by commercial or state media, giving only an illusion of choice; much is tasteless by almost any definition, and some of it is unduly violent. Male leisure continues to reflect a heavy emphasis on the abilities of youth, which leaves older men with less obvious ways to demonstrate maleness in pursuit of it.[46] Relatedly, male leisure has remained unduly circumscribed, with aesthetic outlets particularly relegated to a female sphere; even intellectual activity, touted as male when directed toward work, has not been encouraged as a leisure endeavor, as schools resolutely train for jobs rather than for play.[47] The schools, indeed, promote a male problem in developing a non-work identity, despite the decline of the portion of adult lives that will be spent at work. Not surprisingly, athletics, the recreational focus that meets with greatest public approval and which does receive a huge place in the schools, carries over principles from men's work. It is competitive; it involves discipline and teamwork, thus "building character"; it separates the men from the boys, providing tests of courage, skill, and physical strength. Small wonder that some analysis contends that modern men have lost the ability to play, the ability to use leisure time aimlessly, inventively, as a child does so naturally.[48]

Yet, amid a host of limitations, men have been building a variety of leisure identities in the twentieth century, in both the middle and working classes. Athletics, certainly, has become a fundamental part of communication among boys, differentiating them rather radically from women, whose school socializing is more verbal.[49] More generally, men, including older men, have been using leisure to compensate for some of the blows industrial society has administered to manhood in other respects. This goes beyond a use of leisure simply to fill non-work time. Men are seeking, with a mixture of new and old forms, to recapture their past. Thus in male leisure we see huge traces of a hunting society, beginning with an effort to give bodies an outlet industrial work denies them, but also the work patterns of agricultural society. We see efforts to use leisure to rebuild generational ties now excluded from work itself. The attempt may be inadequate, the motivation not always clear, but the result of associating men and leisure is immensely important.

It is probably true that men do not play much, in the sense of aimless activity. Modern society's redefinition and reduction of childhood make play difficult in any pure sense; since before the advent of industrialization most people seem to have wanted the ambiguous freedoms of adulthood too much to perpetuate an ethic of play. It must be left to others to judge the extent of the loss involved. It is also true that much leisure is passive, not relating to manhood in any distinctive way. Many men still use non-work time simply to rest, sleeping more than necessary and using television or some other device for the near-sleep of purely passive, uncritical spectatorship. Whether the amount, as opposed to the form, of non-work idling has increased in the twentieth century is unclear; probably we sleep less, maintain a passive wakefulness more. But, as with play, the issue is not a specifically masculine one in any event.

The most obviously male aspect of men's leisure pattern in the twentieth century is its relationship to work values, the relationship most directly inherited from the previous century. As they are trained to do in school and family, men apply competitive achievement principles to leisure in many forms.[50] Work addicts justify a great deal of their leisure in terms of its benefits to their job performance, "working out" to improve their health and relieve frustration, and cultivating professional contacts. Businessmen combine work and leisure in terms of organizing their acquaintances around work contacts (no new phenomenon for men, as the recreational role of guilds already suggests) and using recreation to promote business opportunities (the promotional golf game, legally legitimized as a tax deduction). This association raises serious questions about the quality of leisure per se. Many men doutless do deprive themselves of desirable balance in their life interests and the opportunity to relax, to operate according to non-work principles. But the equation can also be reversed. Many men, particularly in the middle class, have introduced a male-game element into work, a sense of jostling camaraderie, from which the work-leisure association is a logical extension. This raises a genuine problem for women who seek comparable work opportunities. For our purpose, however, the point is that leisure, so difficult to define in any pure sense, serves male purposes, and that this has advantages as well as drawbacks.

Many men use leisure to recall other male principles. Suburban men—a type most widespread in, but not unique to, the United States—use a great deal of their weekend time to play lord of the manor, maintaining and improving their personal and family property. (For many urban men, work on the car serves as a limited surrogate.) They can, in this work, relax into an older time frame, working and interrupting work at will; this is not a job in the modern sense. They can satisfy, rather harmlessly, a territorial urge, a desire to bend nature to their will and to glorify a modest family patrimony. Of course there are silly aspects to their devotion to lawnmowing and landscaping—one of the characteristics of free-choice leisure is that people like to laugh at other peoples' choices—but one can argue that leisure is not supposed to be serious.

The zeal for crafts and hobbies reveals another effort to maintain masculine tradition by developing skills and manipulating physical things. A survey of about five hundred British automobile workers around 1960 found almost 10 percent listing furniture-making and model building as a hobby. The more generalized "do-it-yourself" category drew a 50 percent response. Photography, and to a lesser extent other kinds of artistic work, enlist a growing number of men. So do other new skills, notably electrical work. With home and hobby work combined, many men "work" harder in their free time than they do on the job, even viewing the return to official work as a relaxation.[51]

Sports, of course, still serves the even more ancient male function of leisure, to facilitate but also to control male grouping:

> After dinner all the youth of the City goes out into the fields for the very popular game of ball. The scholars of each school have their own ball, and almost all the workers of each trade have theirs also in their hands. The elders, the fathers . . . come . . . to view the contests of their juniors, and in their fashion sport with the young men; and there seems to be aroused in these elders a stirring of natural heat by viewing so much activity and by participation in the joys of unrestrained youth.

This from twelfth-century London by the biographer of Thomas à Becket. Since then, male sports have not only spread, as both participant and spectator activities, they have become more organized and regulated, and on the whole far less violent. Values of teamwork, in which men are trained at school, loom larger. Centuries of government regulation against sports turning into brawls, Puritan disapproval, and middle-class discipline have had their effect. Leading spectator sports, such as American football, clearly ritualize violence. Slightly tamer sports, such as soccer, can evoke a bloodthirst in male crowds, expressed in the brawling on English football trains, or the rioting of Latin American partisans. Yet, more widely than violence, sports serve as an outlet for a physical and mental testing of men, in groups and as individuals. Under the aegis of commercial organization and the increased vitality of sports as part of men's life, levels of performance steadily improve, from the professional match to the sandlot game. In this limited sense, modern men are the best players (and the most informed spectators) in history.[52]

Certain themes can be tentatively sorted out amid the general male emphasis on sports in leisure. Despite all the laments about beer-guzzling spectatorship, rates of participation in sports are steadily rising. A study of English soccer reports mounting levels of formal and informal team play but an apparent decline in direct spectator interest due in part to television, in part to a growing revulsion against crowd hooliganism, but in part to the growing diversity of participatory sports activity among men beyond their youth. The middle class led the working class in the development of individualized sports activity, such as tennis and jogging. Working-class men find social as well as athletic pleasure in group bicycling and fishing, often with a betting component to add competitive zest. But individual sports continue to spread widely. The working-class interest in weightlifting shows an obvious desire to develop the physical attributes of masculinity. Europeans have been held to maintain a greater interest in sports that pit the individual against the natural limits of endurance than Americans—distance running as opposed to sprints, for example. But they too have a fascination with speed, as in bicycle speed racing and car racing. A certain faddism characterizes sports interests on both sides of the Atlantic, the inevitable product of a commercial society. Within this framework, the rise of individualized as opposed to team sports (and the related increase in the cost of sports gear and facilities) and a possible further reduction in sports violence (the decline of boxing), stand out as trends. Overshadowing shifts and variety is the growing use of participant and spectator sports as a male currency, pitting men directly or vicariously against physical limits within a competitive framework.

Like all popular leisure forms, sports has its bitter critics, apart from academics resentful of football ballyhoo and women who prefer less childish (or at least, different) games. Sports are clearly not simply an expression of aggressive frustration under capitalism, for they antedate it and, as the spread of violent modern games to noncapitalist societies suggests, they convey a broader male impulse. Sports may distract from other, more "real," reactions to modern society, but this is not proved; sport and protest groups often intertwine. Sports most clearly represent a male participatory democracy, in which a shared gender expression exceeds class and ethnic boundaries (serving among other things as a mobility ladder for talented but otherwise disadvantaged young men).

Some men devote too much attention to sports at the expense of more balanced interests, including the delights of more purely rational activity. Some men suffer from the bittersweet realization that they cannot be the athletes they strove to be, as they are forced into less satisfactory, if more mature or "realistic" definitions of themselves. This is one reason that spectator-men do not begrudge the huge salaries of those few who can do this male thing so superbly well. Yet for all its limitations, sports represent a basically healthy and supremely entertaining male interest. As men diversify their athletic concerns, as they increasingly pursue sports that can be carried on at various levels of achievement and into later age, they can directly lift the athletic expression into quietly impressive personal fulfillments. They may improve their health and their psyches in the process, the joggers or the iron-pumpers, but most of all they are proving themselves to themselves, which is the purpose which modern leisure can best serve.

In painting a hopeful picture of male leisure and in suggesting that gender interaction in leisure creates a mutually beneficial tension and expansion of interests—indeed, a vital expression of maleness—I do not argue that men *in general* have achieved a satisfactory leisure outlet, that they have been able to build recreational skills and preoccupations into a part of their definition of themselves, although a surprising number of them have. As knowledgeable spectators, as leisure craftsmen, gardeners, fishermen, athletes, and artists, men do a variety of things that not only entertain and pass time, but provide them with sense of purpose.[53]

Given the general uncertainty about how important leisure ought to be, men can usefully devote serious attention to defining and defending their leisure pursuits. They might insist on greater support from the educational apparatus, which trains so narrowly and half-heartedly. They can usefully watch over the delicate balance, traditional in male leisure, between exuberant expression and excessive violence. They can certainly attend more clearly to recreational skills for all stages of life, for the showiest leisure activities remain those of young men, at a time when young men form an increasingly small proportion of the population. The decline of male status in retirement relates to ongoing uncertainties about the validity of play but particularly of gentler play, though the growing popularity of retirement suggests an older-male subculture that provides its own standards.[53] More generally, the dissociation between popular male leisure and explicitly mental activity merits concern. Men have already carved out a significant non-work identity, and they can go further.

The progression of male leisure interests has had some impact even on that traditional resort of men both at and after work, alcoholic drink. Drinking has declined as a male working-class outlet in the last half century. Aided by government action and spurred in turn by middle-class reformers both male and female, the drinking place has faded as a focus of male socializing.[54] Here was, perhaps, a sign also of greater contentment, or at least lessened tension, at work, and both sign and precondition of a wider array of leisure interests. But for certain middle-class businessmen and professionals, as in the United States, male drinking increased. So, more recently, has peer-induced drinking among teenagers, both male and female (and women's drinking generally seems on the rise—one of the ambiguous fruits of entry into the wider world). And many workers still prove their virility by feats of drink. Here is, for some, a joyous, or joy-inducing, diversion which affluence facilitates for an increasing number of groups; and for others, like the growing number of American alcoholics, an obsession which can override work and leisure alike. The balance of life interests between work and leisure, the ability to find self-expression in a complicated world in which a single standard of achievement is too risky for most people, because of the ambiguity yet necessity of work itself, remains particularly difficult for men, and their insecurities can still tumble them.

Few twentieth-century men have tried to pursue a self-identity in a combination of work and leisure alone. They remain men of work; they increasingly have become men at play; but they insist also that they are family men. The definition of the provider role has been fused into a general sense that work is done, sometimes simply endured, for the family. Leisure interests have been modified by family concerns. The decline of corner taverns owes much to the rise of family-based entertainment, notably television, but also to bottles from package stores, which helped bring working-men home as distressed wives had never managed to do. Even in athletics, particularly in the more individualized sports such as tennis or golf, men and women began playing together as never before, at some cost perhaps to strictly male contacts. In many respects the male world became increasingly privatized, family-centered, in the twentieth century, as workers pulled back from social contacts outside the family and many middle-class men retreated to suburban castles. Small wonder that men professed that the family was the center of their being. If work compulsions or individual or male-group leisure seemed to contradict the profession, in fact and in the eyes of many lonely wives, important features of the contemporary male situation suggest that men's well-being depends heavily—perhaps excessively—on their family setting. With difficulty, with some rebel impulses, often ineptly, men have been trying to come home, their day of work and play completed. What they found there, and the style with which they themselves approached the family, have raised the greatest questions about contemporary manhood. Far more than work or leisure, the family challenges modern man, though less to devise his goals than to figure out how to achieve them.

Men and the Contemporary Family: "Friends Always"[55]

The twentieth century has proved an uneasy era in family life. Laments, and sometimes rejoicings, over the breakdown of family ties and allegiance have been almost standard fare. The persistence of concern suggests instability, but it also indicates the need for caution before tossing the final spadeful over the American, much less the Western, family.[56] The modern family has not been overanalyzed—our ignorance on many topics is surprisingly great—but it may have been excessively discussed. Unquestionably, great alterations have occurred. Soaring divorce rates challenge any claim not just to family stability, but to family serenity. Family control over adolescence has declined in favor of a regime of schools and peer groups. Extended family ties have loosened in many middle-class settings where travel—for education, for jobs, and later for retirement—can put huge distances between family members. A rapidly declining birth rate, falling below the level sufficient to maintain population levels in the 1930s and again in the 1970s, suggests growing unconcern with what once was the family's prime function. Experiments with communal living in the 1960s, and in the 1970s a rise in the marriage age, decline in marriage rates, and the increasing popularity of informal relationships, may herald the displacement of the family even as an institution in law.[57] Yet, though obviously subject to change, the family has not yet proved open to revolution, and obituary statements are usually premature.

Marriage rates rose steadily for two decades after World War II. In the twentieth century, a person is more likely to be married by age 40 than in any century since the Middle Ages. (After World War II the age of marriage briefly fell in the middle class—particularly in the United States—as well as in the working class, suggesting that marriage was not only usual but was eagerly anticipated.) Remarriage after divorce or widowage has risen in the twentieth century also, even in older age groups, a sign that instability should not be equated with rejection of the family as an institution. Telephones and automobiles preserve even extended family ties, and grandparenting, particularly grandmothering, has become an ever more common part of family life. The troubled parent-adolescent relationship, never simple, may have eased by the 1970s. It is possible to predict some decline in intergenerational strife, as parents relaxed some of their demands over teenagers and as teenagers found it less possible to shock parents, themselves products of considerable emancipation in behavior, with new forms of self-indulgence.[58] Even the birth rate, a basic measure of traditional family purpose, did not lend itself to facile prediction. Increased infant survival, rising consumer expectations, a possible increase in the cost of each child, new parental selfishness—all pointed to a birth-rate decline, and in the twentieth century this has in fact occurred. But the renewal in the popularity of babies for two decades, beginning in the early 1940s, and, in the late 1970s, a growing interest in having a child or children somewhat later in a marriage (say, in a couple's early thirties) qualify any notion that most families, even middle-class families, will fail to reproduce themselves. They likewise qualify the notion that society will be divided between a minority of (often lower-class) breeders and a majority of childless or near-childless couples who undertake a family, if at all, only for adult companionship and convenience. The family may decline further in importance, even dramatically; a decline in the marriage rate during the 1970s suggests an interesting change, for example. The institution is a troubled one, certainly for many individuals at key points in their lives. Children, parents, even grandparents do think of themselves more as individuals, forming relationships for individual advantage and without loss of identity, than as family members in the traditional sense. The implications of market economic relationships, which first disrupted the family as a producing unit, have certainly extended farther into personal relationships. But the resilience of the family is also striking, and it is misleading to frame a discussion of the contemporary institution in terms of decay or imminent demise.

For men, the subject of the family is particularly complex. The most common impression is, I think, in error. The twentieth century has not seen increasing male neglect of family. Rather, the male interest has been growing.

Aided by television and by better housing, working-class men reduced the leisure time spent outside the home. Classic institutions, notably the neighborhood pub, have declined, as men prefer to sit and drink at home. Not a glorious return to domesticity, perhaps, and not necessarily an active return, but some sort of renewed interest nevertheless. The decline in age at marriage, particularly notable in the college generations after World War II, was primarily a decline among males, suggesting a new eagerness and ability (or believed ability) to get started at the business of having a family. Observers in Europe and the United States generally noted a growing interest in dealing with children, in spending more time with them and in forming closer relationships, among middle- and working-class men alike, after World War II. More recently, a movement to reverse the discrimination against men in child-custody cases, to support the possibility of paternal custody or a parity in custody, reflects the growing paternal concern.[59] More generally still, family outings and vacations have constituted an increasingly important portion of male leisure time allocations; starting with weekend excursions in the nineteenth century, they have become the most important basic innovation in recreational patterns in industrial society.

Men, freer from work in terms of time, often less interested in work as a personal identification, have naturally sought to devote more attention to the family after a century of substantial removal. Their emotional need for family had always been great, even in the nineteenth century, and they have increasing ability now to act on that need. They sought shelter from the harshness of the marketplace. They wanted, in family, a sense of purpose for work that too often seemed meaningless. As a British worker put it, "Everything I do is for my wife and children." And others: "All my life is centered around the home"; "Children and home, that's my life."[60] For many men, there was a real reversal of priorities, accompanying the shift in the allocation of time. Whereas during the nineteenth century pressures at work often had to be brought home to poison family life, now family tensions received top billing, and could spoil a workday. Generations of vigorous mothering also played a role here, enhancing in many men the desire to find, in family, a return to that comforting dependence in which they had been nurtured.

Why, then, the persistent impression that men were still devoting insufficient time to the family? There is of course never enough time, and men obviously retain substantial work commitments outside the home. The prominence of compulsive male workers, who do have limited time, lent credibility to an old female lament about male neglect.[61] Even blue-collar workers, not intrinsically compulsive, might be driven to seek extra jobs or overtime jobs to earn the kind of money they thought their families deserved. In general, however, while men may not have been devoting enough time and attention to their families in the twentieth century, and while individuals have formed families only to leave them to the woman's charge, men have gained new family interest, and for their own good reasons. Their need is not only rhetorical, but also a matter of polishing the family emblem for public, and particularly female, consumption. The family man is the happiest man; he is also the healthiest, for not only widowers but also bachelors are at a considerable disadvantage to married men in longevity.[62] And while a good part of the bliss may consist of finding a woman to do chores and provide emotional support, a concrete translation of the idea of home as shelter from the outside world, men have been increasing their own active commitment to the family as well.

More active interest has not insured effective interest.[63] Many men doubtless expected an ordered house and friendly children to await them when they set aside family time. Their new attention could be irrelevant to the daily routine of the household, failing to reduce a woman's round of labor and involving a desire to play with children more than to discipline or look after them.[64] Hence new male patterns have not necessarily reduced female complaint. Furthermore, the dominant style of the male domestic interest invites confusion about where men are, in terms of family. Men have returned to family without the ability, and possibly without the will, to do what husbands and fathers used to do, and the results bewilder observers and family participants alike.

Two examples. The student upheavals of the 1960s provoked a host of comments about intergenerational tensions and paternal inadequacies. Student rebels, predominantly male, were seen as rebelling against absent, halfhearted fathers, who sired them and then fled to the corporate office. Small wonder that the youth attacked the values of the paternal world, the affluence, the organization-mindedness. They were really bemoaning the neglect which their fathers had visited upon them. (And possibly feminists, on the heels of the student rebels, also reflected the lack of a male presence in the household, and in attacking masculine privilege were protesting male indifference to wives and daughters.)[65]

The unrest of the 1960s yielded of course to greater calm on the campuses, which might seem to cast some doubt on explanations of student unrest that focused on family setting, for no one argues that the family has changed comparably in the interval. But recently critics, again predominantly male, have found another, and very plausible, bone to pick with the contemporary paternal style.[66] Youth today has lost any sense of achievement. They are less rebellious than their counterparts of a decade ago, but little different otherwise, for they have picked up the hedonist strand of the 1960s, the sex and escapism, and eschew effort and sacrifice in favor of contemplation of self. The reason? Their parents—working mothers may come in for some of the attack now, but the blame is primarily paternal—give them little attention, buying off guilt with material opulence, so that children are forced to seek the more shallow satisfactions of peer groups and never receive the intense discipline which real fatherly care should provide.

These arguments reflect the laments for youthful abandon that have been part of intergenerational relations for centuries. They capture disappointment that the protest of the 1960s turned out to be so formless, and that the present student generation has not picked up more positive banners. The critique depends, in other words, on one's sense of political purpose. It also inevitably homogenizes the present generation of adolescents. Christopher Lasch asserts that even class differences among adolescents, and therefore in child-raising styles, are breaking down, because parents in all social situations are neglecting their duties. In fact, the critique may be accepted for some adolescents, including those who form the loudest peer group cultures, but not for all. It is also not clear that lower-class families ever instilled a sense of driving, individual conscience save in isolated cases. If there is a decline in achievement orientation, the sort provided by available paternal example and loving discipline, it has been primarily in the middle class, which of course fits some of the notions of the work-compulsive father whose contact with his children is particularly ephemeral. The claim that a dominant personality style has been changing toward a desire for social ease among one's peers and a narcissistic contemplation of self may have some merit, despite its echoes of conventional blasts at youthful indulgence. Insofar as it is correct, it reflects problems in the contemporary paternal role.

These problems must not be oversimplified. They return us to the real conundrum of twentieth-century men and the family: an increase of interest that has produced doubtful results. Leading student radicals of the 1960s might indeed have been protesting—among many other things—absent, work-compulsive fathers, particularly insofar as they sprang from upper middle-class backgrounds or outright broken homes. But other sons, in the same generation, were complaining that their fathers' affection was almost too cloying, that it was harder to break away from the paternal orbit than in the days of the harsh disciplinarian who provided an obvious target for rebellion.[67] The point—beyond the obvious fact that paternal styles vary greatly and that children are not predictable products of any given style in any event[68]—is that it is more the effectiveness than the amount of the interest contemporary men devote to their families that is at issue.

While men returned to the family in a real sense in the twentieth century, they did not return in traditional male style, for several reasons. It was obviously difficult to regain control over children who were substantially trained in school and lured by the company of their peers. Fathers not only lacked property to bequeath, as a method of control, but also saw the impossibility of passing jobs from themselves to their sons. Only a few blue-collar trades, particularly in the crafts, were really exempt from this. What fathers could transmit was moral guidance and a general orientation toward life, plus funds to support the appropriate education, but both they and their sons could easily find this rather remote.[69] A rethinking of paternal purpose was almost inevitable when the continuity in work between father and son was disrupted. And in the larger setting it was easy to think of one's sons, and daughters as well, as people to woo, to approach as pals, since one had so few of the conventional attributes of paternity to offer and had in addition to compete against children's other interests.[70] It is this good-buddy approach, rather than outright inattention, that most commonly causes symptoms of insufficient paternal guidance, for it is true that the father bent on being friends, and gaining the rewards of childish response, is not primarily or consistently concerned with disciplined guidance.

The renewal of familial interest among men inevitably encountered the entrenched position of women in the home. Even women dissatisfied with their domestic role or those who had entered the workforce could attempt to exclude the husband from the day-to-day authority in the family—including, of course, authority over the children—that served as their power base, and the most obvious source of their self-definition.[71] Here was another encouragement to the man to court his children, and to some extent his wife as well, by playing big pal, likeable even if peripheral. And the male family concern coincided with a female itch to get outside the home: "Honey, I'm back." "I was just leaving." At least until very recently, men were dependent on the family, which in turn depended on women who were implicitly, sometimes explicitly, discontented with this same institution.[72] Both men and women were engaged in a process of rethinking the nineteenth-century division of gender interests, with men reaching for a domestic component and women reaching for something in addition to the domestic component. In the long run, the process may balance out, but for several decades it has not done so very neatly. Men have sought closer family ties, but not as their primary definition, so that they have been unwilling to confront the female domestic authority head on. Women, not satisfied with this degree of interest, and bent on defending familiar authority even as they experimented with new kinds of activities, have not encouraged the full integration of men into contemporary family life. Some men in this situation resort to an older authoritarianism, with physical abuse of wives a continuing result.[73] Others, not innately work compulsives, find solace in their job, putting in hours of overtime at routine work because, given their experience, the job somehow seems more controllable, less anguished, than the domestic sphere. Others of course break up their family or feel that the hopes they had for domestic bliss have been dashed. These latter revert to a companionship with their wives as the best they can get, and so are confirmed in the sense that the proper male role in the family more generally is to serve as chief pal.[74]

Men themselves, encouraged by the situation of their wives and children, decided during the twentieth century that an authoritarian approach was wrong. Sociologists studying British working-class families and French middle-class families suggest that the Depression and World War II provided an important break,[75] causing men to question the older ethic and to seek friendlier contact with family members. In Britain, for example, the prolonged absence of men at war may have completed the erosion of traditional male authority in the household and also reoriented the family interest of the men themselves when they returned. At some point, men decided that they wanted their role as fathers to differ from the fathering they received. This followed from the long decades of declining patriarchalism. Without abandoning a valuation on achievement—men remain more interested in instilling a desire to accomplish, less interested in instilling successful social graces and even "happiness" in their children than women—[76] men strove to gain new pleasure from befriending their progeny. Without jettisoning all claim to head the household, men sought to share more than to boss. The decision to cast off the remnants of patriarchalism as unworkable was essential if men were to gain more active participation in family life, for the bases of tradition had eroded long since.[77]

It can be argued that the friendly approach, save in its more humane contrast to patriarchalism, constitutes the symptom of a profound collapse of masculinity. Men, defeated in the world of work by corporate controls and the sheer dullness of routine, decided that their fathers, similarly defeated, had offered them nothing, and that they could at least gain surface tranquillity in the household. Some observers claim that a new attitude toward daughters is particularly revealing, as fathers abandoned their natural, if hopefully re-strained, sense of sexual control in favor of being pals not only with the daughters themselves but with the daughter's suitors, those natural rivals of real paternal love.[78] There are reports also of continued ill-feeling between fathers and sons, even in the buddy-like atmosphere; one (male) critic of masculinity claims that fathers are reluctant to be seen nude by their sons, lest penis rivalry destroy their fragile relationship,[79] and that in general con-temporary men prefer daughters because sons remind them too vividly of their failures as men. Perhaps. The commentary at least suggests that the new paternal style is ill-defined, inviting a good bit of hogwash. The rise of new manuals for fathers, although a welcome contrast to older parental literature that assumed maternal all-sufficiency, suggests a similar uncertainty, particu-larly as they often begin, rather self-consciously, by defending the idea that there is a paternal role at all.[80] In a period when men have been questioning older family norms, undeniably in conjunction with some uncertainties about their work roles, some have been unable to develop more than shallow innovations.

American men gather, ill at ease, in groups such as the YMCA "Indian Princesses," to discuss how they can ritualize friendliness, in this case with their daughters.[81] And they wait for the girls to go for a snack, so that they can share their firewater. Policemen, yielding to pop psychology, sport bumper stickers about hugging one's kid today. Yet other men suggest that older values can be retrieved along with a new desire for friendliness and the decline of work links. These are the men who school their children in recreation, developing skills and guidance that can join them in play and at the same time, so the men hope, prepare the children for a life of active achievement. There is in this the hint of a fruitful reassertion of a paternal role.[82] It is no accident that successfully achieving women—in contrast to many of the feminist leaders of the previous century—can point to active male as well as female models in their family background or that, despite continued frictions, relations between fathers and sons have improved overall since 1900.[83]

Yet the male approach, partly because it remains inchoate, partly because it is complicated by occasional impulses to assert older forms of authority, is far from completely successful. It can confuse sons. Seeing their fathers still too infrequently, boys also have to reconcile their father in his friendly guise with the kind of values the father seems to be applying to his own work. The approach is, in other words, insufficiently integrated, and the playful father, careful not to be a heavyhanded disciplinarian, may be critical of his son's lack of ambition. More generally, while men continue to believe that emotional comradeship can be found in the family, it has not been a reliable source. Family instability, though by no means the fault of men alone, testifies to continued disparity between what men offer and what women want, and to disparity as well between what men expect and what they get. Men cannot of course cure the ills of the family by themselves, but they must convert their great need and their new interest into more active involvement, indeed assertion, and consider whether a family of pals is family enough.

The failures are truly agonizing.[84] You see them at airports forlornly putting their children on a plane, the occasional fathers whose families have collapsed, who see their children once in a while, at the pleasure of their ex-wives and of judges lulled by the illusions of maternal omnicompetence. Their marriages broke up for any number of reasons, sometimes at their own instigation when the home stopped providing whatever combination of solace and excitement they expected from it. Some tried to retain custody over the children, for a real man is supposed to be a father, and the new-style man wants the easy friendship of his offspring as well. But because of laws and court rulings that reached a high point in the 1930s in many countries and reversed the traditional bias in favor of fathers to one toward mothers, paternal custody has been well nigh impossible unless a mother disclaims interest. Only recently, in some American states and in England, has there been an occasional approach toward equity, in considering a father's case without assuming that children automatically belong to the mother. Other men, just as concerned about their progeny but poorer or wiser, do not try for custody. Some had no interest in the first place; others compensate for their exclusion by avoiding the contact they could have. But the sad ones in the airports preserve what they can, typically exaggerating the sugar-daddy approach to the children when they see them, trying to cram pleasures into a weekend that the father-pal of their imagination would spread over a month. And with luck they are friends, even influences, but when kids leave there is an awful hollowness, a sense of failure. Some partially fill the void with new friends and work. Still more turn to another woman, and more than a few decide to start another full family—like the handful of men now seeking to reverse vasectomies, obtained to please one woman, in order to please another and, with luck and wisdom, to do the fathering right this time.

The majority of men are spared this experience. Many find what they want in marriage, and the proclaimed happiness of married men, ritualistic protests about loss of freedom to the contrary, and the eagerness of men to marry and to remarry caution against an excessively gloomy evaluation of the family from the male standpoint. The biggest male indictments of contemporary family life would include family instability or the fear of instability—though this is, overall, no greater than that which higher mortality rates once provided. The indictments would emphasize, however, the impact of family patterns on sons, prompting too many sons to fail to integrate the restraints which successful manhood requires, with results that range from delinquency to undue dependence on facile emotional ties with women. The specific male complaints about family are not obvious even to many men themselves; women have far more visible charges to levy. It requires more than a superficial grasp of what a man owes to and deserves from family to see the family as a male problem.

Judgment is further complicated by the need to avoid a false comparison between present and past, and by key differences within the Western world. Enduring romantic bliss has been the lot of few men in any period in Western society. It may be more likely in the contemporary era, when both parties are free to express a desire for a romantic basis for a marriage.[85] Relations between fathers and sons always risked tension, and again the conflict was almost certainly worse in the nineteenth century when patriarchalism was under active attack than it is now. The family has changed a great deal, and it is changing still; but to measure quantities of family happiness is a difficult task. Men could definitely, in the eighteenth century, proclaim with greater confidence than their contemporary counterparts that they were heads of family, rulers of the domestic turf. But for many men the pain of surrendering this claim to authority has long passed, and other satisfactions have entered in its stead. Middle-class men in the nineteenth century (nineteenth-century families are in favor now among critics of contemporary degeneracy) did take a more active role in the moral development of their sons, though their effectiveness might be questioned. Certain hallowed kinds of pride, notably the joy of having one's own life confirmed and one's duty done by preparing a boy to follow in one's own steps, are definitely less possible now, and this forces fathers and sons alike to think a bit more explicitly about what work and striving mean, a painful process at best. But contemporary fathers, even those who adopt the shallowest "pals" approach to children, find pleasure in progeny, usually well beyond the demonstration of sexual potency, and there are signs that this pleasure is increasing. In sum, there is much in the contemporary family to cause concern, whether one defends women, or men, or children, or the social interest in the first instance; but this concern should not blind us to the fact that families have never been utopias, marriages never as good as expected, children always disappointing.

The other complication to an analysis of the contemporary family— insufficiently explored even by the insatiable observers of the American domestic scene—is that one cannot posit a clear family type emerging from the contemporary social environment. Class differences remain, despite important common pressures. Indeed, after some suggestion of more uniform fertility patterns during the baby boom years, the middle class has resumed a lead in birth control and delayed marriage. The decline of patriarchalism applies across class lines, but methods of childrearing differ in the two major classes nevertheless, beginning with such basic matters as the timing of toilet training (with working-class families opting for greater rigor).

Along with class and ethnic variables, national contrasts vex any effort to define the family produced by advanced capitalism. European families, taken generally, remain much more stable than their American counterparts. European divorce rates, though they have risen in the twentieth century, do not match American levels and have not followed the same chronological curves. Rates in a number of countries held steady during the 1950s and 1960s, while family dissolutions in America became ever more common.[86] Relatedly, Europeans never married as early as Americans did. They remained, in fact, slightly less likely to marry at all. Middle-class men, most notably, continued to marry in their mid- to late twenties. Europeans thus avoided some of the precarious unions formed in the late teen years. They also preserved more traces of the putative superiority, established in the nineteenth century, that comes with being male *and* older. Contrasting studies of the American and English working classes suggest that, beneath some important common trends such as the increasing employment of women, American working men may have found less active companionship in marriage than their English brethren, though the evidence is a bit sketchy.[87] Certainly the paternal style, though greatly modified in Europe as well as the United States, retained stronger traces of traditional authority, particularly in countries with a Catholic background, such as France.[88] American children, in contrast, seem more ebullient or ill-disciplined (the choice of adjectives depends on the observer). Some factors in the divergent pattern are obvious. Less affluent, Europeans could not afford such early marriage. With more crowded housing, control over children was more important, and this encouraged greater paternal authority. But possibly there were differences in values as well. American men may harbor more romantic expectations about the marital relationship, and so be more easily disappointed. They may preserve, from a frontier mentality, a greater desire to shelter women, and so be more open to confusion as women seek wider roles. This would be consistent with the greater stridency of American feminism. Middle-class Americans opted more eagerly than Europeans for suburban residence, the epitome of family isolation, which if nothing else imposed greater commuting time and left fewer hours for actual male-family interaction. Greater male violence in the United States, including a greater propensity to rape, suggest still broader distinctions in the male mentality.[89] Certainly Europe, with a quieter masculinity and possibly a greater male domestic authority, has not offered the extremes of gender tension characteristic of the United States in the past decade, just as it has avoided the most glaring family instability. American patterns are not necessarily the most desirable; they are not even, inevitably, the wave of the Western future.

With these caveats, we can turn to some common developments in male family behavior. They begin of course with boy meets girl.[90] Courtship became freer with every decade of the twentieth century, as parental supervision and arrangement were progressively reduced in all classes. Courtship imagery continued to depict a marriage-bent female, either starry-eyed or calculating, luring an independent male into matrimony, although the initiative for dating arrangements formally rested with the male. Marriage remained vital for most women, and indeed schoolgirls buzz over boys before the latter, whose conversation sticks to more purely male topics, return the compliment. As sexual contacts between potential marriage partners spread to the middle class, the chances of entrapment of men through pregnancy, though still more common among working-class youth, spread as well, undoubtedly a cause of the reduction in marriage age. With greater use of cosmetics and increasing freedom in costume, particularly from the 1920s onward, women young and old seemed bent on pleasing the male eye, readying themselves for a ritual of romance. (Male costume, though it too relaxed, changed less and later than female costume, and more as a function of new leisure interests than of courtship per se, though on balance a male preening instinct has won growing sway, particularly among working-class youth.[91]) But the male interest in courtship was fully as great as the female and, despite conventional imagery, it may have been even more leavened by romance and its illusions. Contemporary feminists worry, to be sure, about the implications of courtship for women, claiming that women are typically called upon not only to wait for male initiative but also to invest more emotionally, as men retain greater detachment, finding out more about their partners, for example, than they reveal of themselves.[92] But, granting that generalization cannot capture the host of individual combinations, men in the twentieth century have in fact chosen their partners according to more romantic criteria than women. A common economic and social background informs the male as well as the female choice, and in countries like France direct economic considerations—the property a woman brings to marriage—continues to affect the arrangements many middle-class men make.[93] But men increasingly choose by looks, sex appeal (and premarital sexual performance), the stuff of which dreams are made.[94] Women, not immune to these factors, opt more for real or probable economic success. Both partners can err egregiously, of course, when choices are made young, relatively freely and among comparative strangers. But it can be argued that many men set themselves up for particular disappointment in emphasizing physical and emotional characteristics that are often transitory, that the pattern of their often disappointed dependence on family is suggested very early.

Again, the chances of an ongoing love relationship within marriage have probably been better in the twentieth century than before. Surrounded by a romantic public culture, abetted by opportunities for some affluence and mobility, many couples have found love. But married men, though professing happiness, most commonly express a certain disappointment that ardor turned into companionship. "It's more mutual understanding," with older men, particularly, adding "The process of cooling off is a natural thing," or "Not the same thing as when we're young."[95]

Male sexuality has become increasingly unfettered in the twentieth century.[96] The most startling changes have involved youth and the middle class. Cultural criticism and parental control of the sexual practices of young men declined. The pervasive idea of burning oneself out by early sexual activity, such a hallowed part of Western and particularly Victorian ethics, has waned, though it lingers still in the fears of athletic coaches that their young charges may hinder their performance by any contact with women too close to a sporting contest. The intense censure of male masturbation was gone by the 1930s, thanks to more sophisticated sexual studies and the warnings of psychology against undue repression. Increasingly, middle-class as well as working-class youth were told that sexual activity was normal, and they were increasingly inclined to believe that sexual achievement was in fact a key early badge of masculinity. This new freedom was not without drawbacks. Childrearing still involved substantial repression of sexuality. As one doctor has put it, children are in essence told: don't play with it, it's a dirty thing, save it as a gift to your spouse. A great deal of fear remained attached to early sexual contacts, heightened also by the stern warnings against deviant sexuality. Many men found the expectation that they would be zestful sexual achievers another of the manhood tests that they could pass, if at all, only with strain, for sexual criteria for manhood, not part of traditional Western definitions, have gained in importance. The culture of young men therefore involves a great deal of sexual boasting as well as effort at sexual performance.[97]

But the biggest problem involved the partner. Female sexuality simply did not evolve in the same way as did male sexuality. Nature played a trick, of course, by having women reach a peak of sexual activity later than men (late twenties as opposed to late teens), and on the whole Western society has not encouraged the obvious solution of matching young men with older women.[98] Indeed, for middle-class youth the appeal of contact with older women declined. The romance of high school and college, by the 1920s, was a romance of peers in social status and, roughly, in age, though the male-senior might legitimately pick among freshmen women. The acceptability and, almost certainly, the use of prostitutes declined as a prime outlet for schoolboys, in contrast to the nineteenth century, which left men sexually pursuing and wooing the kind of women they might also marry.[99]

With less chaperonage and more blatant attire, proper girls were geared for sexual wooing by the time they were in secondary school. But actual sexual contact, as opposed to the infinite gradations of necking and petting, was far less tolerated for them than for males. The result of redundant sexual revolutions—of the 1920s and 1940s—that raised the level of public frankness about sex was, for many men, an increase of teasing: so far and no further.[100] Both male and female were encouraged to see sex as a contest, even a weapon, with the woman reserving a valuable possession as a lure to marriage, the male seeking to score. Despite important changes in the sexual culture, the image of the woman as passionless and the man as a drooling beast, retained its hold. Tragically often, it could describe behavior, as boys pressed too hard, girls held back too much. Among young men, sexuality in this situation could mean nothing more than penetration and ejaculation. Quick in, quick out, a burst of male triumph was duly celebrated in the demi-pornography that dotted the book stands of drugstores and railway stations and encouraged a lingering fantasy that quantity rather than quality was the key to proving maleness. Of course adolescent sexuality might be more than a unilateral male score. Schoolgirls did become more willing, though a predominant esteem for virginity lasted into the college populations of the early 1960s, and this could encourage something more than a hasty victory. But many men and women entered marriage with a wary sexual eye on their partners. And it was harder, in the middle class, for the male to assume a responsibility for a tender sexual education of a new wife than it was in the nineteenth century, for he was less likely to have a substantial advantage in age, and the wife, the product of a less restricted girlhood, seemed less a tender flower in any event.[101]

It is possible, indeed, that mutual sexual satisfaction in marriage declined in the first half of the twentieth century. The slim evidence on rates of female orgasm in middle-class marriages in the late nineteenth century suggests levels considerably higher than the 40–50 percent standard achieved in Western society in the late 1940s.[102] Certainly the burgeoning advice to women—who were now recognized as sexual creatures of a sort—was counterproductive until the 1960s, in contrast to the marriage manuals that circulated more silently a century or half-century before. The Freudians' low esteem for female sexuality, plus a feeling in the 1940s and 1950s that women were defying their true natures by working outside the home, encouraged promptings of passivity.[103] Women were to lie back and let men do.

Large numbers of married couples did , of course, achieve mutual sexual satisfaction—but not, according to surveys, a majority, and probably only a slight majority even today.[104] Middle-class sexuality was, to be sure, increasingly imaginative by mid-century, involving greater use of oral sex and a wider array of positions for intercourse. Yet for many men the situation was worse than in the nineteenth century in that they had been schooled to have more confidence in their own sexual appetite; when their wives, deriving insufficient pleasure, pleaded reluctance, it seemed downright unfair. Which may be one reason why, to the nineteenth-century arsenal of male sexual outlets of prostitutes and pornography was added increasing tolerance of extramarital affairs and, above all, abandonment of sexually unsatisfactory marriages.

The last decade and a half have brought changes, of course, though some are so recent that the implications are not clear. New sexual research and the feminist movement have greatly increased knowledge of female sexuality. The later twentieth century bids fair to be the era of the clitoris, just as the uterus symbolized the later Victorian period.[105] Younger women particularly are taking new sexual initiatives and are learning to be more active in, and more demanding of, the sexual process. Men who are interested in mutual pleasure—if only to assure continued female interest—are learning better how to assure it. Among young men there may be some reduction in the "score" mentality, in favor of an appreciation of the more sophisticated effort required for mutuality. The need for men to restrain ejaculation, to allow women sufficient time for their own orgasm, indeed appeals to the older idea that masculinity involves natural impulses that a real man can curb.[106] Sexually demanding women—some of them loudly aware that they can out-orgasm men—pose problems of course. American college campuses report new difficulties with male impotence, as men cannot alter their sexuality to deal with women who not only ask much of them in bed but aspire to the same roles in life. Some male students indeed find it easier to accept their female classmates as pals, capable of similar achievements in class and career, than to meet their sexual demands.[107] Some feminists, delighted to repay the long male lament about female sexual sluggishness, talk of an increase in male impotence and the need to seek help in therapy. New female expectations may simply be making male inadequacies more obvious, for when women were meant to be passive a man could often conceal a low level of interest and ability even to himself. (An increase in genuine, durable male impotence would suggest causes deeper than the attitudes of partners.) Despite impotency reports, most men seem to want sex with greater frequency than before.[108] It is clear that sexuality remains something of a battleground, even as the sides choose more sophisticated weapons.

The most recent sexual revolution has yet to be fully understood. It involves increasing sexual activity among young adolescents, leading since 1960 to a massive rise in illegitimacy. The implications of this for later sexual activity on the part of women burdened with painful childhood memories of pregnancy and abortion, are not encouraging. Not all young women, even the college students, are converted to a new sexual style, for women are now held to more rigorous tests of sexual adequacy. An indeterminate number are sitting this sexual revolution out.

The current sexual climate may ultimately encourage greater mutual sexual satisfaction, changing male sexual tactics somewhat but allowing fuller and more regular expression of the sexual drive. For some individuals it has already achieved this goal. There is abundant evidence of an increase in oral sex and an interest in imaginative positions, and without question men have become concerned with their women's orgasms, a concern that rises with a man's educational level. The continued sexual problem that men emphasize is a female unresponsiveness, which has a long history in the behavior and expectations of men as well as women, and it would be rash to predict either that the incompatibility will be resolved or that it will radically change in nature.[109] All we can definitely expect is confusing clamor, as sexual claims move from magazines to trash novels to T-shirt emblems. We would like to think we are sexy, but we are not sure we are.

Women have increasingly joined men in finding that a given marriage is sexually disappointing. Even before the 1960s, increasing numbers of women had extramarital affairs, though with less social approval than prevailed for men. But it is men, still, who are more likely to articulate sexual disappointment. Their looks, in an irony of nature and culture, deteriorate less rapidly than women's. Their sexual expectations in later age may be higher (though this by culture, not nature) as many women see menopause as a terminus of desire (followed by some men whose activity ceases a decade later).[110] Most generally, men still invest sexuality with more romance than women do. The female adepts at more active sexuality, for example, report a more purely physical experience than that of men.[111] Men, conditioned to see sexualtiy as proof of their prowess, do not find marriage a predictably satisfactory outlet, which dilutes the pleasure in family and adds to the difficulty of defining manliness in its context. Again, there is no novel crisis here, and what evidence there is suggests that mutual sexual satisfaction in marriage is improving. But while sexual knowledge and innovation are increasing, some argue that men continue to place a growing stake in the sexual act—as they find manhood more difficult to prove elsewhere—or at least to complicate their definition of sexual achievement by the new stress on female pleasure, that the differential remains between what is sought in sex and what is found. Certainly a majority of men seem to agree that an unresponsive woman remains their key sexual problem, and that what they most want in a woman is a greater willingness to experiment sexually. The definition of the ideal woman has changed, away from passivity: A woman should be uninhibited, willing to satisfy as well as be satisfied, able to enjoy her own sexuality ("not be hung up on guilt or inferiority trips"), and a capacity for innovation is also important. Men are calling more generally for response and approval from the female partner, a sexual demand but also part of the friendly approach to family relationships which can complicate a sense that the sexual ideal has been fulfilled.[112]

While sexuality suggests persistent difficulty amid change, marital power relationships have altered more definitely. Men have abandoned a direct expression of power in the marriage relationship in favor of mutuality. Few now claim to be boss in their household, and many take some pride in pointing out that decisions are fully shared with their wives: "One leg of the trousers for each of us."[113] A few qualify mutuality with a claim to primacy in the big decisions: "Wife is a junior partner otherwise we wouldn't get anywhere." And in one survey, a quarter of those interviewed professed outright male superiority.[114] But the idea of sharing, and a recognition of its novelty, is increasingly common to both middle- and working-class families.[115] It meshes with the general decline of the patriarchal style and even with the growing concern that wives share actively in sexual pleasure. In admitting mutuality, men are in fact recognizing a situation which had long prevailed, in which they had neither time nor the moral authority to rule a household unilaterally; the surrender of male control is no new blow, though of course its recognition is interesting. Mutuality follows also from the prevailing tone of family advice in the twentieth century, which has predominantly urged a companionate marriage, a marriage of mutual friendship and respect, as against masculine hegemony and the dangers of purely romantic attachment alike.[116] The absence of men in war and the erosion of the authority of unemployed men during the Depression have altered men's family position. Still more important, the movement of wives into the labor force automatically lifts their effective voice in the family. The working woman seems uniformly to gain greater respect from the husband, a greater right to participate in family decisions, particularly those relating to the allocation of money and to family recreation patterns.[117]

Yet, though undoubtedly a trend, hailed or noted in all the major family studies and recognized by men themselves, the rise of mutuality may conceal as much as it expresses. Many women could note that male expressions of sharing, the fruit of a new sense that it is improper publicly to claim dominance, have not gone far enough. Figures on wifebeating suggest that an important minority of men depend on the most brutal subordination of their women. A middle-class wife describes a husband who could not be sweeter in public, who would undoubtedly advocate family democracy to any inquiring pollster, but who has to punish her: "He will strike out when he's ready and for whatever reason he has at the moment."[118] Even aside from these extremes, many men cannot shake the sense that they have lost something, in yielding authority, that mutuality is fine as a method of consensus but that in disagreement their will should logically prevail. Still other men, constrained to admit their wives' parity, may feel a frustration in the male family role that will find other outlets, in a diminution of their family interest or in a sense that the family is not providing the satisfaction that they expected from it.

For mutuality, to the extent that it has been achieved, is too often viewed primarily in terms of what women gain. Most clearly, as the male breadwinner role has been dented by external disruptions and by the rise of working wives, the power that men wielded because of their economic control has been reduced. And this, from the male standpoint, raises two related questions: To what extent has there been a corresponding sharing out of women's family power—the other dimension of mutuality—and what, if anything, has compensated men for the power they have (however properly and inevitably) given up? In other words, has mutuality, such a nice-sounding word, improved family life for men, apart from the minority who implicitly or explicitly reject it altogether?

Most aspects of family activity fell under female control during the nineteenth century. Daily decisions about money allocations, the organization of the household, the orientation of children, even, most probably, the number of children to have were de facto wifely responsibilities. When one talks of mutuality the reference is most obviously to important but more occasional items: decisions about big purchases, about moving, about where to send children to school when choice is involved, about career choices of sons—items that traditionally involved male interest (the future of sons) or that in requiring special disbursements gave the breadwinner an obvious voice. And, lest the discussion become ensnarled, it can be granted that matters of this sort do have a fundamental effect on families—where to live, for example; how much the household budget will contain—and represent the most basic kind of power. But the woman's family authority resulted from the division of labor that left her at home with the need to make countless daily decisions. From women have come determinations about how the house would look and how clean it would be. From her most typically have come nightly decisions about whether to use a birth control device or not. Daily routines had more to do with the ongoing conduct of children and with their ultimate personalities than any decisions which men could make. Even those stereotypic suburban families in which wives left disciplining to their husbands reflected female control over what should be disciplined. Routine handling of money gave women prime power over family diet and dress, and their effectiveness as budget managers predetermined decisions about leisure time expenditures or larger purchases in which men might share more directly. Women also developed prime authority over relations with kin, forming orbits based primarily on connections with their family of origin, particularly with their mothers. None of this, obviously, represents some cabalistic undermining of male rights; it all followed from the often arduous chores which devolved on women as specialists in the home.[119]

Inquiries into mutuality have not touched as heavily on the areas—often so prosaic—that became female-dominated.[120] Men have most clearly staked a greater claim to decisions about childrearing as part of their new definition of family. Here is one area where they think they deserve compensation for authority surrendered elsewhere. But most studies of changes in family power resulting from a wife's going to work indicate that decisions on housekeeping and daily finance remain a woman's province. So, in all probability, do decisions about birth control and family size, which are based increasingly on a woman's consideration of child-bearing as one among many options open to her. So do decisions about contact with relatives, which form an important part of the social networks of many people, remain the woman's prerogative. The twentieth-century rise of the grandmother, though in part a function of greater female survival rates, also reflects the continued female orientation of the larger family.[121]

The dominant power of women in the family becomes part of a circle, vicious or benign. Men have not articulated concern about gaining shared authority in the women's areas in part because the decisions, although frequent, are seldom crucial, and because they recognize, and are told to recognize, women's superior expertise. In matters of birth control women have been asserting even stronger rights to control their own bodies. Women have yielded little in matters such as household appearance because men show so few signs of wanting to undertake day-to-day household activity, content largely to carry out what the women tell them. Working wives can easily rephrase the whole domestic power issue. Harrassed by their newly multiple functions of job and housewife, they cry out for greater help from their husbands, for a more equitable sharing of chores. But, as few husbands press forward to exceed their brief, the women rarely reconsider their role in shaping the framework of the household: their plea, understandable enough, is for more help in carrying out what they have decided should be carried out.[122] Mutuality, then, remains subtly incomplete. And while men have gained some new sense of the family as a participatory endeavor, they can still feel, somewhat confusedly, strangers in their homes. They have indeed been told so often that it is their power that is or was abusive—some learned their lessons at a complaining mother's knee—that they have not been able clearly to consider raising demands on the other side of the power structure.

What they have sought from mutuality, whether they granted it willingly or whether a wife's independent earnings thrust it upon them, is a more contented wife. No brief survey can do justice to the myriad family disputes that have been tossed up in the twentieth century. We do not even know that the family has become a less happy institution though we do know that family members have become freer to express their unhappiness. Yet by the middle of the century it was clear that women were far less satisfied with families than men were. The male impulse, quite apart from formal power considerations, was to become in the main friendlier, for this expressed not only their desire but also their need to see the family as a source of warmth and contentment. The comfortably companionable marriage is indeed the most successful form that large numbers of men report, which means that mutuality, giving women an increasing voice in the larger shape of family activities, has paid off from a male standpoint.[123]

Yet the success has been incomplete. Some men may have yielded too much, unable to find new satisfactions in the family to compensate for their partial exclusion from its daily running.[124]

The surrender of social contacts outside the family on the part of many married working-class men has been striking, over the past several decades. Home and family have indeed become the focus of attention outside of work. In many cases, active companionship with the wife has repaid the effort, even after the romance fades somewhat. But in other cases mutuality can increase, in a strict power sense, without bringing husband and wife together. The American blue-collar marriages described by Mirra Komarovsky, in which older men, particularly, depended heavily on family for whatever emotional satisfaction they won, could be bleak even when decision-making was mutual.[125] Particularly in the United States, where mutuality has probably gone farthest, the rising divorce rate attests to the limited impact of power-sharing on family stability, though one could argue that without it instability would have become still more rampant.

Despite immense variation, men do not see the wife as an outlet for the sharing of emotional problems to the same extent the wife views the husband. Emotional mutuality is typically incomplete. Particularly in the working class, men pride themselves on not burdening wives with their problems.[126] They judge their wives' efforts to rely on them emotionally with ambiguity, on the one hand exaggerating the dependence—for it remains pleasant to see oneself as family bulwark—and on the other objecting to the wife's need to be consoled and entertained. Yet many men have not maintained clear emotional alternatives to their wives. They lack frequent contact with other relatives, and they have reduced their social contacts outside the home. In many instances, they seem to perceive the family as a place to rest in, as a supportive context to be alone in.[127] Yet men remain vulnerable to a need for the family which they cannot fully articulate, to which mutuality in power, while not necessarily damaging, is irrelevant.[128]

For women have been finding the family tie decreasingly satisfying, despite the progress of mutuality. To old complaints about male brutality or insufficient attention from men wedded to job or to male leisure were added new ones. The 1920s saw an increasing number of divorces, particularly in white-collar families, based on discontent with living standards.[129] Dependent still on male earnings, many women translated the expectation that the man would provide into an expectation that he would provide generously. Keeping up with the Joneses became written into manhood, as the wife of a New Jersey worker suggested when she complained that he had had ample time to "make a man of himself" by moving out of a low-paying job that he apparently enjoyed. More recently women have become freer to criticize male lack of emotional sharing and sexual incompatibility. Men may be less responsible for female dissatisfaction than women's inability to find in the family an adequate substitute for traditional childbearing.[130] There was no way for women to avoid boredom and frustration at home as their maternal role declined, whether they vented their boredom in nagging, in divorce, or in seeking to develop interests beyond the family. Polls that in the 1950s indicated dissatisfaction with the role of housewife throughout Europe and the United States, with a large minority of women wishing that they were men, revealed the extent of the problem.[131] Increasing mutuality on the part of men was not an adequate answer, though it could help, yet men could easily be confused that their new style was so ineffective. Men were depending on a relationship with women who, because of essential, often mutually-agreed upon changes in family function, had to alter their own role definition, or be dissatisfied, or both. Male inadequacies—too little time for the family, too passive a definition of family role—could add immensely to the problem, and men could claim more than their share of assignable faults. But the fundamental problem of female role definition was not in men's power to control, and this was frustrating in itself.

There have been happy endings, and there may be more as women clarify their own interests. Working women gain alternate sources of activity, while cementing the trend toward mutuality, and it may be that those women who do not work will have explicitly chosen their more traditional role and be less likely to find it obscurely confining. This has demonstrably increased marital happiness in some cases, though the impact on marital stability remains problematic. It remains true that women are changing more rapidly than men's marital reliance on them. It is changing more rapidly than the admission of men into the active shaping of the household, which adds up to considerable burdens on many working women and a potential, if inarticulate, lack of satisfaction on the part of many men, a sense still of being peripheral to an entity they need but do not control. Male dependence on the family may prove to be an anchor on which the institution will survive amid inevitable female experimentation. Yet the male tendency, when the level of dissatisfaction rises too high, to abandon one family in favor of forming another, has obvious drawbacks. Possibly men will opt for a still deeper involvement with family, developing and insisting upon a fuller definition of mutuality. Possibly male reliance on the family will slacken, where men develop their considerable means of finding interests outside the family and reverse any tendency to use the family instead of company with other men to provide social contact. Certainly men stand to gain from articulating their family needs and from taking an active hand in the definition of family activities generally. Mutuality, besides sounding equitable, may prove to be a vital key in improving the family relationship for men. The fact remains, at present, that men are peculiarly vulnerable to expectations from marriage that they do not know how to achieve.[132]

Interaction with children has unquestionably increased as part of the decline of patriarchalism and the rise of mutuality.[133] Here is a potential source of emotional satisfaction that men have become eager to exploit. There is some irony in the new interest in friendship with children, for not only has the number of children declined but also the male ability to determine that number; for many couples a contemporary version of womb envy may prove particularly acute, for the feminist interest in extrauterine conception has, with one partial exception, yet to bear fruit. But greater involvement with individual children has been a normal part of reduction of family size, and contemporary fathers are belatedly participating in a process that, a century before, seemed to entice or ensnare mothers alone. Middle-class fathers have gone somewhat further than working-class in sharing time and attention with their children, but the trends are remarkably compatible. Age differences are more significant. Fathering remains most satisfying in the pre-teen (though post-infant) years of children, and fathers are less likely than mothers to retain or redevelop ties with adult children. The "pals" approach has not removed the peer group or displaced the ultimate primacy of mothers. Fathers are still gingerly moving into an area in which they are loath to claim expertise. There has been no trust-busting in motherhood. Male claims of interest often surpass ability or willingness to perform. Many a father asserts that he fully shares childrearing with his wife, when both the allocation of time and the child's perception argue the contrary. But a new sense of interest and responsibility cannot be denied, beginning in some cases with paternal presence in the delivery room and unprecedented paternal participation in the caring for infants. More clearly than mutualist endeavors in other aspects of marriage, they add up to a definite attempt to broaden the roles of modern masculinity.

Uncertainty about the appropriate manner to assume for the new interest in parenthood lingers. Middle-class men compare their daily attentions to their fathers' remoteness, the gruff pleas of fatigue on return from work. Working-class fathers comment more on the change in authority: "My father had power over us; I can't boss them."[134] They note particularly their growing reluctance to use force, their role as guides rather than dictators. Yet, while these men are convinced that they greatly improved their relationship with their children, descriptions such as "I am like a big brother to them" or "I am like a mother to my children" suggest a lingering confusion. Indeed a distinct paternal role seems to require justification in the eyes of fathers themselves, and men who take primary responsibility for childrearing often think of themselves as male mothers. Men have added pal to boss in the imagery of fathering, but they are hesitant to claim too much for a distinctive male style.[135]

The results of the new concern for fathering remain unclear as well. Many fathers are in fact sporadic in their expressions of concrete interest, flirting with greater parental involvement but easily retreating when there is little immediate feedback. Weekend carriage-pushing or the growing sports involvement of fathers and sons are impressive changes in male-child contact, but they hardly rival motherhood in practice. Individual men who have broken through to really concomitant parenting (mainly young, university-trained men in the United States and northern Europe) are too recent and few in number to allow general conclusions. Certainly, new paternal interest has not, to date, wrought massive improvements in rates of delinquency or in the general social confidence that parenting is being well handled. Men's own uncertainty combines in fact with women's reduction of motherhood to raise new doubts about whether children can be raised right at all, without constant reference to outside experts.[136] Insofar as men have seized on a definition of fatherhood as friendliness, they open themselves to charges that they have exchanged the responsibility of the father to serve as moral mentor to the child for a pleasant but somewhat superficial and indeed unreliable bond of affection. Failing to inspire the deep affection reserved still for mothers, many fathers have difficulty retaining a sense of satisfaction in their progeny when the years of mutual play are over. In settings where fathers and sons can still work together, as in certain factory jobs, sons prefer greater independence, finding their fathers still too demanding—the old complaint—but also now too cloying in their affectionate attention. Most fathers, unable to participate directly in their children's achievements now that generational succession is impossible, cannot define an ongoing link, beyond service as a secondary grandparent. Memories may be more affectionate than they once were, bitterness less likely, but the kind of respect possible for the father who took responsibility for his child's will is less likely, too.[137]

Yet parenting in general has been reduced by outside forces that impinge on the raising of children, and satisfactions are inevitably reduced when children cannot follow directly in parental footsteps. Mothers, in a period of rapidly changing female roles, have at least as hard a lot as fathers. Along with some uncertainty about how to be anything but a friend to a child, men continue to bring some distinctive elements to the childrearing process. They still place considerable emphasis on a child's achievement (which in itself of course leaves them open to disappointment), not only in their stated hopes for a future career or for performance in school or in sports, but in their tendency to insist that a child earn their affection rather than benefit from an automatic, loving embrace. Fathers play a vital role, then, in helping to set standards for both sons and daughters and in providing a different kind of guidance from that of mothers. A distinctively paternal approach remains possible, even though contemporary fathers differ from their predecessors in their hope for more immediate emotional return from children and their reduced ability to take pleasure in discipline.[138] As fathers receive more recognition for their new interest, as indeed they define this interest better themselves, the lingering sense of being a peripheral parent will dissipate further.

Families are in trouble. Men seem to need families.[139] Men's dependence on family has not significantly lessened in recent decades and their desire to use family to broaden their roles and interests has increased. Few men seek to make family their exclusive purpose. Their return to more domestic concerns has not been a flight from male identification with work and leisure, but rather a supplement, and there is evidence that sexuality and successful fathering depend on a wider sense of fulfilled masculinity. Men seem to seek a more abundant emotional life, ranging from more expressive sexuality to the new relationship with children, and in the process they are recalling, if inadequately, an interest in tenderness that had declined in masculine regard in the first reactions to industrialization. Substantially excluded still from certain kinds of domestic power, unsure really how to define maleness in the family, their efforts often have a tentative air. Many men continue to see jobs and male leisure as areas of greater certainty, in which both control and routine are more familiar. A pervasive desire to use the family as a place of rest brings increasing frustration, for obviously it is not a predictably restful place. Nor does it provide an automatic, elaborately sanctioned set of purposes for men. However, though some of their efforts are questionable, men show some signs of coming to terms with their need and of developing family styles that, in expressing some redefinition of role, can be built into articulate statements of male goals. Quite apart from its probable social value, family determines so much of what men are, as well as what they require, that it compels male initiative.

8. Conclusion:
Vive une différence!

These are not easy days for gender relationships in Western society, particularly in the United States. From the standpoint of social analysis, gender differences have steadily lessened over the past half-century, particularly in the workplace. But this is part of the problem, for rhetoric, individual, or even institutional expectations have yet to catch up with reality. They may never do so fully. Economic roles may equalize more fully than ascribed gender characteristics. This study has stressed gender as a means of personal identity, particularly in modern society, and in an age when emotional balance requires explicit attention this has a reality of its own apart from economic gender convergence. Personal identity does not come easily in the contemporary industrial world. Its difficulty increases at least for women, as they flee or are torn from their traditional roles. Gender, for all its insensitivity to individual variation, may serve as a useful personal baseline, when community and family structures are too relaxed to provide norms of their own.

Yet gender identity is itself under attack. Women have to attack it, though they may do so in different degrees. This is a contemporary historic necessity. The starting point of gender relations must be the realization that women cannot rely on hallowed traditional roles alone. They must be something more than mothers, because the decline of motherhood quantitatively (the limited birth rate, frequently compressed into a short period of life) and to some extent qualitatively (the rise of non-parental education) prevents them from filling their days, and so defining their lives, with a maternal function. What they will do instead, and particularly how far they will go toward obtaining a job or professional identity, remains unclear. We cannot even be sure that they will move in uniform directions. Some women may opt for leisure, like those suburban matrons who crowd the tennis courts and bowling alleys during the day, though the tide of feminist sentiment and the trends of the lives of younger women runs against them. Even they, though they cosset their children, are not traditional women despite the fact that they may appeal still to the imagery of the nineteenth century.

But do men need to question the identity which evolving manhood provides them? The pressures here are far less clear, for men were forced into the marketplace over a century ago. Nothing so dramatic as the decline of childbirth has occurred to them since. Men have been changing, modifying some of the rough edges of industrial masculinity, particularly by seeking a non-patriarchal family role and developing leisure outlets for some of the older expressions of manhood, from skilled manipulation of matter to physical competitiveness. But they are simply not in the same historical situation as women. They can in theory adapt their gender tradition, not rewrite it, just as women were more cushioned by custom during much of the nineteenth century. There are important indications that men are attempting just that, quite apart from the promptings of feminism. Some feminists indeed seem to be attacking male images of the past and atypical men of the present rather than the complexity of contemporary manhood itself, which leaves ordinary contemporary men more than a bit bewildered.[1]

There are real problems with manhood. While the genders have drawn closer together, and men have stepped back from the artificial extremes of the nineteenth-century reaction to industrialization,[2] men still maintain an aura of toughness and self-containment that may be harmful to them and unrealistic in the larger society. The dependence of the male role on work and the inability to make work fully satisfying can be a quiet tragedy. Difficulties remain in replacing patriarchalism with an articulated but new approach to the male role. The evolution of society, while changing the nature of men's dilemma, does not promise to remove it. There remains in fact a certain schizophrenia to contemporary manhood, between the aggressive manhood presented to the outside world and the tenderness sought at home. In a sense this has long been implicit in Western masculinity, but it was greatly heightened by the reaction to industrialization.

Overriding the male dilemma is the anger of some contemporary women. Here is the clearest sign that things are not well, but ironically the anger complicates the male reaction. Some men react with hostility, ridiculing feminists in general, seizing on divisions in the ranks of women, and viewing the strivings of women with whom they have actual contact as a personal attack. Still more men are simply confused by the feminist dismay. What could possibly be so wrong? Others, particularly younger, college-age men, feel an active sense of guilt: Something must be amiss with men, with being a man, if our mothers and sisters are so aggressively distressed. Some see active opportunity in the feminist attacks on conventional manhood, to escape or to modify roles and tasks that are seen as unduly burdensome.[3]

I have argued that the first gender reactions to industrialization rather narrowed the range of manly criteria, reducing for example the gentle religious outlet. Over the last century the criteria have widened once again, even apart from class distinctions. The middle class, though drawn to athletic and military achievement along with economic competitiveness, also fostered quiet, bookish, indeed very gentle boys. Feminism promises, at the least, to further this healthy diversity. Men who can express themselves in dance and other aesthetic endeavor, men who adopt new nurturing roles within the family, will win new approval. Changes in the population's age structure, which see an increasing percentage of men middle-aged or older, may have similar effects in reducing the excessive youth orientation of nineteenth-century manhood criteria, as in leisure or sexuality.

But simply to stress an increase in diversity would be an evasion. Many feminists are asking not for diversity, but for replacement of one standard of manhood with another. They are asking indeed for a new male personality.[4] And there are men who say they are right, that a new personality would not only be fairer to women but also would benefit men. Their challenge is not entirely new, but it is certainly vigorous. The whole future of gender is under question, at least at one level of intellectuality, a level important enough to warrant serious attention even if many men and women remain ignorant of the issues.

I have tried to present a historical overview of manhood, however personal some of my interpretations. It is hard to use history to predict or to recommend. There are good reasons to argue that history cannot cast clear light on the future of women or men, for the current and prospective female situation has no real historical precedent. Never have women been so well educated, or so nearly equally educated with men. Never have women been so free from the physical fact of childbearing. We can predict that both trends will continue. Women will increasingly gain on men's educational levels and may even surpass them. Giving birth and, quite probably, caring for the children born will likely command an ever slighter portion of the woman's life cycle, though we cannot know if this trend will proceed without interruption. (Witness the unexpected increase of births in 1977 in the United States, the product of women deciding to have children in their late twenties or early thirties.) Yet even though history most clearly serves to point to the new, the unprecedented, it does at least suggest a definite framework within which questions about gender can be asked. This in turn produces, if not specific recommendations about how men and women should behave—I certainly make no such claims—at least some desirable boundary lines. There are some problems that the two genders have to address; there are others that they may address. Simply sorting these categories out is a useful start.

For gender discussions threaten to become a garbage bag. Precisely because so much is new, or newly questioned, virtually any theory may be proposed. A woman writes Ann Landers saying that 95 percent of all men are competitive aggressors and not fit for the company of women, in bed or out. Other women, and some sociopsychological studies, point to growing male docility and weakness, resulting among other things in rising impotency, which seems to suggest that men are not fit company for women, at least in bed, but for quite different reasons.[5] Maleness is becoming a big guessing game. The chances not just for bad guesses, but for outright idiocy, are legion in this situation.

A host of predictive scenarios can indeed be outlined. There is in contemporary feminism a utopian component. Building on nineteenth-century notions of women's special purity and the twentieth-century reality of the need for new roles, some feminists are suggesting that everything can be tidied up with a few simple, revolutionary strokes.[6] Let women do what men have been doing, but with their distinctive virtues, and let men know the wonder of feminization, thus gaining true nurturing gentleness and the ability to make meaningful friendships. Add perhaps a dash of technological futurism, so that the messiest work does not have to be done by either gender. Free children from the burdens of gender socialization so that they can be their natural selves—and at last we'll be on the right track. All of this is unlikely. Those who do hold out cosmic hopes at the end of a very difficult transitional period for women are often admirably sympathetic people, truly concerned with humanity. I might agree with their goals if I thought we could reach them, but I do not. Their rhetoric complicates the task of sorting out what men and women are likely to do and what changes are realistically possible and desirable. We will come out of the current gender tension a somewhat diferent society, and hopefully a somewhat better one, but not enough better to encourage wild experimentation en route, not enough better to do without some of the established strengths of manhood.

A more prosaic prospect can be suggested. Late twentieth-century society is in many ways trying to redress some of the real or imagined exaggerations of the more exhuberant period of initial industrialization, trying to recapture, by mechanisms new as well as old, values that had been lost or distorted. Ecologists urge a return to resource conservation reminiscent of peasant concern for generational transmission of property. Birth control also can be seen as an attempt to recapture traditional population stability. After a century of distortion, gender relationships are taking on something of a preindustrial balance.[7] Men return to greater and more effective family concern. Women become producers in their own right. Men will remain primary breadwinners, but women's vital contributions (usually in jobs that differ from those the men dominate—building on divisions of white-collar labor that began to emerge a century ago) will give them new, more equal stature in the family. Women will remain more family-focused, and motherhood will still be more important than fatherhood, but men will take a more active role in associating with their children. This notion of a restoration of a preindustrial gender relationship can be seen as returning an important balance to family life and as usefully broadening the base, the range of personal identifications, of men and women alike. Or it can be seen as a loss, not only of an opportunity for a fundamental recasting of gender definitions in the future but also of a strength and intensity which, at its best, the gender relationships of a century past produced, at least in their middle-class versions.[8] Hence the feeling that a vital individualism of character, pervasive in the first industrial century, is being buried amid a new blandness and conformity that recalls the smothering communities of a peasant culture now writ large by media and institutional pressures.

The prosaic view (whether pessimistic or not) has much to recommend it. It cautions against the idea that we are on the verge of a magic new gender mix that can right a host of ancient wrongs. It suggests that some of the extremes of the gender reaction to industrialization, including greater differentiation and the narrow association of men with competitive work and women with perfect motherhood, are being worn away by an effort more to restore an old balance than to cast about for a new one. But a prediction based on "the more it changes, the more it is the same thing" would be off the mark, and no one is suggesting that preindustrial values will be literally recaptured. Men and women have been individuated by the industrialization process. They cannot think of their relationship in terms of the family as a traditional entity. Women's new work outlets only enhance the necessity of their acting individuals. Men cannot return to a definition of self based on proprietorship. Women cannot define their lives in terms of motherhood. If we are not headed toward utopia, neither are we headed back to the bliss or boredom of our rural past.

Men and women are more alike, in role, temperament, even in appearance, than they were a century ago. It is probably easier now for a man to be timid, and it is certainly easier for a woman to be assertive, than it was in the heyday of industrialization. Some women may seem to be describing men as if they were all robber barons, devoting themselves to a seamy competitive chase. Men can still delight in downplaying women's rational capacity, and certainly many are shocked at the recurrent signs that women are not models of purity. It would be possible to argue that passions will ultimately cool, that behavioral trends will ultimately allay the outdated gender images. Even now, most women are not as upset as their articulate spokespeople, and some of course are opposing even a modest gender redefinition. Men have generally been content enough with actual behavioral trends—the wife working, for example—that they have largely ignored the rhetoric. But gender relations will not necessarily fall easily into place, and rhetoric will not necessarily cool. We do not, first of all, know how far the trends will go. Aspects of the current gender prospect have no historical precedent, particularly because of the decline of traditional motherhood. Men cannot help but feel something of a loss as gender roles change or are at least opened to new discussion. That the changes correspond to some preexisting behavioral trends, such as the desire to find new ways to relate to the family, does not assure their easy acceptance, particularly when some women delight in playing on the ambiguities of manhood. (Can't get it up? Can't handle assertive women? Out of touch with your real emotions? Incapable of forming real friendships?)[9] Rhetorical tension is real, which is why I return to it in concluding a brief history and why I hope that the historical framework can serve to help sort out the present and the proximate future.

Is men's traditional dominance in society now doomed? I really do not think we know. (I also do not care too much, though quite conceivably I would if the possibility were closer to reality.) Diligent feminist searching of history and anthropology has produced evidence of no society in which men were not dominant.[10] Certainly, in the Western tradition men's functions have always been socially regarded as more important than women's. So forcefully was this brought home in the nineteenth century, despite the elaborate and by no means entirely insincere bows to motherhood, that articulate women are now paying men the compliment of trying to imitate their performance in almost every aspect of life, while sometimes hoping to retain the evanescent moral superiority of women in the process (an unbeatable combination, if successful). The liberated woman is thus one who can behave quite like a man, in work, play, and personal style, although possibly without some of the recognized drawbacks. Imitation does not of course guarantee widespread success, although it may be sufficient to challenge that majority of men who are not fully successful in their own approximations of the ideal. The historical and anthropological evidence can be cited to suggest that the dominance of male things will be dislodged only with difficulty, and only slowly; it is alive and kicking at present. Bio-psychological evidence, from size and strength to independence from mother, may suggest insuperable barriers to female equality with the male. This is a view now being asserted against some extremes of feminist euphoria.[11] But against this is the fact that we are outside the historical framework, now that technology has so reduced the importance of physical disparities and now that society needs to call on relatively little of a woman's time for mothering purposes. Certainly, male dominance of the nineteenth-century type is being modified. There are far fewer clearly male areas, many more top women who can do better than most men at their own game. How far the modification will go is, I think, impossible to predict.[12]

Will erosion produce backlash? Certainly, to some extent. It must be recognized that some of the measures being urged on men to compensate for partial surrender of their work and power roles would not easily establish new claims to importance; repair work on the family and personal relationships— which is, I think, needed—would be a step back, however limited, from the public spheres in which male dominance has been traditionally asserted. Possibly, men will be able to define new spheres of cultural preponderance. If gentle nurturing were to become male, for example, it might turn out to be a leading attribute just because it is male. But the rules of the dominance game have changed somewhat because of women's liberation from many traditional restraints. We do not know as yet how far women will be willing or able to go in challenging men for a fair share of dominant positions. But there is no reason to posit a massive increase of gender tension.

In what follows, it will be clear that I think men can and should disagree with what some women are currently claiming, though less as to roles than as to the male personality. I think there are certain things men should do for their own benefit. I admit that some of these could be factors in dominance competition. But I do not see the utility of a battle model as a focus for some final comments on the contemporary gender situation. I hope indeed that feminists can see the utility, if not of disagreement per se at least of expressing certain views of masculinity that, left unarticulated, could fester beneath a humorous tolerance of feminist rhetoric. Men have been strangely silent on gender issues, largely because the greatest compulsion to seek change affects women and partly because, as the feminists point out, men are less gifted at verbal self-analysis. If they cannot claim credit for initiating contemporary gender assessment, men must begin to discuss what is being said about them.

I see neither need nor use to complicate a statement with a pervasive sense of guilt. Articulate women, like any group with goals not yet attained, can be inclined to develop elaborate systems of blame for human impediments—in this case, men. But the female situation does not historically resemble that of other minorities, in that the rules of the game have so clearly changed within the last half-century or so. Men do not have to apologize for past dominance or immerse themselves in the sins of history. For the oppression of women was primarily biological, which is not to deny important individual abuse along the way. Men and women simply elaborated on the physical constraints of motherhood. Women may of course inform themselves of past oppression that they now wish to avoid.[13] But to go on to sweeping gender blame is anachronistic, and I suggest that men are under no obligation to buy the approach. Men who continue to apply past views of female roles to women in the age of birth control are increasingly at fault, though their lag is to some degree understandable since many women seek to perpetuate older self-definitions as well. But there is no need to approach the question of current and future gender relationships with a reverent desire to right ancient injuries. Guilt is not a very effective social motivation in any event.

Women absolutely require, and have every right to insist upon, a redefinition of their roles in life. There is no way realistically to devote one's life to maternity if one has only one or two children. Many husbands like and seek a certain amount of mothering. A family focus of a broader sort, combined with friendships and leisure activities, may continue to satisfy some women. But that is their business, and men should try not to build on this narrow structure or to base their own economic and political roles on any pattern of exclusion of women. The historic transformation of women must in this sense be recognized. Otherwise we as a society are in for needless injustice and bitter haggling.

There may of course be losses in the female transformation. Gentle femininity has contributed powerfully to the beauty of life. It has been pleasant, if unrealistic even a century ago, to think of women as a haven, defending aesthetic and moral purity. Certain reform impulses may be lost if women largely redefine themselves in more masculine terms. Patronage of the arts and humanities, already declining, could be hurt further if women in school adopt the same curricular preferences as men, seeking economic opportunity more than aesthetic satisfaction. Developments of this sort are at this point possibilities, not predictions. Women have not yet opted for the same patterns as men in education. But they may do so. The nineteenth-century division of gender labor, already severely modified, may collapse.

Men must, in the long run, stand back to let women develop their redefinitions as they wish, recognizing that the old patterns simply cannot persist without change. This means in turn that men must be ready to take up their share of the slack in areas which have been disproportionately left to women that still remain socially desirable or necessary. This could mean more male humanism, a good thing in itself. It could mean that if men do in fact need some special comforts, some lifelong mothering, they will have to provide it themselves or strive to rearrange their outer world so that it requires less domestic solace. There is opportunity in the reshuffling. As the feminists point out, men can gain from venturing into fields that they left to the care of women, from certain of the arts to the nurturing of children, broadening their own horizons as they do their share toward the social good.[14] And there is challenge as well. Men will have to figure out how much they had been leaning on women, depending on set role definitions both to prove their masculinity and to gain the comforts required to bolster their strengths; and they will have to provide alternatives. The task will not be easy. But manhood has always involved challenge, and this one could be truly interesting.

How far women's role redefinition will go is anyone's guess at this point. Women themselves are in sharp disagreement. Quite possibly the long-run result will prove rather a major readjustment than an upheaval, with most women taking jobs as a supplementary self-definition, and men taking on some additional family tasks as a supplement of their own. Quite possibly women, at the summits of achievement (which are few enough for men) will not be able to match the male pattern or, more probably, will not choose to, save in selected instances. It is not easy to wait for women to decide. It might be nice to be able to plan on a certain percentage of women in each job slot and thus figure what the precise male occupational role will be. But quite apart from women's right to take some time to work out their own definitional adjustments, there is simply no way to avoid a transitional process. What I hope will happen is that men can eventually give women the breathing room they need without too much anxiety about the outcome. This means an adjustment to some shifts in family arrangements. It means flexibility on the job, with men willing to define their occupational roles for themselves, and not in terms of what women do not or "cannot" do. It means, ultimately, a willingness to compete. Men owe women a clear shot. Ideally, this will involve some reconsideration of extrinsic jobs hurdles—drinking bouts to prove that one is a good union member or the kind of fraternity man an alumnus-employer can trust, or some of the other hazing competitions in professional schools—that have not been good for men themselves. Minimally, it means an acceptance of women at various levels of the occupational hierarchy without a sense of male degradation. We do not have to be sure at this stage if women can make it to the top in a fully male way, for most men do not make it either. Maybe the top mathematicians will still be disproportionately male. Maybe the brightest women will not choose traditional male fields. Maybe women—as some doctors predict, in a field where the eye-catching prediction is still untrammeled by solid information—will learn to run as fast as men. Maybe they won't, or won't want to. Maybe men will learn to run faster. The male gender definition need not depend on precise outcome.

Will men be able to deal with the implications of the transition? With wives who are professional successes, with women supervisors, with women jocks? The omens are diverse. An increase in crimes against women may well signify a substantial male minority that feels desperately threatened. Middle-class male culture suggests substantial receptivity to change, as it did earlier with regard to the increased educational opportunities for women on which the current female challenge is so clearly based. There are fights and frustrations in the offing, without question, but an expectation of something less than an all-out gender war is not hollow optimism.

This is true particularly because men stand to gain in certain respects from the female transition. A further loosening of male hazing rituals, a trend already visible for the last several decades, can be all to the good. Women may add useful variety to the personality types that now dominate the professions. Medical practice, for example, may come to depend more on sympathetic warmth and less on driven, arrogant claims to infallibility, as femininity supplements the male professional style. Above all, men can benefit as they adjust to women's new economic roles. Most women, even married professional women, are still supplementary breadwinners; less than 10 percent of wives outearn their husbands. Most men still make it a point of pride to claim primary responsibility for family income. It is premature, given the relative newness of married women's work and the continued barriers to equality of earnings, to predict equalization of the breadwinning role. But what men will have the increasing right to claim is an increase in the flexibility of their role. They can use the growing female earning power to create a greater freedom of choice for themselves. Some may want to stick to their job for economic reasons. For at least a generation, women do have catching up to do—completing their education a bit later in life, having supported the husband through his own; compensating for still unequal job and mobility opportunity—that suggests the desirability of primary male provision for the family. But in the near future, men will have both right and possibility to reassess this situation, to claim, if they choose, something of same opportunity for changing jobs, returning for retraining, or simply trying to improve the intrinsic satisfaction of an existing job that many of their wives now have. Proper provision for the family remains a source of satisfaction, and at this stage, again, one can neither predict or urge that it be more than modified, until we see how far role adjustment goes. But in this process of role adjustment it is important that men perceive, discuss, and where appropriate insist upon their own right to benefit. Breadwinning, apart from its difficulty for many men, can be a trap, tying men to choices that were made in haste. Its loosening can prove a vital instrument in the future definition of masculinity at work.

What can be suggested, then, is that men, in their family and work roles, give women freedom to maneuver while maintaining a sense of their own rights, including some new ones. Some men may wish to stand back a bit from women as roles are sorted out. Feminists who argue that what they wish to do is enjoy the fruits of sisterhood, to exploit the new opportunities opening to women without involving men are a bit naive—it is hard for men to feel unaffected—but should be taken at their word to a substantial extent. The decline in the marriage rate and increase in marriage age, particularly in the middle class, over the last decade suggest that some men and women are taking a hard look at the tie that conventionally unites them. (Here again, there may be a return to a more normal Western diversity in marital status, against the rush to marry that corresponded to the first stages of industrialization.) Within or without marriage, men who are troubled by women's strivings after new roles would do well to bolster their own groupings, simply to be less affected by what is in fact a difficult struggle on the part of women against male impediments but even more against their own past standards. I think it is clear that, from the nineteenth century onward, men have tended to become excessively dependent on women for routine creature comforts and emotional support. To this extent they need to pull back, for their well-being and women's as well.

But other men may be able to serve women as emotional supports and take pleasure in so doing. For as women move more fully out into the industrial world, they, like their male counterparts a century or more before, need a support apparatus. For all the occasional stridency of feminism, for all the male-baiting, women are undertaking a very difficult task at present, and only a few can do it without qualm. To add to responsibilities while seeing conventional responsibilities carried out by others is no easy matter, however vigorously the right to do new things is asserted and felt. To expect men to replace women as emotional havens is unrealistic, for it was unrealistic to build the imagery even for women. But some men may have the strength to offer at least as much as they demand. Yet this relationship to women who are in the process of redefinition is not an essential obligation, and should be undertaken as carefully and consciously as possible. Even if it cannot be maintained, and it is quite difficult, men are best served by seriously supplementing this particular emotional focus. Again, the main point is to accept both novelty and uncertainty in the female role and to avoid self-definition in a job or in family life that precludes the ability to stand back from the experimentation that women must undertake on their own account.

However, if men must accept growing role equality—can indeed learn to benefit from it—it does not follow that they owe women, society, or themselves a basic redefinition of manhood or of the male personality. We are not compelled to become androgynous, and there are good social as well as gender reasons to resist androgyny as anything like a common male pattern. As roles draw closer together, so of course do personal attributes; men and women are less different in character than they were a century ago. Possibly there are still some generalized male characteristics that impede women's own role redefinition; these would at least bear reexamination.

There are, certainly, more than a few horrible men: insensitive competitors, physical brutes, the disproportionate number of male criminals. They require regulation and policing, to a greater extent than do women whose excessive femininity leads them more to vacuity than to criminality. The male principle is not easy. There are, additionally, masculine pleasures that are simply funny—football or automobile addictions or compulsive bookwriting. But many feminine things are funny as well. Unisex, even if possible, would be humorless. None of this intrinsically calls for a sweeping redefinition of the male personality.

There are feminists and male liberationists who are arguing for a feminization of the male character.[15] Masculinity distorts an individual's nature. It puts him out of touch with his emotions[16] Men do not cry. They do not touch each other. They do not form real friendships. They are too silent. They are aggressive, achievement-oriented, competitive bullies. Their artificiality depends on the victimization of women. If they do not themselves rape, they tolerate rapists. They are sick; they die early; they do not handle disease well; they flood our mental institutions. But they are savable: they have only to look at the female model, which providentially offers healthy emotionality, true friendship, noncompetitive achievement, long life, and mental health. And we are now offered books on how to raise androgynous children.[17]

The causes of the resulting plea for androgyny, for a change in male character, are numerous. The concept of women as more natural than men relates to obvious differences in physical functioning, which make women inevitably more conscious of their bodily workings, and it is very old. So of course is the idea that women are more emotional than men, though this used to be directed to women's disadvantage. More generally, nineteenth-century women were schooled to believe in their moral superiority. Even as they copy many male standards of behavior, contemporary women can easily indulge the belief still. Revulsion against an intensely physical masculinity has been a recurrent theme in Christianity and grew up again amid the gentler male rationalists of the nineteenth century. Small wonder that some male academics now find it particularly congenial. But the plea has more immediate origins as well. As women find their role redefinition difficult, and job opportunities often blocked by men, they can easily wish that men were more accommodating types. They are, without question, trying to develop commonly male characteristics such as assertiveness, and it can easily seem not only helpful but simple justice for men to meet them halfway. The attempts of fathers to approach their children as pals, over the past few decades, may have created confusion among those children, once grown up, when they encountered less friendly male characteristics, in the workplace and even in competitive leisure activities; here is another basis for pleading for a further reassessment of maleness.

Finally, aided by the spur of feminism, many men and observers of men have directly complained of the damage inflicted by trying to live up to male traits. A handful of men now literally renounce manhood each year by sex change operations. Larger numbers report on the constraints they have felt in trying to be men in the conventional sense, lamenting hollow friendships with other men in the absence of being able to express real feelings (and in fear of being thought homosexual). A number of psychiatrists comment on the psychic fragility of manhood, leading at an extreme to insanity and the high male rate of suicide, and more commonly to a comparative male intractability and resentment toward therapy.[18] Some of the critique relates primarily to roles, not to personality itself: the difficulties of breadwinning, the problems of dealing with role changes among women, the friction between bread-winning demands and any artistic bent. Some observers use the current gender furor to make masculinity the symbol of everything wrong with contemporary Western society—too rationalistic, militaristic, materialistic, and competitive—an approach which is not necessarily wrong but which buries masculinity amid such a host of pleas for change as to risk unmanageability.[19] But there are abundant signs that some ordinary men, not just intellectual dissidents from modernity, find the masculine personality too stressful, assuming not only a level of achievement but also a godlike control over one's fate that simply escapes most male mortals, and they seek not so much roles but personalities that will allow for greater emotional content, greater serenity.

A reassessment of the male personality follows thus from certain kinds of American feminism; from some psychiatric findings; from events (Vietnam, Watergate) that at least temporarily seemed to undermine stock masculine traits; and from philosophical dissent against the dominance of activism-rationalism in Western culture. It relates also to the qualifications of the nineteenth-century masculine image that men themselves have been introducing over the past several decades. The friendly approach to children, displacing patriarchal authoritarianism, suggests already a gentler male. Expressive physical activity, as in athletics, already modifies rationalism. Even the male aesthetic sense has broadened somewhat since the heyday of business philistinism. Some of the criticisms of the male personality do ignore the changes that have occurred, and seem rather to be fighting the ghostly stereotypes than to be building on ongoing trends. It remains true, however, that the typical male emotional style differs from an androgynous model, particularly in the area of emotional expression, and it is not clear that this is changing. The partisans of a personality change, though they may recognize some encouraging trends and certainly take note of signs of male distress, are explicitly arguing against what most men define as manly: They want less competition, more asethetic contemplation; less thought, more emotion; and a standard of moral and psychic balance that is still taken from a somewhat idealized womanhood. In urging their case, the most far-reaching advocates of androgyny clinch their argument by claiming that most men are simply unaware of what is wrong with them, so incapable are they either of feeling or of being able to express their feelings.

Despite the passion of the pleas and the cleverness of argument, advanced consistently in male-liberationist gatherings and literature, it is impossible to add androgyny to the list of changes men are making, will make, or should male. (It is worth noting that the androgynous movement is largely American, despite the fact that broader trends in gender behavior have affected Europe almost equally. The milder definition of male stereotypes in Europe, the lower intensity of feminism, possibly also a more restricted maternal role in rearing male children probably account for the difference.) What the advocates of androgyny are doing is building an elaborate superstructure on some very real but limited changes in contemporary manhood, though their prime impulse comes from the intensity of American feminism. They offer deceptively simple panaceas: Troubled about being a man? Just relax, and stop trying. But they pose a distraction not only in assessing what men are and should be—their ultimate impact is not likely to be great—but also in establishing the proper approach for interpreting the context of manhood, in a field where serious study is in its infancy. Here too they simplify, in this case the constraints of history, which is why their approach demands a final set of comments. That many men can usefully continue to modify not only their social roles but also their behavioral style is unquestionable. That some require a much broader behavioral range than that stereotypically permitted to men is unquestionable. The range of permissible activities is already growing, and intelligent critique of gender limitations will hopefully expand the choice still further. But a move toward androgyny, is, I think, a red herring, unlikely and possibly harmful, distracting men from coming to grips with real difficulties.

Male-liberationists' appeals for androgyny are frequently couched in terms of allowing men to express their own nature (in contrast of course to mentally healthier women, who are closer to this nature). We are, admittedly, rather far from a natural man, and some of the imagery developed in the past—the godlike patriarch of rural Protestantism, the heroic business warrior of the nineteenth century—removed those men who took their images literally too far from a balanced personality. But invocations of nature are not the answer, and they jar particularly in a period when women are necessarily moving further from natural functions than ever before. The question is really what kind of social artifices are most serviceable. Gender is one. We cannot quickly cut through centuries of accrued definition of masculinity even if we want to. It is proving difficult enough to do this with femininity, even with the spur of a much greater functional change. Some of the statements of the androgynists assume, against all historical and anthropological evidence, that men's nature, back then somewhere, was like woman's. It was not. It has always been to some extent culturally produced, following from the physiological distinctions and the need to differentiate boy from mother. We may now, as a society, choose to try to alter the culture. We may try to differentiate girls as fully as boys. But a natural man, in the same sense as a natural woman, is simply an impossibility. It would be well to drop the concept with its misleading implications about gender psychology and the gender past. If masculinity unbalances some men, then the problem can be discussed in these terms. Androgyny would be a different, indeed more radical, way to tamper with man's nature, and it additionally assumes some constancy in the feminine principle in a period when women's characteristics are changing very rapidly. This is not the time to play a game of more natural than thou.

Nor has it proved terribly useful to play crossculture games, one step removed from the nature arguments.[20] Western maleness is unquestionably not the only form. There have been a few primitive societies in which men seem to have played nurturing roles rather close to those of women though some of these same societies engaged in other practices such as headhunting. There have been a number of societies in which masculinity was less aggressive than it has typically been in the West, though usually these societies (the bulk of the major agricultural civilizations) involved much more rigid subordination of women than that which the West has tolerated. Human society has always involved gender distinctions, indeed male dominance in some form. Civilized societies have always imposed female subordination, the West far less than any other. Contemporary Western society need not exactly follow historical patterns, of its own or of any other area; indeed it cannot fully, given the tremendous changes springing from the reduction of the birth rate. It may in this connection be mildly useful to pull out selective traits of men in other societies, just as it was, a generation ago, mildly useful to know that Samoans handled adolescent sexuality differently from beleaguered Americans. But we are in fact stuck with our own historical context, and in the case of gender it is not such an awful context in fact. We cannot import another set of norms by fiat, and the fact is that we would not want to even if we could. No more than nature is the record of other societies going to tell us what to do, much less how to effect change given our own past.

I believe that the moral superiority notions of androgyny are off the mark as well. It is no longer useful, if indeed it ever was, to think of women, and therefore a female principle, as bearers of unique moral purity. This was an understandable but unfortunate gambit of the nineteenth century, and it undoubtedly allowed many men to ignore their own unethical behavior in the world outside the home, confident that home life and the little woman would restore purity. It is certainly clear that morality should be androgynous, and that no differentiation of gender roles should assign disproportionate moral responsibility to one gender or the other. But none of this means that men would become more ethical persons by becoming more androgynous. It is increasingly clear that much of the brutality of the outside world, the world of business and politics, had little to do with the fact that it was a male world. As women shake the remnants of their home-centered, pre-industrial ethic and explicitly renounce the constraints of maternal morality, they show every sign of succumbing to many of the same pressures and temptations that men have done since industrialization first started to shape the world in which they operated. For example, rising female rates of drug and alcohol dependence (or the increasing public knowledge of these rates) suggest that we cannot rely on femininity to keep us pure. Certain feminists, bearers of the older hope that women were better, deplore this, and may urge sensitive men to join their crusades in the effort to salvage something of their vision. Some articulate women may be able to set and maintain styles of behavior, while taking over previously male roles, that men will wish to copy; indeed I hope this will be so. But at present we cannot count on androgynous personalities to save us, for feminine traits are no guarantee of virtue. Androgyny certainly promises no guarantee against the rogue males who so distort masculine aggressiveness and strength; they need in fact more acceptable male outlets, not fewer. Manhood in general has not benefitted by the sense that it is less virtuous than womanhood, and it will not be made more virtuous by abandoning gender.

Few are arguing that men and women become exactly alike, aside from an appendage or two. Insofar as individual men have found benefit in a reduction of competitiveness, in a conscious search for gentleness, there can be no quarrel. At this same practical level, however, it should be recognized that other men—I have encountered a number in the college classrooms—are either needlessly antagonized or needlessly confused by the androgynous pleas. The desirable male flexibility in reconsidering gender role allocation may be reduced, not enhanced, if it is accompanied by blasts against the masculine personality. Feminist critiques of masculinity are unavoidable. They are part of the movement's history and are a logical concomitant of a painful role adjustment. Men can listen, and what they cannot learn from, endure. But promptings of androgyny should not stand alone in discussions of appropriate contemporary maleness. Most men must believe themselves masculine, which means they can at best only be bewildered, at worst repelled, by a thorough attack on an identification they cannot escape. Whether desirable or not—and I will argue that it is not—there is no way that we can raise a new generation of nicely androgynous boys. Indeed the belief among some feminists that they can predictably mold the personalities of their offspring is a distressing flight from reality, apparently following from some belief that what is male is bad.

For what are the advantages of androgyny, were it even possible? First, women might like men better, or so some believe. Not undesirable, though the implications of androgyny for sexuality are genuinely unclear, as complaints about rising impotence suggest. It is not certain that women are best served by men who resemble them, as opposed to those who attract by some contrast. Second, men would become healthier. A good bit of the androgynous litera-ture seeks to attract men to the goal of woman-like longevity. And yet here is much of the logical and practical drawback of the appeal. We do not know how much of the female longevity advantage has resulted from role differen-tials, not personality differentials. Indeed, we do not know whether men can "naturally" expect to live as long as women once the latter's childbearing is dramatically restricted. The health of men has not generally been deteriora-ting. Industrial masculinity has not hurt men measured by their own standard.

Most important, it is not clear that optimal longevity is the greatest goal for men to strive for in any event. The stereotypic male attitude to health has much to recommend it. Endure, even enjoy, a bit of stress for the sake of achievement, don't worry about every pain signal, even maintain some skepticism in the face of omnipresent recommendations of caution and self-preservation. This is not the only legitimate attitude to take toward health (nor is it of course the one that all men in fact adopt),but I would argue that it is *a* legitimate attitude.[21] We do not, as a society, need more docile patients. It is not clear that health should be an overriding goal, as opposed to some of the dash and just plain stubbornness most commonly associated with masculinity. Androgyny might not help men anyway; it is being preached without full consideration of a complex set of facts and speculations. It might, if seriously practiced, reduce a vigor, even a daring, that remain legitimate, even socially desirable. It would by definition reduce the range of personal expression, and to that extent it would quite simply be dull, in a society that does not need more monotony.

What the present moment of history suggests is that men should strive to maximize their flexibility with regard to new roles and personality characteristics among women, but not through a self-conscious renunciation of the whole set of distinctive male traits that the Western tradition offers or by imitating an equally stereotypic feminine personality. Women have legitimately tired of men defining their characteristics and setting norms for their sanity. Men can legitimately return the compliment. It was absurd, a generation ago, to assume that women were disturbed who were not passive, housewifely types. But it would be absurd, and socially dangerous, to see men who preserve a competitive, achievement orientation as disruptive brutes who need another round of therapeutic domestication. Male values need not be seen in new or intense disarray. Indeed, as male roles broaden, the values can usefully be applied to a host of new activities.

A single male norm is not the point, of course. Nor is immunity from criticism. Nor is criticism of women or of feminism. There are drawbacks to any personality style, and certainly to any tendency around which individuals group. There is a good bit that is wrong or confusing about contemporary manhood, and only some of this derives from the changes taking place among women. But the basic concept of manhood, severely challenged and modified by industrialization, is not in a new, fundamental crisis. Problems arise mainly from excesses or limitations of past adaptations, plus of course the shifts among women. It is analytically messy to claim that genders undergo basic transformations at different points, though in practice it may prove a blessing. The adaptations that men are called upon to make, apart from those involving new female roles, are more subtle than the appeals for an androgynous revolution can allow, more selective—and also more attainable—than pleas for a merger of gender personalities. In response to the industrial challenges to traditional criteria of manhood, men have created some new standards, in some areas some new realities, that allow them to continue to gain identity.

The adequacy of these efforts is still being tested, quite apart from women's new strivings, and men must still ask if they have defined a set of traits that allows them sufficient coherence among their various roles.

What men rather generally have been searching for, in the later twentieth century, is less a new personality than a new balance in life, different from that imposed by industrialization, different also from that of traditional society though recalling some of its elements. They seek meaning, some kind of manly identity, in a series of activities, leisure as well as work and family, now that the omnipresence of work has been removed and the unity that patriarchalism provided between work and family has been disrupted. That the efforts, viewed collectively, have been somewhat disjointed is not surprising. Yet men have not fully failed in any area, either, and many men will doubtless do well to keep plugging at the uneasy combination. The work compulsives, who can carry an achievement drive into competitive leisure, perhaps come closest to an integrated approach, just as they most resemble earlier male ideals, but their leisure activities can be criticized as far too limited and their recent record in family life is not encouraging. Still, without pretending a magic improvement just around the corner, or indeed any compelling single formula, some comment on areas open to attention is possible.

Whether men can strive for greater intrinsic pleasure at work, going beyond the present somewhat resigned tolerance, must be open to serious question. In a way they do well to combine a pride in breadwinning and some sense of skill, of physical or mental expression, to be able to convey at least surface satisfaction. Beyond this, it is hard to fault the present impulse to reduce work time and to seek earlier retirement. It would be well if men could voice more dramatic demands for improvement in the work itself, but this has been said so often during the course of industrialization, with so little impact against the partial satisfaction that men do derive and the other demands they must levy against the job, that it would be idle to hope too much. Possibly, if inflation is kept within some bounds, a gradual acceptance of a female breadwinning status could reduce the pressure for instrumental gains, and balance attention to the paycheck with attention to the quality of work itself. But for men to surrender their prime breadwinning claims will be difficult, for this is one of the rewards that now makes the job endurable.

There are more precise tasks within the contemporary framework of manhood and work. The present small trend toward career changes can be encouraged, though it is easier to state the problem than to produce change.[22] By all evidence, most men, apart from the minority of unskilled, need not be unduly pitied during their first decade or two of work commitment. Some young workers indeed display unusual consciousness of their need for dignity at work, and can be urged to defend themselves. Others find themselves on a ladder of advancement that provides its own entertainment for a time. But the widespread sense of malaise among men around the age of forty, cutting across class lines, deserves more coherent, even institutionalized expression.

Middle-class women, whose mid-life crisis remains to be as fully docu-
mented, do point the way with their pursuit of new levels of education in their
middle years. They express the fact that they had often been denied interesting occupational outlets before; it remains to be seen if the pattern will persist,
among women who are now staking out a job identity earlier in life. But
women have also benefitted from the sense that their work commitment was
supplementary, forming only one of several supports for their identity. A
career change, a return for additional education, has been unusually possible
as well as unusually necessary. Men can legitimately insist on equal time, on
the opportunity temporarily to relax their earning obligation in order to
develop a more meaningful job experience for their later lives. They have
every reason to insist on equal ability to return for additional education, not
just to add earning capacity or embellish a career line chosen in later youth,
but to develop a new tack, a fuller sense of job commitment if and as the first
choice palls. In this area and possibly others, men can and should combine
an identification of a characteristic male problem (whether distinctively male
or not is of no moment) and the new economic position of women to
experiment with new patterns of behavior. If mid-career evaluations put some
pressure on employers to increase the intrinsic interest of the original job in
order to retain valued workers, so much the better. Given the incomplete
success of collective protest in improving the quality of work, individual
action may prove essential. Mid-career decisions can also condition the
retirement experience, directing men who would find complete retirement
trying into work that can be continued longer. Probable pressure to modify
widespread retirement, in light of the aging of the population of industrial
societies, and the resulting cost to social insurance funds, makes this flexibility for men particularly desirable.

How many men can shake the sense of routine, and the satisfaction of a
fairly regular paycheck, to modify their lifetime work pattern, remains to be
seen. This is a case where a specific problem, far more manageable than work
in general or the male personality in general, needs widespread attention and
comment from men themselves, and toward the solution of which it is
legitimate to seek a firm economic commitment from wives. The return of
wife as well as husband to a producing function within the family can here be
a new opportunity for greater individual expression, including a more flexible
contact with higher education, of both men and women. The result need not
damage a male breadwinning role over a whole lifespan, and indeed may
enhance it during the second half of life.

Successful work-compulsive men, already differentiated from most men in
their stance toward work, have less need of this kind of formal option. They
even age fairly well, either continuing their work into later life or adapting to a
busy retirement. Yet for them too, there are questions about the future, in
terms both of what will be and what should be. There is a strong current
feeling that work compulsion will fade somewhat. The evidence is slim,
coming mainly from testimony by young managerial and professional types

that they will be less amenable to corporate whims, more concerned about their non-work lives and the work opportunities of their wives. Possibly a recognition of the narrowness of the work compulsion of older men, the fathers of the new generation, and the need for greater sensitivity to parallel wifely careers is beginning to effect a modification of the type. Possibly also, a generation of milder parenting, including friendlier fathering, and a re-placement of guilt-induced work goals with more pleasure seeking is pro-ducing even more fundamental effects. (It is also possible to imagine one group of men modifying work compulsion, only to be rivaled by groups from a lower social level who only wait the chance to develop work-defined lives, and the power that goes with this, a pattern of partial replacement of elites that is not new to Western history.) Again, firm prediction remains impos-sible; we can at best know what to watch for.

A statement of desirability is harder still. Against the pleas for a modera-tion of work compulsion, for the sake of manly health, the well-being of men's families, or more subtly still for the quality of leadership that at present reflects too narrow a range of interest—too much efficiency, too little poetry—is the concern of those who see achievement of any sort, not only within the current set of work and economic values but also toward the inevitably arduous displacement of these values, being undermined by hedon-ism. Is it brash to suggest that the achievement-oriented male, though definitely not the only desirable character type, has been sufficiently success-ful, socially as well as personally, that it would be unwise to discourage his perpetuation in a period of some uncertainty of male purpose? If indeed the more sensitive, men as well as women, are encouraged to eschew the work-defined life, they may leave the achievement orientation to those who are most careless about how achievement itself is to be defined. At the profes-sional and managerial level, industrial society may be producing more, not less, work to be done, and while some of this will be taken up, possibly with some distinctiveness of style, by achieving women, there is no reason to reduce the male potential. Nor is there personal reason to attack a style of life that has provided successful, even engrossing self-definitions for an important minority of men. Indications are that the type deserves more support than scorn, which is not at all to say that the existing framework of work compulsion, the goals to which it is directed, should be uniformly defended. That Western man has long thought of work too much in terms of activity than of contemplation, and more recently in terms of bureaucratic ladders and earning power, is undeniable. But the belief of slightly old-fashioned radicals, work compulsives themselves, that it will take a lot of effort to deflect this bent is surely correct.

Yet all this is, for the foreseeable future, for a minority of men, just as only a minority of women will find long-term purpose in using work as primary self-definition. While urging some balance in the attacks on the work compulsives, attractive non-work options are important for them as well, even if they will view them largely as supplementary to the main life task. Leisure will surely become increasingly important to manhood. Men's efforts in this area over the past century clearly point in this direction, though they have often fallen short of adequacy. There is reason to hope that leisure will gain respectability as a social concern, just as it has already become a major form of expression for many individual men. Leisure is capable of serving many of the same purposes that work once served, and with greater freedom from material compulsion and organizational dictates: expressions of physical prowess, of distinctive skill, of male bonding, and transmission of values from father to son. How well it can serve these purposes, in a society undeniably still reluctant to legitimate leisure, and amid immense commercial pressures toward the regimentation of taste, remains, of course, uncertain. The historical precedents are remote and incomplete, consisting most obviously of aristocratic codes which touted male leisure activities as the most complete expressions of human value, as in ancient Greece and, less fully, in the Western aristocratic ethic from the later Middle Ages to the nineteenth century. To predict mass conversion to a similar leisure sense would be foolhardy, given our nagging devotion to work, though an increasingly clear articulation of existing leisure interests can be expected.

While awaiting a full definition of the role of modern leisure, men can, as with work, strive toward certain goals in relationship to their current needs. The desirability of fuller leisure training has already been suggested. Too much male leisure revolves around the special requirements and capacities of youth for courtship and physical distraction, reducing older men to nostalgia and spectatorship. With the numerical importance of youth declining, a greater focus on more durable leisure outlets is already being suggested, as individually competitive sports rival team efforts and less competitive endurance running attracts the attention that, in the United States, was once reserved for the record dashes of young men.[23] Still, an emphasis on wider participant activity as opposed to passive spectatorship, remains highly desirable. A broader definition of popular leisure, to include for men not only physical activity and craft skills or even entry into aesthetic outlets such as the dance but also more intellectual interests, becomes increasingly essential. Too many men are schooled to regard the mind as a tool for work, not for recreation; yet in all societies in which a full leisure ethic was elaborated, mental pastimes, even intellectual development played a vital role. Male leisure in modern Western society has evolved in rather piecemeal fashion, on the fringes of a primary work experience and from popular traditions of male recreation that are now too limited. Again, the educational conditioning of men needlessly perpetuates the limitations. Here is a clear task for men, in terms of their own needs, beginning with demands that they can place on the educational apparatus, for themselves and for their sons. It calls essentially for a broadening of the successful association of manhood and rational endeavor into a recognition of the potential of the mind for play.

While leisure serves a host of male interests, and can be made to serve still more in the future, allowing demonstrations of manhood vital to a sense of value and identity in a contemporary life, there is no need to assume a set of leisure virtues that are distinctively male. Women have been participating in traditionally male enjoyments, from the sensual through the athletic, with gusto and skill. We seem fairly well beyond the eyebrow-raising stage. Female leisure prowess no longer has a great deal of shock value. Whether a larger numerical entry of women into male leisure areas will cause a sense of loss remains to be seen; there is no reason to predict it.

But men may want to preserve some separate leisure groupings and even place new emphasis upon them. In most human societies, and indeed those of the primates as well, males need opportunities for separate gathering. During the past two centuries, work could serve this purpose for most men, and considerable non-work time could therefore readily be devoted to the family or other mixed company. With work roles increasingly shared, men may need to define leisure groupings that are distinctively male in composition if not in distinctive activity, though possibly in both. This could rouse female concern, the conventional worry of the wife that male fellowship jeopardizes a marriage and the newer objection of feminists that male gatherings can serve to promote male power wielding. In a period when articulate women are vaunting their own sisterly unions, and sometimes deriding a male inability to form close bonds, the maintenance and even enhancement of male leisure groupings, even all-male places, can be fully justified. Leisure, long vital to manhood particularly in the period of transition from youth to adulthood, will predictably fill broader needs in the defining and maintenance of male personality types, sharing and possibly surpassing the role of work and serving, as necessary, to give men some regular opportunity to be with their own kind, with the mixture of fellowship and mutual testing that has served to link males since prehistory.[24]

The tasks of men in work and leisure involve a continued, if hopefully more sophisticated effort along lines dictated by industrialization itself, to find outlets for man's physical exuberance and his desire for manual skill and mental mastery. Despite important critiques, the goals derive still from the traditions of manhood, beginning with some of the physical imperatives of the hunting animal and extending, shorn of territorial proprietorship, to the competitive and rationalist images of the past century. They are, of course, embellished by the growing addition of leisure identifications to those of work. It may be hoped that a growing range of expression, and a reduction of youthful emphasis toward greater manly fulfillment throughout the life cycle—both already suggested by recent trends among men—will facilitate the approach to the thornier issue of man in the family.

For recent history suggests that men need a different kind of reliance on the family from that which they have been encouraged to develop, in some cases a lessened reliance, while taking a more active role in the family in other respects. Here is the most subtle challenge to contemporary manhod, the one least clearly hinted at in current male behavior patterns. Whereas trends in work and leisure suggest further tasks, men have yet to develop some of the basic questions about the family role. On the one hand, evidence points to an excessive dependence on a family framework, excessive particularly in a period when women are redefining their own goals. On the other hand, men must ask if they have reentered fully enough into actual family functioning, not just in fairness to their women, though this is important enough, but in fairness to themselves. They must ask if they have found an adequate family style to replace patriarchalism; indeed the biggest work issue for many men is less the job itself than the inability to carry the competitive work style over into family relationships while avoiding total reliance, in the nineteenth-century fashion, on the women to set an alternative tone. Decreased dependence is not incompatible with increased activity and an effort to go beyond the good-buddy approach to other family members. Indeed the various parts of the equation are essential to the whole. But the combination will be difficult; and in the interim, that many men, like many women, are growing slightly warier of family formation is not surprising, for this at least reduces the dependence.

Aside from sheer material support, men have been relying more on family than women have for at least the past half century, and this is dangerous to men and unhealthy for both genders. Studies of divorce reveal men more bereft than women, despite the economic disadvantages of the divorced woman and her typical lack of employment experience. Apparently it is easier to cope in the outside world than in the domestic world. The correlation of male health with family status is still more striking when compared to female patterns. For the last hundred years in France, married men in the older age categories were only a bit more than half as likely to die as widowers, and the rate for bachelors, by the 1960s, was as dismal as that of widowers. But while married women in the nineteenth century had a similar longevity advantage over spinsters and widows, by 1963 this had dwindled to 19 percent. The lesson, for men, is clear: to maximize both professed happiness and long life, get married, stay married, and remarry should something happen to the wife. And within limits, this is surely unobjectionable. But the very fact that the situation differs for women raises problems. Surely, without touting longevity as the best measure of fulfillment for men, the degree of dependence on marriage, given the chanciness of life situations plus the new strivings of women, is not optimal.[25]

Women, trained for household responsibility even if remaining single, comforted by household routines if widowed, have an ability to care for themselves and a controlled continuity that men typically lack. This can be remedied, at least in part, though it undeniably goes against the male grain. Household chores can be learned—men have, after all, long claimed that they were not all that difficult, and used, in fact, to delegate many of them to male servants until imposing/accepting a female monopoly: boys can be taught, married men can share. Whether this *will* happen is another question. ("Today, masculinity is not threatened in the supermarket, kitchen or nursery," an enlightened maternity pamphlet states,[26] perhaps too hopefully.)

Families in which both husband and wife have strong career commitments seem to prefer to return to reliance on female domestic servants. Even career women have difficulties surrendering their responsibility for household management, preferring to believe that men cannot match female standards of cooking and cleanliness and often viewing the more successful male efforts as threats to their special domain. Nevertheless, the inducements of equity to working wives, a desire for new competences and moderate physical exercise, and above all a more enlightened sense of self-preservation may lead more men into the kind of skills that, although historically degrading for men, can be important for survival in a womanless setting, important perhaps in attracting and maintaining a modern woman in the first place.

How much of the special family dependence of men goes beyond routine, to emotional need, is hard to calculate. So often heavily mothered, since the nineteenth-century division of family labors, men can easily fall into the rhetoric of the family haven, the woman-directed shelter from the pressures of the outside world. Finding the haven has of course been another matter, as women's discontent with a purely family role has grown in the present century, but this does not necessarily daunt the search. Hence the pattern of often quick male remarriage after divorce, the divorce perhaps caused by the failure of the first family to live up to expectations. Happy those men, of course, who find in a family the softness and satisfaction that can balance their lives. But there must be concern about the men who cannot, and their apparent disorientation after failure. It seems clear that men must plan to bring to the family, beyond the conventional obligation of breadwinning, a sense of active role, not the expectation of repose, when they opt for family at all.

And this is where, from the standpoint of adult men themselves, the let's-be-pals approach is questionable. Women argue that men fail to do their share not only with the routine chores but with the emotional nurturing associated with infancy, and it is true that it is hard to be buddies with a very young child. The female argument is muddied because many women are now discussing mothering as a rather annoying chore that men must share as a matter of equity, freeing women for their due allotment of the more important things in life, while trying also to say that men will improve their own existence by gaining the nurturing qualities that women have developed in mothering. Nor is it clear whether men can play the same kind of role with infants that mothers do. Their omissions here were considerable even before industrialization took them farther from home. Nevertheless, this may be another case in which historical patterns must be defied in the interest of a more balanced parenting. Equity must be given women as they develop their new roles outside the home, and some definable needs of men themselves must be met. Western men, and American men particularly, may lack sufficient human contact in the most literal sense, the sense of touching. We know that male children are touched less than females, we know that a dominant adult male style shuns touching unless acceptably sexual. There is no need to assume androgynous infancies and exactly equal parenting styles between the two genders to urge that men could usefully develop a greater sense of physical nurturing in dealing with infants, and that male infants would grow into a less restricted arsenal of expressive modes as a result.

The larger problem with the pals approach, however, is that it has left men too peripheral to family activities. Now that men cannot train their sons for work, and work with them during an overlap of careers, it has been difficult to find an alternate style which will produce guidance and authority, though not necessarily with the harsher aspects of patriarchal discipline. Leisure activities, to which men now resort for so many of the satisfactions of manhood, have been the best surrogate, for they combine friendly association with training in skills and, where the father keeps up his own abilities, with the possibility of ongoing contact. But is there not, still, too often a gap between the criteria urged for manhood and the principles, not always easy to instill, that fathers are actually willing to inculcate in their sons? Lack of time remains an inhibition, of course, and is the source of much paternal guilt and the cause of some of the influence that peer groups gain with boys. But the desire not to impose too much, not to force an authority or abuse a friendly relationship, has its effect as well. Part of the coming decisions of manhood involve not only an articulation of what a man should be, given changes in his role and function, but also a decision to take serious responsibility for the resulting orientation of sons.

For fathering still involves a responsibility for guiding children toward achievement in the world outside the home. Feminist mothers may play a new role in this same direction, particularly toward daughters (there is considerable feminist uncertainty about sons, apart from the androgynous interest of some). And fathering need not preclude a friendly relationship with children. It certainly should not preclude the kind of tenderness that is all the more impressive because it is combined with expectation. Of course there neither will nor should be a single style of fathering. But there is more to the desiderata of the role than simply urging fathers to spend more time with their children. The decline of patriarchalism and the rise of the friendly approach have, in the last several decades, reduced some of the worst tensions between fathers and sons, though as always in this relationship, they can easily boil up again and there are strong signs of new turmoil among younger teenagers. But there is reason for fathers to move more actively against the continuing generational separation, which can, among other things, make a mockery of a quest for friendship with one's children, and at least to pay attention to the serious concern now being expressed about the decline of individual purpose and conscience in the dominant psyche of the young.

The family is, or should be, a field of male action in which men insist on defining a clear role for themselves, including a style of parenting. Women complain that despite important strides to mutuality, men actually remain dominant in more cases than not. This is doubtless true in many aspects of husband-wife relations. But it is less likely true in areas of family activity, including childrearing, over which women have long maintained a virtual monopoly. Unquestionably it is difficult for women to surrender a claim to special expertise, even as they march off to work with a desire for job parity with men. Men, in the converse dilemma, are finding it difficult to grant women job equality even as they themselves turn from a primary work definition. Unquestionably it is still pleasant for men to hope for a household that will sustain them, providing not only creature comforts but satisfactory sex and the friendship of children. Clearly, not only the future probability of increasing outside commitment on the part of women but also the record of the recent past, in terms of the actual rewards and products of family life, suggest that this hope is too risky. Men must actively shape their family role and, through this, the family itself. This does not necessarily suggest a wave of domestic battles for power or a new assertion of male primacy. It does, however, involve some insistence and a drive for active parity. It means, for men, some return to the sense that the family is a product of their efforts, and not simply by indirection through their economic provision which is, anyway, less necessary than before.

This is deliberately vague, because while problems in the family and in its present rewards to men are abundantly clear there is no way to predict what will occur in the future or to recommend precise modes of action. It has a reactionary tone: I do think that both men and families have suffered from a decline in male influence and that while this influence cannot return in exactly the old ways, and should not, the past in this regard had some advantages over the present. The suggestion of renewed male authority risks antagonizing women, in principle and in practice. For though it follows to some extent from the pleas of women that men take a more equal role, it suggests both that they should do this in a style rather different from the maternal style and that this will cost even those women who profess to seek reorientation of their roles a certain amount of domestic security. The idea of new male assertion can certainly disturb those who already find men insufficiently passive. But there is no plea for a more assertive masculinity overall, simply for less passivity within the home. And the male products of a more definite fathering, the boys raised by men more regularly conscious of their need to guide, and not just to compete with mothers for daily affection, might just be more socially useful, less dependent on a set relationship with women because they are less anxious to return to a real or imagined mothering, than those currently being turned out. Men now have the time for a new family role. Whatever their desire for a conflict-free home life in which they are called on for little emotional initiative, they have every reason to see that, in general, it has been a long time since this life was seriously available, that their image of family and the reality they have encountered are too different to be acceptable. They need, then, to make emotional investments of their own, and not expect facile love and friendship to result from their labors in the job world. Insofar as they need to arrange work, leisure, and male ties to provide the emotional support they require for real family participation, they have considerable latitude to do so.

Of course, they have not been totally laggard; there is no reason to mount a total attack on the current male family style. Nor is a new male initiative going to bring social or psychic utopia. But it just might bring a better balance to family life and to manhood. It definitely fits the real need for men to take more responsibility for the definition and perpetuation of manhood, in a social and not just biological sense.

The call, then, is not for a specific set of criteria by which boys can be socialized or resocialized, if only because the products of childrearing so often defy any formulas, but for a reassertion of a paternal style. Not a patriarchal style: quite apart from the effective disappearance of the proper-tied weapons of the patriarch, there is no way to justify a return to this formal dominion. But paternalism, modestly construed as an expectation of achievement cushioned by a responsible willingness to provide guidance and support, has both a firm basis in male tradition and a present utility. As with many of the important criteria of manhood, it expresses tension between judgment of performance and a loving association with the performer: one measures one's son and tries to help him through the measurements. Paternal love can be more satisfying as well as more useful than friendly affection. The paternal style can call on the best in the male tradition, binding men not just by their physical nature or their reaction to women but by the positive historical experience of manhood. Properly applied, it has the potential to reduce the ongoing gulf between generations that so bedevils industrial society, a gulf expressed not only in emotional and ideological gaps but in an unwillingness of one generation to take responsibility for the next, to assure personal and social continuity. Men can no longer pass on a total way of life or expect to see their children follow literally in their footsteps, but they can pass on a style. The paternal style may also reduce the disparity between criteria of manhood in work and leisure, on the one hand, and those of manhood in the home. It can reduce the atomized approach to achievement outside the home, in which a man hacks out his own competitive way in an alien jungle, by extending guidance and support among men, just as it superimposes a sense of standards on a purely friendly approach to family members. The paternal style can, in other words, link unduly disparate elements of the male experience; it builds not only on traditions of manhood but on types of men that flourish still, and impulses that men even more generally sense in themselves.[28]

Men have some rather subtle tasks and opportunities before them. Some may usefully contemplate grand personality changes, but I suggest that this is more likely to be individual than general, however attractive the notion of getting rid of norms of gender behavior may be. The return to a greater array of male roles, a more diverse male balance, already being sought by large numbers of men in the twentieth century, will also reemphasize the traditional Western tension among desirable male traits. The paternal image, of solidity and tenderness, shorn of the excesses of patriarchal power, involves men effective in the world and in the home, and as men gain new domestic initiative while hopefully not losing a commitment to achievement in work and leisure, they may indeed themselves develop traits, and breed sons who find the traits still more natural, that involve renewed validity for the gentler emotions. Some of the tension between strength and tenderness was indeed downplayed during industrialization, as a result of the division of gender labor and the imagery most commonly associated with masculinity, though the subordinate religious theme and the middle-class invocation of restraint kept it alive to an extent. Western men can find in their own tradition, as part of the effort to find balanced foci for their lives, the security that will allow them to be gentle, even loving guides. This will not create emotional androgyny or a single standard of therapeutic emotionality for men and women. It will not encourage male passivity, for rather it requires a new range of strengths.

But in all this is opportunity, for both genders and society more generally. Increasing overlap of roles can benefit from diverse gender styles. Greater variations around a standard gender personality can be expected. Whether we will gain the tolerance accompanying new variety is open to question. As they explore new traits along with new roles, women are not producing models of intragender courtesy, and the history of Western manhood does not encourage hope for new breakthroughs in accepting a full range of character-istics (even the male liberationists tend to ask for new norms, not new diversity). For men, however, the issue is less one of tolerance than the renewed acceptance of essential tension within the modal personality itself. What men can do for the family is redevelop an appropriate male style, using friendliness but calling on older traditions as well, to provide an approach different from the maternal style: no better, not simply supplementary in the sense of doing a fair share of the woman's work in the woman's way, but different, in a manner that will give children a greater range of choice in their own personal styles than the maternal monopoly has normally allowed.[28] Work, in turn, can benefit from the application of different gender styles, if women are not forced or enticed into adopting largely masculine modes. Societies have always built on the genetic model of two gender principles, encouraging the interaction of different if overlapping sets of traits. Con-temporary Western society can and must build differently, relying less on distinctions of role resulting from motherhood, but it requires still the vigor that comes from sanctioned gender diversity. Diversity often means bickering and mutual misunderstanding. We have never had perfect gender harmony in the Western tradition, and there is no reason to want it. Each gender is entitled to vaunt virtues that the other lacks in the same measure. Within this framework, men can have real confidence in their own.

It may be that men can usefully group more explicitly to discuss their own situation, in frank imitation of the feminists and of the more modest efforts of the minority of men who claim liberation from masculinity. Some men will doubtless group in defense of rights, for although the gender situation is hap-pily not primarily political or legal it does impinge on these spheres. The unfairness of current child custody favoritism toward the maternal side can stir legalistic passion, though I fear there is no wisdom of Solomon to be found. Men could legitimately claim the right to disavow paternal responsibility up to the third month of a woman's pregnancy, along with those women who work for the corresponding natural right to terminate pregnancy, in lieu of a male right directly to share in abortion decisions.[29] Legal issues relating to gender on the job, though of much greater legitimate concern to women, could prompt some collective male watchfulness. But questions of law and a defensive stance in general are not of prime importance, though they can usefully group men and encourage some discussion of broader reactions to the current gender situation. Men have been groping in considerable isolation toward redefinitions of their roles, though their quest for a new balance displays substantial implicit unity. The decline of many forms of collective male activity, and the feminist attack on male exclusivism, may have left men too removed from each other, too dependent on family units that are not even primarily male. Feminists, delighting in the mutual ties that collective striving produces, are claiming that men lack the female ability to form friendships, and some men agree that male bonds are now too superficial, too competitive to produce real emotional sharing. It is not clear that men need or want the same kind of links that some women now possess (and feminists themselves wonder if their ties are not slackening among younger women). Men, not called upon to meet the same role challenges as women in the present moment, are quite literally schooled to different patterns of association from childhood, but no less intense for being more athletic, less verbal. It may be, nevertheless, that their links are not fully adequate after youth. A men's movement clearly is not required. But the need to be men may now involve a return to more male formats, for the deep jostling warmth that male ties can provide. And there are tasks, as in patterns of education provided to men, quite different from beleaguered defensiveness, that legitimately call for attention.

Strength, solidity, gentleness, achievement, physical prowess—men still have an awesome array of traits to strive for, to blend into a personality. Manhood is a solemn thing. It is not purely natural, for like most of the attributes of civilized society it has to be taught. Even appropriate sexuality requires encouragement, at least in Western culture. The internal tensions of manhood in the culture have always been difficult to reconcile, though immensely rewarding when combined. A better balance among functions, with family elevated along with work and leisure, necessitates a return to this tension, for too many men have felt free to express an undiluted toughness in their work role, expecting tenderness to be provided for them in the home. Some of their strength is essential to the family, and more gentleness can be devoted to the job, in a paternal style, shorn of the harshness of patriarchalism, now applied more uniformly to the life of men. But an equilibrium of traits along with functions will not be easy to achieve, particularly when some of the badges of manhood, already more difficult to acquire in contemporary industrial society, yield to the diminution of the visible distinctions between men and women.

Fathering is a staggering responsibility. So is achievement in the world of work or leisure, particularly achievement without a compulsive frenzy. Manhood involves restraint. It involves building on the rudimentary courage that boys are taught, not to falter when weak and, anomalous as it may seem in an age of loudly precarious mental health, not always to admit fear. It involves also, however, the courage and the sense of security to admit pain and vulnerability. But manhood is also exuberant, outrageous, and these are traits that must not be lost to the attacks on masculinity or to the solemnity of the paternal role. There is sheer pleasure in triumphing over a physical task, an intellectual problem or over other men; there is pleasure in male humor, in the fellowship of others. The joys of men need not be abusive, yet they involve surges of mental or physical energy that are no less than thrilling. Sorry the man who, in some corner of his existence, cannot prove himself.[30] Western manhood wars with manly moderation, and he is wise who lets neither pole triumph. No man can consistently fulfill all the requirements of his gender. Collectively, however, men can take new responsibility for defining their gender and for transmitting it. It is tough to be a man, and not only in the obvious physical and martial tests that we hope our sons may avoid. But when a man reaches toward his own standards, he can ride high in his own soul. When the laughter surges, when the intractable yields just slightly, when the child excels, and yes, when the woman glows, it can fill a man to bursting.

Notes

Chapter 1

1. Jack Nichols, *Men's Liberation: A New Definition of Masculinity* (New York, 1975); Joseph H. Pleck and Jack Sawyer, eds., *Men and Masculinity* (Englewood Cliffs, N.J., 1974).

2. Philip Wylie, *Generation of Vipers* (New York, 1942).

3. The basic statements remain Simone de Beauvoir, *The Second Sex* (New York, 1962), and Betty Friedan, *The Feminine Mystique* (New York, 1963). See also Shulamith Firestone, *The Dialectic of Sex* (New York, 1970); Kate Millett, *Sexual Politics* (New York, 1970); Janet Chafetz, *Masculine/Feminine or Human? An Overview of the Sociology of Sex Roles* (Itasca, Ill., 1974).

4. Maureen Green, *Fathering* (New York, 1976); Ferdynand Zweig, *Workers in an Affluent Society* (New York, 1962).

5. Florida Scott-Maxwell, *Women and Sometimes Men* (New York, 1971). This is a theme also in the literature that seeks to prove that women "modernize" better than men; Patricia Branca, *Women in Europe Since 1750* (London, 1978), pp. 204ff.

6. See, for example, Lionel Tiger, *Men in Groups* (New York, 1969).

7. For an intelligent version of this, see Michelle Z. Rosaldo, "Woman, Culture, and Society: A Theoretical Overview," in *Woman, Culture, and Society*, ed. Michelle A. Rosaldo and Louise Lamphere (Stanford, 1974), pp. 17–42. See also Margaret Mead, *Male and Female* (New York, 1949). J. Nichols, *Men's Liberation*, pp. 45–55, 311–323; see also Warren Farrell, *The Liberated Man* (New York, 1975).

9. Eleanor Maccoby and Carol Jacklin, *The Psychology of Sex Differences* (Stanford, 1974).

10. Sigmund Freud, *Civilization and Its Discontents* (New York, 1962), p. 51.

11. Tiger, *Men in Groups*, pp. 46ff.

12. Carol Smith Rosenberg, "The Female World of Love and Ritual: Relations between Women in Nineteenth-Century America," *Signs* 1 (1975):1–30.

13. Criminality, a clear and interesting case of biopsychological attributes and cultural role combined, will not receive a great deal of attention in this book since most men have not been criminal; but it must be mentioned as a fascinating, if rarely endearing, part of masculine history. Two useful discussions of gender criminality in the past are John Beattie, "The Criminality of Women in 18th-Century England," *Journal of Social History* VIII (1975):80–118; and Carol Z. Wiener, "Sex-Roles and Crime in Late Elizabethan Herfordshire," *Journal of Social History* VIII (1975):38–66.

14. Rosaldo and Lamphere, "Introduction," pp. 1–16, and Joan Bamberger, "The Myth of Matriarchy," pp. 263–280, both in *Woman, Culture, and Society*.

15. There is a resurgence of emphasis on the biological attributes of gender, however, with stress on the naturalness and utility of male aggressiveness (and female nurturing). See Steven Goldberg, *The Inevitability of Patriarchy* (New York, 1973).

16. Mead, *Male and Female*, passim.

17.   See E. K. Childs et al., "Women and Sexuality: A Feminist View," in *Female Sexuality*, ed. Sue Cox (Chicago, 1976), pp. 52–75, which argues that women are not innately less aggressive than men. There is a tendency in some analysis to prove that basic gender traits are *partly* socially determined, this in a tone that seeks to persuade us that since they are partly determined they might as well be entirely determined. See also Judith M. Bardwick, *Psychology of Women* (New York, 1971), pp. 242ff.

18.   Peter Filene, *Him/Herself: Sex Roles in Modern America* (New York, 1975).

19.   John Gillis, *Youth and History: Tradition and Change in European Age Relations, 1770–Present* (New York, 1974), for example, talks only of boys—and says so—but generalizes as to age group rather than gender. The existence of this sort of study, however, like those on the working class, provides, along with the abundant materials generated by recent work on women's history, an extensive array of data and concepts for use in direct efforts to establish a history of men.

20.   See, e.g., Edward Shorter, "Illegitimacy, Sexual Revolution, and Social Change in Modern Europe," *Journal of Interdisciplinary History* II (1971): 251–253; idem, *The Making of the Modern Family* (New York, 1975). Disagreements with Shorter's hypothesis have centered almost exclusively on women. See Louise Tilly, Joan Scott, and Miriam Cohen, "Women's Work and European Fertility Patterns," *Journal of Interdisciplinary History* VI (1976), 447–476.

21.   On the popular export of the cowboy, see Ronald A. Fullerton, "Toward a Commercial Popular Culture in Germany: The Development of Pamphlet Fiction, 1871–1914," *Journal of Social History*, XII (1979):493ff.

22.   For an introduction, see Aileen Kraditor, ed., *Up from the Pedestal* (Chicago, 1968), pp. 137–147 et passim.

23.   There has, of course, been an excessive combing of the literature to discover male absurdities about women, without much attention to typicality. See G. J. Barker-Benfield, *The Horrors of the Half-Known Life: Male Attitudes toward Women and Sexuality in Nineteenth-Century America* (New York, 1976); for a more level-headed study, see Katherine Rogers, *The Troublesome Helpmate: A History of Misogyny in Literature* (Seattle, 1966).

24.   An explicit, pronounced statement of this sort is Caroline Hennessey's *I, B.I.T.C.H.* (New York, 1970).

Chapter 2

1.   Walter C. Langer, *The Mind of Adolf Hitler* (New York, 1973).

2.   Bamberger, "The Myth of Matriarchy," in *Woman, Culture, and Society*, pp. 263–280.

3.   Konrad Lorenz, *On Aggression* (New York, 1974).

4.   Nancy Chodorow, "Family Structure and Feminine Personality," in *Woman, Culture, and Society*, pp. 43–66; idem, "Oedipal Asymmetries and Heterosexual Knots," *Social Problems* 23 (1974):541–568; Dorothy Dinnerstein, *The Mermaid and the Minotaur* (New York, 1966).

5.   Rosaldo and Lamphere, "Introduction," in *Woman, Culture and Society*, pp. 1–16.

6.   Tiger, *Men in Groups*.

7.   C. T. Wright, "The Amazons in Elizabethan Literature," *Studies in Philology* 28 (1940):103–146.

8. On the hunting tradition in Western society, see E. P. Thompson, *Whigs and Hunters* (New York, 1976); Edward, 2nd Duke of York, *The Master of Game* [the oldest English book on hunting, reissued with a foreword by Theodore Roosevelt] (New York, 1910); Nicholas Cox, *The Gentleman's Recreation, in Four Parts (viz.) Hunting, Hawking, Fowling, Fishing* (London, 1674); Douglas Hay, "Poaching and the Game Laws on Cannock Chase," in *Albion's Fatal Tree: Crime and Society in Eighteenth-Century England*, by Douglas Hay et al. (New York, 1976), pp. 38–62.

9. It must be stressed that this courage is quite compatible with male gentleness, assumption of many household functions, and so forth. See Rosaldo, "Woman, Culture, and Society: A Theoretical Overview," in *Woman, Culture and Society*, pp. 17–43.

10. See, as a parody on this fascinating question, Diana Shard, "The Neolithic Revolution: An Analogical Overview," *Journal of Social History* VI (1974):165–170.

11. This is discussed in Eleanor Leacock, "Women in Egalitarian Society," in *Becoming Visible: Women in European History*, ed. Renate Bridenthal and Claudia Koonz (New York, 1977), pp. 11–35.

12. Yolanda Murphy and R. F. Murphy, *Women of the Forest* (New York, 1974); Rayna Reiter, *Toward an Anthropology of Women* (New York, 1975).

13. J. G. Peristiany, ed., *Honour and Shame: The Values of Mediterranean Society* (Chicago, 1968).

14. Randolph Trumbach, "London's Sodomites: Homosexual Behavior and Western Culture in the Eighteenth Century," *Journal of Social History* XI (1977): 1–34.

15. Frederick Engels, *The Origins of the Family, Private Property and the State*, trans. E. Leacock (New York, 1972); Robert Ardey, *The Territorial Imperative: A Personal Inquiry into the Animal Origins of Property and Nations* (New York, 1971).

16. Sarah B. Pomeroy, *Goddesses, Whores, Wives and Slaves* (New York, 1975).

17. Marilyn Arthur, " 'Liberated' Women: The Classical Era," in *Becoming Visible*, pp. 60–89.

18. Philip J. Greven, Jr., *Four Generations: Population, Land, and Family in Colonial Andover, Massachusetts* (Ithaca, N.Y., 1970); David Hunt, *Parents and Children in History: The Psychology of Family Life in Early Modern France* (New York, 1970).

19. This was, however, compatible with considerable power for women; a Germanic as well as a Christian contribution to the Western gender mix deserves attention. See Jo Ann McNamara and Suzanne Wemple, "The Power of Women through the Family in Medieval Europe, 500–1000," in *Clio's Consciousness Raised*, ed. Lois Banner and Mary Hartman (New York, 1974), pp. 103–118.

20. Peristiany, *Honour and Shame*, passim.

21. François Rabelais, *Gargantua and Pantagruel*, trans. J. M. Cohen (Baltimore, 1955).

22. Erik H. Erikson, *Childhood and Society* (New York, 1963), pp. 109ff.

23. R. W. Southern, *The Making of the Middle Ages* (New Haven, 1953).

24. Kramer and Sprenger, *The Hammer of Witches* [an Inquisition handbook by two Dominican monks, first published 1484].

25. Trumbach, "London's Sodomites," pp. 1–34; Arthur Gilbert, "Buggery and the British Navy," *Journal of Social History* IX (1976):72–98.

26. Carol Z. Stearns, "Punishments of Parents of Bastards in 17th-Century Hertfordshire," unpublished article.

27. Sidney Painter, *French Chivalry* (Baltimore, 1940); F. X. Newman, ed., *The Meaning of Courtly Love* (Albany, N.Y., 1968).

28. Peter Laslett, *Family Life and Illicit Love in Earlier Generations* (Cambridge, Eng., 1977); Lawrence Stone, *The Family, Sex, and Marriage in England, 1500–1800* (New York, 1977); J.-L. Flandrin, *Familles: parenté, maison, sexualité dans l'ancienne société* (Paris, 1976).

29.   Lynn White, *Medieval Technology and Social Change* (New York, 1966); for an explicit contrast, see Traian Stoianovich, "Material Foundations of Preindustrial Civilization in the Balkans," *Journal of Social History* IV (1971):205–262.

30.   Henri Noilhac, *Histoire de l'agriculture à l'ère industrielle* (Paris, 1965), p. 406.

31.   André Biéler, *L'Homme et la femme dans la morale calviniste* (Geneva, 1963).

32.   Erik H. Erikson, *Young Man Luther* (New York, 1958).

33.   Philip J. Greven, Jr., *The Protestant Temperament* (New York, 1978).

34.   Greven, *Four Generations*, pp. 72–102.

35.   Antoinette Chamoux and Cécile Dauphin, "La Contraception avant la Révolution française: l'exemple de Chatillon-sur-Seine," *Annales: économies, sociétés, civilisations* 24 (1969):662–684; E. A. Wrigley, "Family Limitation in Pre-Industrial England," *Economic History Review* 19 (1966):82–109; idem, *Population and History* (London, 1969).

36.   Richard Vann sees in this the origins of mother as love figure and father as disciplinarian in early modern Europe, though this clearly picks up on earlier Christian imagery. "Toward a New Lifestyle: Women in Preindustrial Capitalism," in *Becoming Visible*, pp. 192–216.

37.   William G. McLoughlin, "Evangelical Child-Rearing in the Age of Jackson: Francis Wayland's View on When and How to Subdue the Willfulness of Children," *Journal of Social History* VIII (1975):21–34.

38.   Philippe Ariès, *Centuries of Childhood* (New York, 1962).

39.   Edward Shorter, "Illegitimacy, Sexual Revolution, and Social Change in Modern Europe," *Journal of Interdisciplinary History* II (1971):237–253.

40.   Robert W. Malcolmson, *Popular Recreations in English Society, 1700–1850* (Cambridge, Eng., 1973).

41.   Hunt, *Parents and Children*, pp. 145ff.

42.   Cissie Fairchild, "Masters and Servants in 18th-Century Toulouse," *Journal of Social History* 12 (1979):368–393; J. Jean Hecht, *The Domestic Servant Class in Eighteenth-Century England* (London, 1956).

43.   Peter N. Stearns, *Old Age in European Society* (New York, 1977), p. 41.

44.   Henri Noire, *La Retraite d'un cultivateur* (Moulins, 1914), p. 3.

45.   C. L. Lougee, *Les Paradis des femmes* (Princeton, N.J., 1976); on patriarchalism, see David Herlihy, "Family Solidarity in Medieval Italian History," *Explorations in Economic History* VII (1969): 173–184; Stone, *Family, Sex, and Marriage*.

46.   Peter Laslett, *The World We Have Lost* (Boston, 1965).

47.   Stone, *Family, Sex and Marriage*; passim, Randolph Trumbach, *The Rise of the Egalitarian Family: Aristocratic Kinship and Domestic Relations in Eighteenth-Century England* (New York, 1979).

48.   Ester Boserup, *Women and Economic Modernization* (London, 1970); see, also, Joan Scott and Louise Tilly, "Women, Work and the Family in Nineteenth-Century Europe," *Comparative Studies in Society and History* XVII (1975): 36–64.

49.   Natalie Z. Davis, "Women on Top," in *Society and Culture in Early Modern France* ed. Natalie Z. Davis (Stanford, 1975), pp. 124–151.

Chapter 3

1. Wil Jon Edwards, *From the Valley I Came* (London, 1958); Adolf Levenstein, *Aus der Tiefe: Arbeiterbriefe* (Berlin, 1908); David Crew, "Definitions of Modernity: Social Mobility in a German Town," *Journal of Social History* VII (1973):51–74; Peter N. Stearns, *Lives of Labor: Work in a Maturing Industrial Society* (London, 1975), pp. 19–44.

2. Narcisse Faucheur, *Mon histoire: à mes chers enfants et petits enfants* (Lille, 1886), pp. 377–382; Jean Lambert, *Quelques familles du patronat textile de Lille-Armentières (1789–1914)* (Lille, 1954); Lee Holcombe, *Victorian Ladies at Work: Middle-Class Working Women in England and Wales, 1850–1914* (New York, 1973).

3. Branca, *Women in Europe Since 1750.*

4. Stearns, *Lives of Labor*, pp. 19–44; Patricia Branca, "A New Perspective on Women's Work: A Comparative Typology," *Journal of Social History* IX (1975):129–153.

5. Gillis, *Youth and History*, passim; David Hackett Fischer, *Growing Old in America* (New York, 1977), pp. 87–90. Specifically female costume has, of course, received the most attention; see Ruth Finley, *The Lady of Godey's* (Philadelphia, 1931) and Aileen S. Kraditor, ed., *Up from the Pedestal*, pp. 122–136.

6. Stearns, "Working-Class Women in Britain, 1890–1914," in *Suffer and Be Still*, ed. M. Vicinus (Bloomington, Ind., 1972), pp. 100–120; Arthur Ponsonby, *The Decline of the Aristocracy* (London, 1912); G. M. Young, *Early Victorian England*, 2 vols. (Oxford, 1934).

7. T. M. Parssinen, "Popular Science and Society: The Prenology Movement in Early Victorian Britain," *Journal of Social History* VIII (1974):1–20.

8. Herbert Gutman, *Work, Culture and Society in Industrializing America* (New York, 1978), pp. 3–78; David Landes, *The Unbound Prometheus: Technological Change and Industrial Development in Western Europe from 1850 to the Present* (Cambridge, Eng., 1969).

9. Laura Oren, "The Welfare of Women in Laboring Families: England, 1860–1950," in *Clio's Consciousness Raised*, pp. 226–244.

10. Daniel Walkowitz, "Working-Class Women in the Gilded Age: Factory, Community and Family Life among Cohoes, New York Cotton Workers," *Journal of Social History* V (1972): 464–490; Peter N. Stearns, *Paths to Authority: The Middle Class and the Industrial Labor Force in France* (Urbana, Ill., 1978), pp. 57–88.

11. William Reddy, "Family and Factory: French Linen Weavers in the Belle-Epoque," *Journal of Social History* VIII (1974): 102–112; Margaret Hewitt, *Wives and Mothers in Victorian Industry* (London, 1958); June Sochen, *Herstory: A Woman's View of American History* (New York, 1974), pp. 116ff.

12. Patricia Branca, *Silent Sisterhood: Middle-Class Women in the Victorian Home* (Pittsburgh, 1975), pp. 62ff.; John S. Haller and Robin M. Haller, *The Physician and Sexuality in Victorian America* (New York, 1977).

13. Robert Wells, "Family Size and Fertility Control in Eighteenth-Century America," *Population Studies* 25 (1971): 73–82; idem, "Quaker Marriage Patterns in a Colonial Perspective," *William and Mary Quarterly* 29 (1972): 436–439; Branca, *Silent Sisterhood*, pp. 74–115; Barbara Welter, "The Cult of True Womanhood, 1820–1860," *American Quarterly* 18 (1966): 151–174.

14. Joan Scott and Louise Tilly, "Women's Work and the Family," *Comparative Studies in Society and History* 17 (1975): 36–64; Stearns, "Working-Class Women," p. 106. Cf. R. Seebohm Rowntree, *Poverty: A Study of Town Life* (London, 1901), p. 55: "If there's anything extra to buy, such as a pair of boots for one of the children, me and the children goes without dinner—or mebbe only 'as a cup o' tea and a bit o' bread, but Jim ollers takes 'is dinner to work, and I never tell 'im."

15. Edward Shorter, "Illegitimacy, Sexual Revolution and Social Change in Modern Europe," *Journal of Interdisciplinary History* II (1971): 237–253.

16.   Michael Anderson, *Family Structure in Nineteenth-Century Lancashire* (Cambridge, 1974); Michael Gordon, ed., *The American Family in Social-Historical Perspective* (New York, 1973).

17.   Mirra Komarovsky, *The Unemployed Man and His Family* (New York, 1940).

18.   Stearns, *Lives of Labor*, pp. 45–84, 121–147.

19.   J. Michael Phayer, "Lower-Class Morality: The Case of Bavaria," *Journal of Social History* VIII (1974): 79–95; Louise Tilly, Joan Scott, and Miriam Cohen, "Women's Work and European Fertility Patterns," *Journal of Interdisciplinary History* VI (1976): 447–476.

20.   Shorter, *Making of the Modern Family*, pp. 120–168. Basic marriage-rate information is available in government statistical publications of the major industrial countries; see, e.g., Statistique de la France, *Mouvement général de la population,* pp. 1855ff. For the United States, see Thomas P. Monahan, *The Pattern of Age at Marriage in the United States* (Philadelphia, 1951). For England, see the *Fifth Annual Report of the Registrar General of Births, Deaths, and Marriages in England* (London, 1843), et seq.

21.   Clancy Segal, *Weekend in Dinlock* (Cambridge, Mass., 1960).

22.   Michael Katz, "The Entrepreneurial Class in a Canadian City," *Journal of Social History* IX (1975):1–29; Stearns, *Paths to Authority*, pp. 15–34.

23.   Nancy Cott, *Bonds of Womanhood* (New Haven, 1977).

24.   Robert Tressell, *The Ragged Trousered Philanthropists* (London, 1955); Branca, *Silent Sisterhood*, pp. 15–34.

25.   Anderson, *Family Structure*, pp. 43–78.

26.   Gareth Stedman Jones, "Working-Class Culture and Working-Class Politics in London, 1870–1900," *Journal of Social History* IV (1974):460ff.

27.   Mary K. Matossian and William D. Schafter, "Family, Fertility, and Political Violence, 1700–1900," *Journal of Social History* XI (1977):137–178; the same point is made in a more impressionistic fashion by Ferdynand Zweig, while discussing the working-class past. See his *Worker in an Affluent Society*, pp. 20–26.

28.   Gillis, *Youth and History*, pp. 37–94; Filene, *Him/Herself*, pp. 77–104.

29.   Kraditor, *Up from the Pedestal*, pp. 189–203; Joseph P. Kett, *Rites of Passage: Adolescence in America, 1790 to the Present* (New York, 1977).

30.   Gilbert and Sullivan's *Patience* is characteristic of this attitude; see Cesar Grana, *Bohemian versus Bourgeois* (New York, 1964); and Theodore Roszak, "The Hard and the Soft," in *Masculine/Feminine*, ed. Betty and Theodore Roszak (New York, 1969), pp. 93ff.

31.   Adrien Dansette, *Religious History of Modern France* (London, 1962).

32.   Barbara Welter, "The Feminization of American Religion, 1800–1860," in *Clio's Consciousness Raised*, pp. 137–157; Ann Douglas, *The Feminization of American Culture* (New York, 1977); J. Michael Phayer, *Sexual Liberation and Religion in Nineteenth-Century Europe* (Totowa, N.J., 1977).

33.   The idea of a distinctive female, and therefore male, outlook toward health seems valid for the twentieth century; see Christopher Lasche, *Haven in a Heartless World* (New York, 1977), pp. 167ff. For strong evidence of gender differences in health outlook during the nineteenth century, see Regina Morantz, "The Lady and Her Physician," in *Clio's Consciousness Raised*, pp. 38–53; Branca, *Women in Europe since 1750*, pp. 112–121; Peter N. Stearns, *Old Age in European Society* (New York, 1977), pp. 119–124.

34.   Gillis, *Youth and History*, pp. 95–132.

35.   Heinrich Herkner, *Probleme der Arbeiterpsychologie* (Leipzig, 1912).

36.   Foster Rhea Dulles, *A History of Recreation* (New York, 1965); Peter McIntosh, *Sport in Society* (London, 1963).

37.   This is not to ignore important currents of pacifism, inspired by Christian teachings, among men, and middle-class desires to tame their own and working-class youth. The conversion

of British ideal-typical character to an image of nonviolence, for men as well as women, began in the nineteenth century, though behavior lagged. Male gentleness remained an important alternative. See Geofrey Goren, "English Character in the Twentieth Century," *Annals of the American Academy of Political and Social Science* 44 (1967):77ff.

38. For information in this paragraph, I am indebted to Professor Julie Roy Jeffrey, who allowed me to consult the manuscript of her book *Frontier Women: The Trans-Mississippi West, 1840–1880* (New York, 1979). See also Henry Nash Smith, *The American West in Symbol and Myth* (Cambridge, Mass., 1950); and John Faragher, *Women and Men on the Overland Trail* (New Haven, 1979). On the European fascination with these same themes, and the overwhelming popularity of the Western motif and the pervasive tough guy in mass fiction, see Ronald A. Fullerton, "Toward a Commercial Popular Culture in Germany: The Development of Pamphlet Fiction, 1871–1914," *Journal of Social History* XII (1979):490ff.

39. E. P. Thompson, "Time, Work-Discipline, and Industrial Capitalism," *Past and Present* 38 (1967): 127–156; Stearns, *Paths to Authority*, pp. 89–106.

40. Branca, "New Perspectives," pp. 129ff.

41. L. Noirot, *L'Art de vivre longtemps* (Paris, 1868); Stearns, *Old Age*, pp. 18–41, 80–118.

42. Jack D. Douglas, *The Social Meaning of Suicide* (Princeton, 1967); A. Alvarez, *The Savage God: A Study of Suicide* (New York, 1972), pp. 201ff.

43. Matossian and Schafter, "Family, Fertility," pp. 137ff.; Dinnerstein, *The Mermaid and the Minotaur*, passim.

44. Cott, *Bonds of Womanhood*, pp. 62–68. For contemporary theory, see Dinnerstein, *The Mermaid and the Minotaur*, pp. 28–199; Nancy Chodorow, "Family Structure and Feminine Personality," in *Women, Culture, and Society*, pp. 43–66; idem, "Oedipal Asymmetries and Heterosexual Knots," *Social Problems* 22 (1976): 454–468.

45. Barker-Benfield, *Horrors of the Half-Known Life*, passim; Haller and Haller, *Physician and Sexuality*, passim.

46. William Chafe, *Women and Equality* (New York, 1977).

47. Branca, *Women in Europe since 1750*, pp. 73ff. For an interesting portrayal of divergent male reactions to women and feminism, see Constance Rover, *The Punch Book of Women's Rights* (South Brunswick, N.J., 1967), who calls forth a lot of laughter, some fear, but considerable sympathy.

48. See footnote 20 for documentation on marriage patterns; see, also, Etienne Van De Walle, *The Female Population of France in the Nineteenth Century* (Princeton, 1974). For a more qualitative discussion, see Theodore Zeldin, *France, 1848–1945: Ambition, Love and Politics* (Oxford, 1973); André Toledano, *La Vie de famille sous la restauration et la monarchie de juillet* (Paris, 1943); and Peter T. Cominos, "Innocent *Femina Sensualis* in Unconscious Conflict," *Suffer and Be Still*, pp. 155–172.

49. Page Smith, *Daughters of the Promised Land: Women in American History* (Boston, 1970), p. 66.

Chapter 4

1. This is a hope also shared by a number of feminists. See Firestone, *Dialectic of Sex*, pp. 119–141 et passim.

2. On the shrinking but persistent father-son world of the crafts, see Joan Scott, *The Glassworkers of Carmaux* (Cambridge, Mass., 1974); Robert Bezucha, *The Lyons Revolts of*

1834 (Cambridge, Mass., 1974); E. P. Thompson, *The Making of the English Working Class* (New York, 1964); Alan Dawley, *Class and Community: The Industrial Revolution in Lynn* (Cambridge, Mass., 1976); Gutman, *Work, Culture and Society*, pp. 49ff.

3. Stearns, *Lives of Labor*, pp. 45–84. The attitude still persists; see, e.g., J. H. Goldthorpe et al., *The Affluent Worker in the Class Structure* (Cambridge, Eng., 1969); Dorothy Wedderburn and Rosemary Crompton, *Workers' Attitudes and Technology* (Cambridge, Eng., 1972); and Sar A. Levitan, ed., *Blue-Collar Workers* (Cambridge, Mass., 1972).

4. Adolf Levenstein, *Die Arbeiterfrage* (Munich, 1913), p. 107 et passim.

5. Gillis, *Youth and History*, pp. 37–94.

6. Stearns, *Lives of Labor*, pp. 45–84.

7. British Steel Smelters, Mill, Iron and Tinplate Workers Association, *Monthly Reports*, 1913; Arthur Pugh, *Men of Steel* (London, 1951). J. R. Clynes, *Memoirs*, 2 vols. (London, 1937), I, p. 57, described how agitation among cotton piecers was often dampened by the criticism of the spinners, who were characteristically their fathers or uncles.

8. Gillis, *Youth and History*, pp. 37–94; F. A. McClintock and N. H. Avison, *Crime in England and Wales* (New York, 1969).

9. Emile Coornaert, *Les Compagnonnages du moyen âge à nos jours* (Paris, 1966), pp. 77ff.; Eric Hobsbawm, "The Tramping Artisan," *Labouring Men: Studies in the History of Labour* (London, 1964); Douglas Lamar Jones, "The Strolling Poor: Truancy in Eighteenth-Century Massachusetts," *Journal of Social History* VIII (1975): 1–27.

10. Edward Shorter, "Female Emancipation, Birth Control, and Fertility in European History," *American Historical Review* 78 (1973): 605–640. See, also, Peter Laslett, *Family Life and Illicit Love*, passim; and D. S. Smith and Michael Hindus, "Premarital Pregnancy in America, 1640–1971," *Journal of Interdisciplinary History* VI (1975):537–570.

11. J. Michael Phayer, "Lower-Class Morality: The Case of Bavaria," *Journal of Social History* VIII (1974): 79ff.

12. Shorter, "Female Emancipation," pp. 605–640, idem, *Making of the Modern Family*, pp. 80–167.

13. Along the same lines, see Louis Chevalier, *Dangerous Classes and Laboring Classes* (New York, 1976); Theresa McBride, *The Domestic Revolution: The Modernisation of Household Service in England and France* (New York, 1976), pp. 99ff.; Joan Scott and Louise Tilly, *Women, Work and Family* (New York, 1978). See also Lee Rainwater, "Some Aspects of Lower-Class Sexual Behavior," *Journal of Social Issues* 22 (1966):96–108; idem, "Sex in the Culture of Poverty," in *The Individual, Sex and Society*, ed. C. B. Broderick and J. Bernards (Baltimore, 1969), pp. 129–140.

14. L. R. Villermé, *Tableau de l'état physique et moral des ouvriers employés dans les manufactures de coton, de laine, et de soie*, 2 vols. (Paris, 1840), I; Georges Boussinesq, *Reims à la fin de la Monarchie de Juillet* (Angers, 1923); Judith R. Walkowitz and Daniel J. Walkowitz, " 'We Are Not Beasts of the Field': Prostitution and the Poor in Plymouth and Southampton under the Contagious Diseases Act," in *Clio's Consciousness Raised*, pp. 192–225.

15. Moritz Bromme, *Lebensgeschichte eines modernen Fabrikarbeiter* (Jena, 1905); see the exceptionally good discussion in R. P. Neuman, "Industrialization and Sexual Behavior: Some Aspects of Working-Class Life in Imperial Germany," in *Modern European Social History*, ed. Robert Bezucha (Lexington, Mass., 1972), pp. 270–298.

16. Neuman, "Industrialization and Sexual Behavior," pp. 270–298.

17. Gareth Stedman Jones, "Working-Class Culture and Working-Class Politics in London, 1870–1900," *Journal of Social History* VIII (1974):460–508.

18. Neuman, "Industrialization and Sexual Behavior," pp. 288ff.

19. Tressel, *Ragged Trousered Philanthropists*, p. 49.

20.   Fritz Shumann, *Auslese und Anpassung der Arbeiterschaft in der Automobilindustrie* (Leipzig, 1911), p. 106.

21.   Segal, *Weekend in Dinlock*, p. 28 et passim.

22.   Levenstein, *Aus der Tiefe*, passim.

23.   Bromme, *Lebensgeschichte*, pp. 58–124; see also Adolf Levenstein, *Proletariers Jugendjahre* (Berlin, 1909); and Stearns, *Lives of Labor*, pp. 41–85.

24.   Stearns, *Lives of Labor*, pp. 300–334.

25.   Neuman, "Industrialization and Sexual Behavior," pp. 270–298.

26.   Paul Göhre, *Drei Monate Fabrikarbeiter* (Leipzig, 1913); E. H. Phelps Brown, *The Growth of British Industrial Relations* (London, 1959), pp. 16ff.

27.   Phelps Brown, *Growth*, pp. 11ff. The best survey of working-class birth control practices and tensions is R. R. Neuman, "Working-Class Birth Control in Wilhelmine Germany," *Comparative Studies in Society and History* 20 (1978):408–428.

28.   Anderson, *Family Structure*, pp. 43–161.

29.   Dora Landé, *Arbeits- und Lohnverhältnisse in der Berliner Maschinenindustrie* (Berlin 1906); Peter N. Stearns, "Adaptation to Industrialization: German Workers as a Test Case," *Central European History* III (1970):326.

30.   M. Loane, *Next Street But One* (London, 1907); idem, *The Queen's Poor* (London, 1905); and idem, *From Their Point of View* (London, 1908); see also Peter N. Stearns, "Working-Class Women in Britain, 1890–1914," in *Suffer and Be Still*, pp. 100–120.

31.   Tressell, *Philanthropists*, p. 58.

32.   Florence Bell, *At the Works* (London, 1907); Stearns, "Working-Class Women," pp. 105–112.

33.   Wenzel Holek, *Lebensgang eines deutsch-tschechischen Handarbeiters* (Jena, 1909); Ernst Dükerstoff, *How an English Workman Lives*, trans. C. H. Leppington (London, 1899), p. 40 et passim.

34.   Nancy Tomes, "A 'Torrent of Abuse': Crimes of Violence between Working-Class Men and Women in London, 1840–1875," *Journal of Social History* XI (1978):328–345.

35.   Edward Cox, *Principles of Punishment* (London, 1877), p. 102.

36.   Tomes, " 'Torrent'," pp. 328ff.; Stearns, "Working-Class Women," pp. 102–103.

37.   Levenstein, *Arbeiterfrage*, passim; Herkner, *Probleme der Arbeiterpsychologie*, p. 289.

38.   Peter N. Stearns, "The Unskilled and Industrialization: A Transformation of Consciousness," *Archiv für Sozialgeschichte* 16 (1976):249–282.

39.   Stearns, *Lives of Labor*, pp. 121–238; Wedderburn and Crompton, *Workers' Attitudes*; J.-R. Tréanton, "Les Réactions à la retraite," *Revue française du travail* IX (1958):156; Zweig, *Workers in an Affluent Society*, pp. 53–88; Levitan, *Blue-Collar Workers*, passim; Heinrich Popitz, *Das Gesellschaftsbild des Arbeiters* (Tübingen, 1957); H. De Man, *Joy in Work* (London, 1928).

40.   Eric Hobsbawm, "Custom, Wages and Work Load," *Labouring Men*, pp. 344–370; Stearns, *Lives of Labor*, pp. 269–299, 335–355. A classic contemporary case of instrumentalism is described in *Affluent Worker*, passim.

41.   Segal, *Weekend in Dinlock*, p. 66.

42.   Komarovsky, *Unemployed Man and His Family*, passim; Lee Rainwater, R. P. Coleman, and Gerald Handel, *Workingman's Wife* (New York, 1959).

43.   Zena S. Blau, *Old Age in a Changing Society* (New York, 1973); Herman J. Loether, "The Meaning of Work and Adjustment to Retirement," in *Blue-Collar World*, ed. A. Shostak and William Gomberg (Englewood Cliffs, N.J., 1964) pp. 525–533.

44.   Tressell, *Philanthropists*, pp. 494–797.

45. W. H. Warburton, *The History of the Trade Union Organization in the North Staffordshire Potteries* (London, 1931); Barbara Drake, *Women in Trade Unions* (London, 1921); Alice Henry, *Women and the Labor Movement* (New York, 1923).

46. Patricia Branca, "A New Perspective on Women's Work: A Comparative Typology," *Journal of Social History* VIII (1975): 129–153.

47. Auguste Bebel, *Die Frau und der Sozialismus* (Berlin, 1961).

48. William Chafe, *The American Woman* (New York, 1972), pp. 48–88; Maureen Greenwald, "Women Workers and World War I: The American Railroad Industry—A Case Study," *Journal of Social History* VIII (1975): 154–177; Dorothy Richardson, "The Long Day: The Study of a New York Working Girl," in *Women at Work*, ed. William L. O'Neill (Chicago, 1972), p. 3ff.

49. Frederick Rogers, *Labour, Life and Literature* (London, 1913); London Society of Compositors, *To the Workmen of the United Kingdom* (London, 1892); Friendly Society of Ironfounders (Sheffield Branch), Strike Committee Minute Book, 1912–1913.

50. The best study of the human dynamic of strikes is by Michelle Perrot, *Les Ouvriers en grève*, 2 vols. (Paris, 1974).

51. Peter N. Stearns, *Revolutionary Syndicalism and French Labor* (New Brunswick, N.J., 1971).

52. Philipp A. Koller, *Das Massen- und Führer-Problem in der Freien Gewerkschaften* (Tübingen, 1920); Branko Pribićević, *The Shop Stewards Movement and Workers' Control* (Oxford, 1969).

53. Malcolmson, *Popular Recreations*; Laslett, *The World We Have Lost*, pp. 20ff.; Mack Walker, *German Home Towns: Community, State and General Estate* (Ithaca, N.Y., 1971); André Varagnac, *Civilisations traditionelles et genres de vie* (Paris, 1948). One aspect of the destruction of traditional leisure is treated by Robert Storch, "The Policeman as Domestic Missionary: Urban Discipline and Popular Culture in Northern England," *Journal of Social History* IX (1976):481–509; see, also, T. F. T. Dyer, *British Popular Customs Present and Past* (London, 1876).

54. Villermé, *Tableau*, I, p. 235.

55. Michael R. Marrus, "Social Drinking in the *Belle Epoque*," *Journal of Social History* VIII (1974):115–141.

56. Idem, *The Rise of Leisure in Industrial Society* (St. Louis, 1976); Wolfgang Nahrstedt, *Die Entstehung der Freizeit* (Göttingen, 1972); James Walvin, *Football: The Peoples' Game* (London, 1974); Alasdair Clayre, *Work and Play; Ideas and Experience of Work and Leisure* (London, 1974); Max Kaplan, *Leisure in America: A Social Inquiry* (New York, 1960).

57. Albert Cauvin, *La Durée du travail dans les houillères de Belgique* (Paris, 1909); Stearns, *Lives of Labor*, pp. 241–268.

58. Stearns, *Paths to Authority*, pp. 111–140.

Chapter 5

1. Cott, *Bonds of Womanhood*, pp. 64–69; William Chafe, *Women and Equality*, pp. 15–22.

2. Bernard Murstein, *Love, Sex and Marriage through the Ages* (New York, 1974); Duncan Crow, *The Victorian Woman* (New York, 1971); Barbara Welter, "The Cult of True

Womanhood, 1820–1860," *American Quarterly* 18 (1966): 151–174; Zeldin, *France, 1848–1945*, I, pp. 343–364.

3.   Branca, *Silent Sisterhood*, pp. 123ff.; Carl Degler, "What Ought to Be and What Was: Woman's Sexuality in the Nineteenth Century," *American Historical Review* 79 (1974): 1469–1490. See also F. Barry Smith, "Sexuality in Britain: Some Suggested Revisions," in *A Widening Sphere*, ed. Martha Vicinus (Bloomington, Ind., 1977), pp. 182–198.

4.   R. P. Neuman, "Masturbation, Madness, and the Modern Concept of Childhood and Adolescence," *Journal of Social History* VIII (1975); 1–27; E. H. Hare, "Masturbatory Insanity: The History of an Idea," *Journal of Mental Sciences* 16 (1962): 1–12; Peter Cominos, "Late Victorian Sexual Respectability and the Social System," *International Review of Social History* VIII (1963): 18–24, stresses the particularly Victorian pattern of control in which sexual restraint merged with sobriety, savings, and other aspects of self-containment in the middle-class male. See also Ronald Waters, *Primers for Prudery: Sexual Advice to Victorian America* (Englewood Cliffs, N.J., 1974).

5.   Cott, *Bonds of Womanhood*, pp. 64ff.; Chafe, *Women and Equality*, passim.

6.   Murstein, *Love, Sex and Marriage*, pp. 260–276; see also Barker-Benfield, *Horrors of the Half-Known Life*, pp. 45–60.

7.   Faucheur, *Mon Histoire*, pp. 377–382.

8.   Stearns, *Paths to Authority*, pp. 15–34; Gaston Motte, *Motte-Bossut: un homme, une famille, une firme* (Tourcoing, 1944).

9.   Richard Hofstadter, *Social Darwinism in American Thought* (New York, 1959).

10.   Sidney Pollard, *The Genesis of Modern Management* (Cambridge, Mass., 1965).

11.   Jules Burat, *Exposition de l'industrie française, année 1944*, 3 vols. (Paris, 1845), I, p. 8.

12.   A manufacturer in Rheims discussed the difficulty of getting businessmen together save for an occasional charity dance; he claimed that manufacturers were so secretive that "one would think they were looking for the philosopher's stone." Arnold Aronssohn, *Projet d'organisation d'une société industrielle pour la régénération industrielle et morale du commerce de la ville de Rheims* (Rheims, 1833), p. 3.

13.   Cott, *Bonds of Womanhood*, passim; Carol Christ, "Victorian Masculinity and the Angel in the House," *A Widening Sphere*, pp. 146–162.

14.   Mrs. Hugh Gaskill, *Mary Barton* (New York, 1961) and idem. *Wives and Daughters* (New York, 1969); see, also, Helene E. Roberts, "Marriage, Redundancy of Sin: The Painter's View of Women in the First Twenty-Five Years of Victoria's Reign," in *Suffer and Be Still*, pp. 45–76. A good bit of nineteenth-century art was caught between the image of woman as a symbol of purity and motherhood and woman as prostitute and debauched soul. Roberts comments on male sexual interests as well as the constraints of unrelieved motherhood.

15.   H. C. Emmery, *Amélioration du sort des ouvriers dans les travaux publiques* (Paris, 1837), p. 57.

16.   Stearns, *Paths to Authority*, p. 133; Jules Puech, *La Vie et l'oeuvre de Flora Tristan* (Paris, 1925), p. 211.

17.   On paternal uncertainties, see Caroline M. Hallett, *Fathers and Children* (London, 1909); Lloyd de Mause, ed., *The History of Childhood* (New York, 1974). Tellingly, much of the burgeoning childrearing literature omitted fathers; see, for example, H. A. Allbutt, *Every Mother's Handbook* (London, 1897); Lydia Child, *The Mother's Book* (Boston, 1834), Elizabeth Blackwell, *Counsel to Parents on the Moral Education of Their Children* (London, 1878). Mothers, of course, were not always tender; John Wesley's mother was but one parent who rode herd on her sons' wills; but after the early nineteenth century, the impression of maternal tenderness increased, and the sternness in the family was increasingly left to the man.

18.   Barker-Benfield, *Horrors of the Half-Known Life*, pp. 80–134; Ann D. Wood, " 'The

Fashionable Diseases': Women's Complaints and Their Treatment in Nineteenth-Century America," in *Clio's Consciousness Raised*, pp. 1–22.

19.   Barbara Welter, "The Feminization of American Religion, 1800–1860," in *Clio's Consciousness Raised*, pp. 137–157.

20.   Kraditor, *Up From the Pedestal*, p. 137ff.; Sochen, *Herstory*, pp. 119–152; Filene, *Him/Herself*, pp. 77–109, picks this theme up for the turn-of-the-century.

21.   See Louis Henry, *Anciennes familles genevoises* (Paris, 1956), on an early case of bourgeois family limitation; R. V. Wells, "Family Size and Fertility Control in Eighteenth-Century America," *Population Studies* 24 (1971): 73–82.

22.   *Nicolas Schlumberger, 1782–1867* (Microfilm in the Archives Nationales, France, 33MI-3).

23.   Some students of the English middle class have pinned the birth-rate decline to the 1870s, but this is clearly in error since the birth rate of the entire population—of which the middle class was only a minority—began to fall at that point. See J. A. Banks, *Prosperity and Parenthood* (London, 1964); idem, and Olive Banks, *Feminism and Family Planning in Victorian England* (New York, 1964).

24.   Analysis that has recently underscored this pre-1850 change has also switched attention away from female sexual passivity, stressing devices that women could choose without their husbands' knowedge and while maintaining sexual pleasure. This version of "domestic feminism" goes too far. Male participation in birth-control decisions, and female restraint in helping carry out the decisions, are necessary to explain middle-class demography up until the later nineteenth century; see Branca, *Silent Sisterhood*, pp. 114–143.

25.   Robert V. Wells, "Family History and Demographic Transition," *Journal of Social History* IX (1975): 1–20; Ansley J. Coale and Melvin Zelnik, *New Estimates of Fertility and Population in the United States* (Princeton, 1963); Marcel Reinhard and André Armengaud, *Histoire de la population mondiale* (Paris, 1961); Charles Morazé, *La France bourgeoise* (Paris, 1952).

26.   Lewis Perry, " 'Progress, Not Pleasure, Is Our Aim': The Sexual Advice of One Antebellum Radical," *Journal of Social History* XII(1979): 354–367.

27.   Chevalier, *Dangerous Classes*; McBride, *Domestic Revolution*; Leonore Davidoff, "Mastered for Life: Servant, Wife, and Mother in Victorian and Edwardian Britain," *Journal of Social History* VII (1974): 406–428.

28.   Degler, "What Ought to Be," p. 147ff.; Richard Carlile, *Every Woman's Book: Or, What Is Love* (London, 1825); A. Debay, *Hygiène et physiologie du mariage* (Paris, n.d.); Nicolas Venette, *Tableau de l'amour conjugale* (Paris, 1907).

29.   Degler, "What Ought to Be."

30.   Zeldin, *France*, p. 295ff.

31.   Ibid., p. 299ff.

32.   Gustave Droz, *Monsieur, madame et bébé* (Paris, 1866), p. 112.

33.   French Institute of Public Opinion, *Patterns of Love and Sex: A Study of the French Woman and Her Morals* (Paris, 1961); Jacques Baroche, *Le Comportement sexuel de l'homme marié en France* (Paris, 1969).

34.   Barker-Benfield, *Horrors*, pp. 163–88; Neuman, "Masturbation," pp. 1–27; idem, "The Sexual Question and Social Democracy in Imperial Germany," *Journal of Social History* VIII (1974): 271–286.

35.   Sir Jacob Paget, *Clinical Lectures and Essays* (New York, 1875), pp. 284–285.

36.   Edmond Desmoulins, *Anglo-Saxon Superiority: To What It Is Due* (New York, 1898), pp. 135–159.

37.   Gaston Motte, *Les Motte: Etude de la descendance Motte-Clarisse* (Roubaix, 1952), contains revealing letters of advice to sons; typical boys' literature (i.e., moralistic and popular)

for the century was written by Orison Swett Marden: *Making Life a Masterpiece* (Boston, 1896); *Character: The Greatest and Grandest Thing in the World* (Omaha, Neb., 1904); *Architects of Fate; or Steps to Success and Power, a Book Designed to Inspire Youth to Character Building, Self-Culture and Noble Achievement* (Boston, 1895).

38.   René Sédillot, *La Maison de Wendel de mil sept cent quatre à nos jours* (Paris, 1958), p. 162; Jules Sengenwald, *De l'industrie dans le Haut-Rhin* (Strasbourg, 1837), p. 16; A. Egron, *Le Livre de l'ouvrier, ses devoirs envers la société, la famille, et lui-même* (Paris, 1844), pp. 31, 373.

39.   Michael Katz, "The Entrepreneurial Class in a Canadian City," *Journal of Social History* VIII (1975): 1–29.

40.   Stearns, *Paths to Authority*, pp. 89–106; Ludwig Poppke, *Sozialpolitik und soziale Anschauungen frühindustrieller Unternehmer in Rheinland-Westfalen* (Köln, 1966).

41.   William G. McLoughlin, "Evangelical Child-Rearing in the Age of Jackson: Francis Wayland's View of When and How to Subdue the Willfulness of Children," *Journal of Social History* IX (1975); 21–34; see, also, Charles Strickland, "A Transcendentalist Father: The Child-Rearing Practices of Bronson Alcott," *Perspectives in American History* (1969): 5–73.

42.   Greven, *The Protestant Temperament*, passim. Greven describes the two major middle-class family styles (plus a discreet upper-class style) coexisting in the eighteenth century; of course, patterns of parenting are never uniform. But it still seems probable that there was a shift away from breaking the will. Greven himself suggests this in his book entitled *Childrearing Concepts, 1628–1861* (Itasca, Ill., 1973). See, also, Marion Lochhead, *Their First Ten Years: Victorian Childhood* (London, 1959), and Ivy Pinchbeck and Margaret Hewitt, *Children in English Society*, vol. II (London, 1973). Lasch, *Haven in a Heartless World*, passim, praises the paternal style he sees in the mid-nineteenth century. For a more qualified judgment, see Stephen Kern, "Explosive Intimacy: Psychodynamics of the Victorian Family," in *The New Psychohistory*, ed. Lloyd de Mause (New York, 1975).

43.   Mary K. Matossian and William D. Schafter, "Family, Fertility, and Political Violence, 1700–1900," *Journal of Social History* XI (1977): 137–178.

44.   Hofstadter, *Social Darwinism*, pp. 31–50.

45.   R. V. Clements, *Managers: A Study of Their Careers in Industry* (London, 1958).

46.   Daniel T. Rodgers, "Socializing Middle-Class Children: Institutions, Fables, and Work Values in Nineteenth-Century America," *Journal of Social History*, in press.

47.   David Montgomery, "Workers' Control of Machine Productivity in the Nineteenth Century," *Labor History* 17 (1976): 484–487. For a broader discussion of paternalism's decline, see David J. Rothman, "The State as Parent," in *Doing Good: The Limits of Benevolence*, ed. Willard Gaylin et al., (New York, 1978), pp. 67–98. The reasons for the decline of male schoolteaching were numerous, but one of them was the argument on the special suitability of women; it was advanced by men who stood to lose by the admission and has been rated a significant factor in the relatively easy acceptance of women into teaching ranks in France in the later nineteenth century. See Peter V. Meyers, "Women's Entry and the Professionalization of Primary Schooling in France," paper presented at the Society for French Historical Studies, 1979.

48.   Haller and Haller, *Physician and Sexuality*, pp. 45–88. Needless to say, the vociferousness of some intellectuals and professions on the subject of female inferiority has clouded hosts of issues on nineteenth-century gender, for, as has already been noted, there were other male views.

49.   Maccoby and Jacklin, *Psychology of Sex Differences*, passim.

50.   Cincinnati School Board, minutes of meetings, 1846–48.

51.   J. H. Plumb, "The New World of Children in 18th-Century England," *Past and Present* 67 (1975): 67ff.

52.   *The Galveston Daily News*, 1942.

53. Gillis, *Youth and History*, pp. 95–132; James Walvin, *The Peoples Game* (London, 1974); Philip Goodhart and Christopher Chataway, *War without Weapons* (London, 1968); Peter McIntosh, *Physical Education in England since 1800* (London, 1969); H. D. Sheldon, *Student Life and Customs* (New York, 1901); Dulles, *History of Recreation*, pp. 182–200; Thomas Hughes, *Tom Brown's School Days* (London, 1858); T. W. Bamford, *Thomas Arnold* (London, 1960).

54. Frederick Rudolph, *The American College and University* (New York, 1965); Dennis Lawrence and Joseph Kauffman, eds., *The College and the Student* (Washington, D.C., 1966); Kett, *Rites of Passage*, pp. 173–214.

55. Joseph R. DeMartini, "Student Culture as a Change Agent in American Higher Education: An Illustration from the Nineteenth Century," *Journal of Social History* IX (1976): 526–541. For a mid-nineteenth century expression of the tension between boys good at games and more cerebral, sensitive souls, see Hughes, *Tom Brown's School Days*; see, also, Samuel Butler, *The Way of All Flesh* (New York, 1966).

56. Cincinnati School Board, Minutes of Meetings, 1862–63.

57. The male reaction to feminism remains to be fully traced; see William O'Neill, *Everyone Was Brave: A History of Feminism in America* (New York, 1971); Filene, *Him/Herself*, pp. 77–104.

58. Julius Sachs, "Co-Education in the United States," *Educational Review* 33 (1907): 300 et passim.

59. I am grateful to Mr. Jay Devine for information on this subject.

60. Edward H. Cooper, *The Twentieth-Century Child* (London, 1905).

61. Angus McLaren, "Contraception and Its Discontents: Sigmund Freud and Birth Control," *Journal of Social History* XII (1979): 505ff; Banks, *Prosperity*, passim; Banks, and Banks, *Feminism and Family Planning*, pp. 69–84; Branca, *Silent Sisterhood*, pp. 114–43; Norman Himes, *Medical History of Contraception* (Baltimore, 1970); Peter Fryer, *The Birth Controllers* (London, 1965); Linda Gordon, *Woman's Body, Woman's Right: A Social History of Birth Control in America* (Boston, 1976).

62. Zeldin, *France*, 297ff.; Stephen Marcus, *The Other Victorians* (London, 1966); Harold J. Dyos, *Victorian Suburb: A Study of the Growth of Camberwell* (Leicester, 1961); Richard Sennett, *Families Against the City: Middle-Class Homes of Industrial Chicago, 1872–1890* (New York, 1974).

63. Louis Seraine, *De la santé des gens mariés* (Paris, 1865), pp. 112–116. See, also, Paul Janet, *La Famille* (Paris, 1861), who urges the husband's family leadership on the grounds of superior rationality. Writing at about the same time, Amédie de Margerie, *De la famille* (Paris, 1878), saw women as the preponderant influence in the family because of their moral superiority. See, also, Edward R. Sullivan, *Woman, the Predominant Partner* (London, 1894); Harry Horseman, *The Husband To Get and To Be. Homely Homilies for the Home. The Young Man's Model and the Young Woman's Ideal* (Paisley, Eng., 1901).

64. Filene, *Him/Herself*, pp. 7–78; Sochen, *Herstory*, pp. 199–262; Branca, *Women in Europe*, pp. 161ff.

65. Birth control could take its toll directly on men as well as women. Freud reported frequent male anxieties after coitus interruptus; in a case of depression following coitus with a condom, Freud wrote of his patient: "The preparations for using a condom are enough to make him feel that the whole act is partly forced on him, and his enjoyment of it something he was persuaded into." Sigmund Freud, *The Standard Edition of the Complete Psychological Works*, 24 vols., trans. J. Strachey, (London, 1966), I, pp. 196–197.

66. Filene, *Him/Herself*; William O'Neill, *Divorce in the Progressive Era* (New Haven, 1967).

67. Cominos, "Late Victorian Respectability," pp. 18–44, develops the idea that before 1900 middle-class men needed to strive for greater family success to compensate for failure to achieve manhood in the business world.

68. Stearns, *European Society in Upheaval* (New York, 1975), pp. 183ff.; Michael Young and Peter Wilmott, *The Symmetrical Family* (London, 1973).

69. David Lockwood, *The Blackcoated Worker* (London, 1958); Jürgen Kocka, *Unternehmensverwaltung und Angestelltenschaft am Beispiel Siemens* (Stuttgart, 1969).

70. On problems of male friendship, see Marc Fasteau, *The Male Machine* (New York, 1974); Pleck and Sawyer, *Men and Masculinity*, pp. 74–93.

71. This must be stressed against some of the more extreme statements of gender pathology that have normally offered a psychohistorical gloss on a whole culture, in my view, by seizing on loud but atypical voices and asserting that they represented widely held views and, indeed, actual behavior. Both genders have been tainted by this approach, which at its worst makes museum pieces of Victorian men and women; in the case of women, the distortions can, of course, be the fault of men (or male doctors). See Barker-Benfield, *Horrors of the Half-Known Life*, pp. 80–308; and idem, "The Spermatic Economy: A Nineteenth-Century View of Sexuality," *Feminist Studies* (1972): 45–74.

72. Filene, *Him/Herself*, pp. 77–104; Robert Graves and Alan Hodge, *The Long Weekend: A British Social History, 1918–1939* (New York, 1941).

73. W. Andrew Achenbaum, "The Obsolescence of Old Age in America," *Journal of Social History* Vol. (1974): 48–62; Fischer, *Growing Old in America* passim and Stearns, *Old Age in European Society*, passim, deal variously with this question, but all suggest serious problems in any linkage of maleness and old age.

Chapter 6

1. Stearns, *Lives of Labor*, pp. 121–229.

2. Lois Banner, *Women in Modern America* (New York, 1974); Branca, *Women in Europe since 1750*, pp. 191–216; Scott and Tilly, *Women, Work, and Family*, passim.

3. Chafe, *American Woman*, passim; Frank Stricker, "Cookbooks and Law Books: The Hidden History of Career Women in Twentieth-Century America," *Journal of Social History* X (1976): 1–19.

4. Young and Wilmott, *Symmetrical Family*, passim.

5. Donald Bogue, *Principles of Demography* (New York, 1969); William Petersen, *Population* (London, 1969); Wrigley, *Population and History*, pp. 111ff.; Donnella H. Meadows et al., *The Limits to Growth* (New York, 1972).

6. Filene, *Him/Herself*, passim.

7. Erich Maria Remarque, *All Quiet on the Western Front* (New York, 1974).

8. David Schoenbaum, *Hitler's Social Revolution: Class and Status in Nazi Germany* (New York, 1966); Ralf Dahrendorf, *Society and Democracy in Germany* (Garden City, N.Y., 1968).

9. See, for example, Hennessey, *I, B.I.T.C.H.* Lest I be accused of inconsistency, I recognize that the book stands to feminism approximately as the advocates of widespread ovariotomies stood to nineteenth-century medicine; but it is fun reading, and a few of its elements have some currency; see, also, Firestone, *Dialectic of Sex*; pp. 199–200, 202.

10. O'Neill, *Everyone Was Brave*, pp. 361ff. et passim.

11. Del Martin, *Battered Wives* (San Francisco, 1976).

12. Susan Brownmiller, *Against Our Will: Men, Women and Rape* (New York, 1975). The point about rape is tough. That many women have become far more sensitive to rape as a

basic indignity is unquestionable; hence more reporting, from one year to the next, and quite possibly a widening of the definition of what rape is (rape in marriage, for example). That some men rape women, and that still more men have been unconcerned about rape, are also undeniable. But we literally do not know whether male acts and attitudes are changing or not, despite a firm belief on the part of some feminists that things are getting worse. Brownmiller's important book attempts no analysis of trends or an overall assessment of rape in industrial societies, but offers instead more limited portrayals of great vividness.

13.   Nichols, *Men's Liberation*.

14.   This, of course, the feminists realize, as they direct most of their attention to the limitations of other women. See Friedan, *Feminine Mystique*; Sharon L. Sutherland, "The Unambitious Female: A Data-based Discussion of Women's Low Professional Aspirations," *Signs: Journal of Women in Culture and Society* III (1978): 774–794; Rachael Patai, ed., *Women in the Modern World* (New York, 1967), especially the essay on Germany by Helge Pross; Evelyne Sullerot, *Women, Society and Change* (New York, 1971).

15.   Robert Smuts, *Women and Work in America* (New York, 1959); International Labor Office, *The War and Women's Employment* (Montreal, 1946); Chafe, *American Woman* and *Women and Equality*; Evelyne Sullerot, *Histoire et sociologie du travail féminin* (Paris, 1969); Joseph Schoonbroodt, *Les Femmes et le travail* (Brussels, 1973).

16.   Howard Gadlin, "Scars and Emblems: Paradoxes of American Family Life," *Journal of Social History* XI (1978): 320–322; Martha Fowlkes, "The Wives of Professional Men: A Study of Inter-Dependency of Family and Careers" (Ph.D. diss., Univ. of Massachusetts, 1977).

17.   George C. McGlynnis, *Issues in Physical Education and Sports* (New York, 1974).

18.   *Newsweek*, Jan. 30, 1978, p. 9. See, also, O'Neill, *Everyone Was Brave*, p. 368.

19.   The KKK, certainly no friend to feminism, nevertheless does not like to list women among its host of targets, which does make the movement unique among twentieth-century challenges to the mainstream in the United States. The women of the KKK, based in Little Rock, Arkansas, actually advocated extensions of women's activities between the wars; see "The Sphere of Woman in Our National Life," *The Torch*, Dec. 1930, pp. 21–22.

20.   Lasch, *Haven in a Heartless World*, p. 171 et passim; John R. Seeley, R. Alexander Sim, and Elizabeth Loosley, *Crestwood Heights: A Study of the Culture of Suburban Life* (New York, 1956), esp. chaps. 11–12.

21.   Rosabeth Moss Kanter, "Work in a New America," *Daedalus* 107 (1978): 47–78; but see Jean Baker Miller, *Towards a New Psychology of Women* (Boston, 1976), pp. 94–95, for more clearly stated female goals.

22.   Between 1950 and 1960 American men increased their involvement in primary-school teaching and librarianship by about 50 percent; they also gained a better hold on secondary-school teaching and social work. See Sol Swendloff, "Job Opportunities for Women College Graduates," *Monthly Labor Review* 87(1964): 397. Susan Householder Van Horn discusses the resultant confusion of gender roles in her dissertation, "Women's Work and Fertility, 1900–1979" (Carnegie Mellon University, 1979).

23.   Herbert Goldberg, *The Hazards of Being Male* (Los Angeles, 1977).

24.   See "Dress and Male Liberation: Symbols of Sex Roles," in *Readings in Introductory Sociology* ed. Jan L. Flora and C. B. Flora (Boston, 1973), pp. 3–19; Gillis, *Youth and History*, passim; and Lawrence and Kauffman, *The College and the Student*, on changes in youth groupings. Jesse Pitts, "Continuity and Change in Bourgeois France," in *In Search of France*, ed. Stanley Hoffman (Cambridge, Mass., 1963), pp. 135–304, pointed to increased gender mixing even in informal groups at least three decades ago. Decline of working-class male groupings is noted in Goldthorpe, *Affluent Worker*, passim, and J. Kingsdale, "The 'Poor Man's Clubs': Social Functions of the Urban Working-Class Saloon," *American Quarterly* (1973), 472–489.

25. Hennessey, *I, B.I.T.C.H.*

26. Nichols, *Men's Liberation*; Goldberg, *Hazards*; Lasch, *Haven*; Fasteau, *Male Machine*; Pleck and Sawyer, *Men and Masculinity*, esp. Ruth E. Hartley, "Sex-Role Pressures and the Socialization of the Male Child," pp. 7–13; Arlie Hochschild, "Inside the Clockwork of Male Careers," in *Crisis in American Institutions* ed. V. Skolnik and E. Carne (Boston, 1976), pp. 251–265.

27. Lewis Feuer, *The Conflicts of Generations* (New York, 1969); Kenneth Keniston, "The Sources of Student Dissent," *Journal of Social Issues* 23 (1967): 108–137, and idem, *Young Radicals: Notes on Committed Youth* (New York, 1968); Richard Flacks, "The Liberated Generation: An Exploration of the Roots of Student Protest," *Journal of Social Issues* 23 (1967): 52–75; Tarig Ali, ed., *New Revolutionaries: Left Opposition* (New York, 1965).

Chapter 7

1. Against too facile an impression of crisis, however, it must be remembered that they had never been easy. Current laments about manhood stem mainly from people in American academic/professional circles, although they generalize about the gender more widely; and on the surface at least the laments relate less to new difficulties in fulfilling manhood than to a sense that the game was never worthwhile. See the section "Men," a regular feature of *Ms.* magazine; Jeff Keith, "My Own Men's Liberation," *Win* 7 (1971): 22–26; Jerry Farber, "Growing Up Male in North America," idem, *The University of Tomorrowland* (New York, 1972), pp. 93–113; *Unbecoming Men: A Men's Consciousness-Raising Group Writes on Oppression and Themselves* (New York, 1971); Myron Brenton, *The American Male* (New York, 1966); "The Embattled Human Male" [entire issue], *Impact of Science on Society* 21 (1971); "What's Next For Manhood?" *London Sunday Times Magazine*, April 23, 1972 [entire issue].

2. Komarovsky, *Unemployed Man*, pp. 23, 29, 41, 44.

3. Friedan, *Feminine Mystique*.

4. Ralph Turner, "The Male Occupational Role," idem, *Family Interaction* (New York, 1970), pp. 255–266; Mirra Komarovsky, *Blue-Collar Marriage* (New York, 1967).

5. Elaine Tyler May, "The Pressure to Provide: Class, Consciousness, and Divorce in Urban America, 1880–1920," *Journal of Social History* XII (1979): 180–193.

6. Erik Gronseth, "The Husband-Provider Role: A Critical Appraisal," in *Family Issues of Employed Women*, ed. A. Michel (Leiden, 1971), pp. 11–31; idem, "The Breadwinner Trap," in *The Future of the Family*, ed. L. Howe (New York, 1972), pp. 175–191; C. Wright Mills, *White Collar: American Middle Classes* (New York, 1951); Michel Crozier, *The World of the Office Worker* (Chicago, 1971).

7. Henri Mendras, *The Vanishing Peasant* (Cambridge, Mass., 1970); but here a fascination with machines, as well as earnings, has risen instead. See Lawrence Wylie, *Village in the Vaucluse* (Cambridge, Mass., 1967). On general structural change, see Ralf Dahrendorf, *Class and Class Conflict in Industrial Society* (Stanford, 1957); Daniel Bell, *The Coming of the Post-Industrial Society* (New York, 1973); Henry Jacoby, *The Bureaucratization of the World* (Berkeley, 1973), esp. pp. 79–83.

8. S. Schuman et al., "Young Male Drivers: Impulse Expression, Accidents, and Violations," *Journal of the American Medical Association* 200 (1967): 1026–1030.

9. S. M. Lipset and Reinhard Bendix, *Social Mobility in Industrial Society* (Berkeley,

1959). Mobility, of course, increased in the United States and Europe in the first two decades after World War II; the current laments about masculinity may well reflect its cessation, which does not deprive them of deeper significance, particular as we have no assurance that mobility will resume.

10.   Robert Blauner, *Alienation and Freedom* (Chicago, 1964).

11.   Robert E. Gould, "Measuring Masculinity by the Size of a Paycheck," *Ms.* 3 (1973): 18ff.

12.   Wedderburn and Crompton, *Workers' Attitudes*, pp. 118ff.

13.   John T. Dunlop, "Past and Future Tendencies in American Labor Organizations," *Daedalus* 108 (1978): 79–96.

14.   Joseph Pleck, "Is Brotherhood Possible?" in *Old Family/New Family: Interpersonal Relationships* ed. Nona Glazer Malbin, (New York, 1974); Lige Clark and Jack Nichols, *Roommates Can't Always Be Lovers—An Intimate Look at Male/Male Relationships* (New York, 1974); R. Useem et al., "Functions of Neighboring for the Middle-Class Male," *Human Organization* 19 (1960): 68–76; Fasteau, *Male Machine*.

15.   Jon M. Shepard, *Automation and Alienation* (Cambridge, Mass., 1971); Harvey Swados, *On The Line* (Boston, 1957).

16.   Fernando Barolome, "Executives as Human Beings," *Harvard Business Review* 50 (1972): 62–68; Michael Maccoby, *The Gamesman: The New Corporate Leaders* (New York, 1976).

17.   Goldthorpe, *Affluent Worker*.

18.   See *Work in America* (Cambridge, Mass., 1972), pp. 13ff.; Levitan, *Blue-Collar Workers*, p. 89 et passim; Zweig, *Workers in an Affluent Society*; J. R. Tréanton, "Les Réactions à la retraite," *Revue française du travail* 14 (1958): 156.

19.   Studs Terkel, *Working* (New York, 1975); C. Tausky, "Meanings of Work among Blue-Collar Men" *Pacific Sociological Review* 12 (1969): 49–55; Zweig, *Workers*; Marc Fried et al., *The World of the Urban Working Class* (Cambridge, Mass., 1973), pp. 160ff.

20.   Zweig, *Workers*.

21.   Ibid.

22.   Goldthorpe, *Affluent Worker;* J. Useem and R. Useem, "Social Stresses and Resources among Middle-Management Men," in *Patients, Physicians, and Illness*, ed. E. Jaco (Glencoe, Ill., 1958), pp. 74–91; Peter Wilmott, "Family, Work and Leisure Conflicts among Male Employees," *Human Relations* 24 (197): 575–584.

23.   Tréanton, "Réactions"; Caisse nationale de retraite des ouvriers du bâtiment et des travaux publiques, *Réalités du troisième age: Enquête sur les ouvriers retraités du bâtiment et des travaux publiques* (Paris, 1968); Stearns,*Old Age*; Blau, *Old Age*; R. C. Atchley, *The Sociology of Retirement* (Cambridge, Mass., 1976); L. F. Cooley, *The Retirement Trap* (New York, 1965); D. Cogwell and N. Bauleh, "The Use of Leisure Time by Older People," *The Gerontologist* 9 (1965); G. Streib, *Retirement in American Society* (Ithaca, N.Y., 1971); "Les Cadres retraités vus par eux-mêmes," *Revue française du travail* 24 (1968):468–482.

24.   Joan Aldous, "Occupational Characteristics and the Male's Performance in the Family," *Journal of Marriage and the Family* 31 (1969):707–712; David Guttman, "The Premature Gerontocracy," in *Death in American Experience*, ed. Arien Mack (New York, 1973), pp. 184–213.

25.   Young and Wilmott, *Symmetrical Family*.

26.   Fowlkes, "Wives of Professional Men"; Howard Gadlin, "Scars and Emblems: Paradoxes of American Family Life," *Journal of Social History* 11 (1978): 320–322.

27.   Aldous, "Occupational Characteristics," p. 708.

28.   Sharon L. Sutherland, "The Unambitious Female: A Data-Based Discussion of Women's Low Professional Aspirations," *Signs* 3 (1978):774–794.

29. Lasch, *Haven in a Heartless World*, suggests elements of this in his fascinating critique of the American family, though his judgment of work is far more pessimistic than mine.

30. Will Clopton, "Personality and Career Change," *Industrial Gerontology* 7 (1973): 9–17; Maccoby, *Gamesman.*

31. Lasch, *Haven*; Charles Reich, *The Greening of America* (New York, 1971).

32. Feuer, *Conflict of Generations*; Richard Flacks, "The Liberated Generation: An Exploration of the Roots of Student Protest," *Journal of Social Issues* 23 (1967):52–75.

33. College Entrance Examination Board, *On Further Examination* (New York, 1977); Gene Chenoweth, "The Cultural Bind on the American Male," *National Association of College Admissions Counselors Journal* 8 (1969):6–9.

34. Marya Mannes, "How Men Will Benefit from the Women's Power Revolution" in *Subject and Structure: An Anthology for Writers*, ed. John M. Wasson (Boston, 1972), pp. 168–187; Miller, *Towards a New Psychology.*

35. Edward Shorter and Charles Tilly, *Strikes in France, 1830–1968* (Cambridge, Eng., 1974).

36. Goldthorpe et al., *The Affluent Worker*; Robert McKenzie and Allan Silver, *Angels in Marble: Working-Class Conservatives in Urban England* (Chicago, 1968).

37. Annie Kriegel, *The French Communists: Profile of a People*, trans. E. Halperin (Chicago, 1972).

38. Peter Chew, *The Inner World of the Middle-Aged Man* (New York, 1976); Carol Kelleher, "Second Careers—a Growing Trend," *Industrial Gerontology* (1973): 1–8.

39. Eli Ginzburg, "The Job Problem," *Scientific American*, Nov. 1977, pp. 43–51; Dennis F. Johnston, "The Future of Work: Three Possible Alternatives," *Monthly Labor Review*, May 1972, pp. 3–11.

40. See the Jan. 16, 1978, issue of *Newsweek*, pp. 52–61, on male adaptations to women's work, particularly in the professional ranks.

41. Paul J. Andrisani, "Job Satisfaction among Working Women," *Signs* 3 (1978): 588–607.

42. Chafe, *American Woman* and *Women and Equality*. I am also grateful to Susan Householder Van Horn, who has shown me her studies of American working women.

43. Michael Smith, Stanley Parker, and Cyril Smith, *Leisure and Society in Britain* (London, 1973); Sebastian De Grazia, *Of Time, Work, and Leisure* (New York, 1962); Robert Havighurst, "The Leisure Activities of the Middle-Aged," *American Journal of Sociology* 63 (1957): 152–162; Eva Rabbon, "Recreations with the Aged," *The Federalist* (1947): 13–15; E. Larrabee and R. B. Meyerson, eds., *Mass Leisure* (Glencoe, Ill., 1957); Nels Anderson, *Man's Work and Leisure* (New York, 1977); Donald W. Ball and John Loy, *Sport and Social Order* (Boston, 1975); Kaplan, *Leisure in America*; G. S. Kenyon, *Aspects of Contemporary Sport Sociology* (New York, 1968); George H. Sage, ed. *Sport and American Society* (Boston, 1975); Joffre Dumazedier, *Towards a Civilization of Leisure* (New York, 1967), and idem, *Sociologie empirique du loisir: critique et contre-critique de la civilisation du loisir* (Paris, 1974); Clayre, *Work and Play.*

44. Lasch, *Haven*, for example, dismisses contemporary leisure as hollow.

45. G. Vinnai, *Football Mania* (London, 1973).

46. Maccoby and Jacklin, *Psychology of Sex Differences*; Ruth Hartley, "Sex-Role Pressures in the Socialization of the Male Child," *Psychological Reports* 5 (1959): 457–468; Brian Allen, "Liberating the Manchild," *Transactional Analysis Journal* 2 (1972): 68–71; H. Biller and L. Borstelmann, "Masculine Development: An Integrative Review," *Merrill-Palmer Quarterly* 13 (1967): 253–294; P. H. Mussen, "Long-term Consequents of Masculinity of Interests in Adolescence," *Journal of Consulting Psychology* 26 (1962): 435–440.

47. Julius Fast, "The Predator with a Brain: How Men See Themselves," idem, *The*

Incompatibility of Men and Women (New York, 1972), pp. 95ff.; N. Elias and E. Dunning, "Dynamics of Group Sports with Special Reference to Football," *British Journal of Sociology* 17 (1966): 388–401.

48.   McGlynnis, *Issues in Physical Education*, pp. 128ff.

49.   Johann Huizinga, *Homo Ludens: A Study of the Play Element in Culture* (Boston, 1955); but see Maccoby, *Gamesman*; S. B. Linder, *The Harried Leisure Class* (New York, 1970).

50.   See Howard Michel, "Going Beyond Competition," in *The Complete Runner* (New York, 1978), pp. 5–6; Robert Daley, *The Bizarre World of European Sports* (New York, 1963).

51.   Zweig, *Workers*.

52.   Walvin, *Peoples Game*; Ian Taylor, "Soccer Consciousness and Soccer Hooliganism," in *Images of Deviance*, ed. S. Cohen (London, 1971).

53.   This relates, of course, to the extent of successful retirement; see footnote 23. Herbert Askwith, *Your Retirement: How to Plan for It; How to Enjoy It to the Fullest* (New York, 1974), pp. 59ff. René Berthier, *Nouvel âge de vie* (Paris, 1973); M. Shrem, *Des Années, Oui; Vieillir, Non!* (Neuchâtel, 1965); L. Chaflen, "Leisure Time Adjustment of the Aged," *Journal of Genetic Psychology* 88 (1956): 261–296; C. DeGrucky, *Creative Old Age* (San Francisco, 1946); B. Gelb, "Getting Ready for Retirement," *International Teamsters Magazine* 74 (1977): 788; H. D. Shapiro, "Do Not Go Gently," *New York Times Magazine*, Feb. 6, 1977.

54.   Brian Harrison, *Drink and the Victorians* (Pittsburgh, 1971); Thomas Coffey, *The Long Thirst* (New York, 1976); J. C. Burnham, "New Perspectives on the Prohibition 'Experiment' of the 1920's," *Journal of Social History* 2 (1968): 51–68; Jack Wiener, *Drinking* (New York, 1976).

55.   The slogan, richly symbolic in suggesting the new male family approach, was adopted in a YMCA father-daughter group formed in 1926 to "restore" family contacts disrupted by urban life. Charles C. Kujawa, *The Father and Daughter Y—Indian Princess Manual* (New York, 1976), p. 3 et passim.

56.   Lasch, *Haven*; Shorter, *Making of Modern Family*; Susan Gettleman and Janet Markowitz, *The Courage to Divorce* (New York, 1974); R. Thamm, *Beyond Marriage and the Nuclear Family* (San Francisco, 1975); R. D. Laing, *The Politics of the Family* (New York, 1971); David Cooper, *The Death of the Family* (New York, 1971); and, perhaps reflecting the European experience against the crisis thesis, Philippe Ariès, "The Family and the City," *Daedalus* 107 (1977): 227–237.

57.   James R. Smith and Lynn G. Smith, *Beyond Monogamy* (Baltimore, 1974).

58.   See the concluding section in Gillis, *Youth and History*; Pitts, "Continuity and Change," pp. 194–204. But see Herbert Hendin, *The Age of Sensation* (New York, 1975), and Edgar Z. Friedenberg, *Coming of Age in America* (New York, 1965).

59.   Zweig, *Worker;* Goldthorpe, *Affluent Worker;* Pitts, "Continuity and Change," pp. 194–204; O. S. English and C. J. Foster, *Fathers Are Parents Too* (London, 1953); Paul Bohannan, *Divorce and After* (New York, 1970); Stephen Koch, "The Guilty Sex: How American Men Became Irrelevent," *Esquire* 84 (1975): 53–57; John M. Mogey, "A Century of Declining Paternal Authority," *Marriage and Family Living* 19 (1957): 234–239; Walter Mischel, "Father Absence and Delay of Gratification," *Journal of Abnormal Psychology* 63 (1961): 116–124; John Nash, "The Father in Contemporary Culture and Current Psychological Literature," *Child Development* 36 (1965): 261–297; R. A. Elder, "Traditional and Developmental Conceptions of Fatherhood," *Marriage and Family Living* 11 (1949):99.

60.   Zweig, *Worker*.

61.   D. Aberle and K. Naegele, "Middle-Class Fathers' Occupational Role and Attitudes Toward Children," *American Journal of Orthopsychiatry* 22 (1952): 366–378.

62.   Statistique, *Mouvement général*, pp. 1930ff.

63. Lasch, *Haven*; Alexander Mitscherlich, *Society without the Father* (New York, 1970).

64. F. I. Nye, *Role Structure and Analysis of the Family* (Beverly Hills, Calif., 1976).

65. Feuer, *Conflict of Generations*; Kenniston, *Young Radicals*; Richard Flacks, "The Liberated Generation," 52–75.

66. Lasch, *Haven*; p. 171ff.; see, also, Friedenberg, *Coming of Age*; David Riesman, *The Lonely Crowd* (New Haven, 1950).

67. Zweig, *Worker*, pp. 61–84, notes that this is a common complaint among young British workers.

68. This is a very important point against the idea that parenting is predictable and that childhood events are the principal motor of cultural change. See Howard Gadlin, "Scars and Emblems: Paradoxes of American Family Life," *Journal of Social History* 11 (1978): 315; Jay E. Mechlin, "Advice to Historians on Advice to Mothers," *Journal of Social History* 9 (1975): 44–63.

69. Eva Figes, *Patriarchal Attitudes* (New York, 1970).

70. See the second chapter in Martha Wolferstein and Nathan Leites, *Movies: A Psychological Study* (New York, 1970).

71. W. G. Dyer and Dick Urban, "The Institutionalization of Equalitarian Family Norms," *Marriage and Family Living* 20 (1958): 53–58; David Heer, "The Measurement and Bases of Family Power," *Marriage and Family Living* 25 (1963): 133–139.

72. Patai, *Women in Modern World*; Chafe, *American Woman*.

73. Del Martin, *Battered Wives*; R. J. Gillis, *The Violent Home* (London, 1972).

74. For a not entirely satisfactory overview, see Young and Wilmott, *The Symmetrical Family*.

75. Pitts, "Continuity and Change," pp. 194–204; Zweig, *Worker*; see, also, Komarovsky, *Unemployed Man*.

76. See chapters 11 and 12 of Seeley, *Crestwood Heights*.

77. Fried, *World of Urban Working Class*, pp. 121–151. Zweig, *Worker*; Colin Rosser and Christopher Harris, *The Family and Social Change* (New York, 1965).

78. Wolferstein and Leites, *Movies*.

79. Nichols, *Men's Liberation*, pp. 164ff., 264ff.

80. For an overview, see Leonard Benson, *Fatherhood: A Sociological Perspective* (New York, 1967); Fitzhugh Dobson, *How To Father* (Los Angeles, 1974); J. G. Howells, "Fathering," *Modern Perspectives in International Child Psychiatry* 3 (1969): 124–138; Green, *Fathering*.

81. See footnote 55.

82. Green, *Fathering*; Chew, *Inner World*, pp. 76–100.

83. Mary K. Matossian and William D. Schafter, "Family, Fertility, and Political Violence," *Journal of Social History* 11 (1977): 137–178.

84. Robert S. Weiss, *Marital Separation* (New York, 1975); Morton M. Hunt, *The World of the Formerly Married* (New York, 1966).

85. Shorter, *Making of Modern Family*; but see John H. Schoor, *Escape From Authority: The Perspective of Erich Fromm* (New York, 1961); Lasch, *Haven*; E. W. Burgess and A. J. Locke, *The Family: From Institution to Companionship* (New York, 1945); Willard Waller, *The Family* (New York, 1938); Robert Blood and Donald Wolfe, *Husbands and Wives: The Dynamics of Married Lives* (Glencoe, Ill., 1960).

86. Good twentieth-century divorce history is still lacking. Elaine Tyler May's forthcoming book should help greatly; see, idem, "The Pressure to Provide: Class, Consciousness,

and Divorce in Urban America"; O. R. McGregor, *Divorce in England: A Centenary Study* (London, 1947).

87.   Rosser and Harris, *Family;* Zweig, *Worker;* Komarovsky, *Blue-Collar Marriage;* Peter Wilmott and Michael Young, *Family and Class in a London Suburb* (New York, 1965), and idem, *Family and Kinship in East London* (London, 1957).

88.   John Ardagh, *The New French Revolution* (New York, 1969); Pitts, "Continuity and Change," pp. 194–204; Wylie, *Village in the Vaucluse.*

89.   Brownmiller, *Against Our Will.*

90.   Willard Waller, "The Rating and Dating Complex," *American Sociological Review* 2 (1937): 731ff.; Francis E. Merrill, *Courtship and Marriage* (New York, 1959); Bernard I. Murstein, *Who Will Marry Whom?* (New York, 1976).

91.   "Dress and Male Liberation: Symbols of Sex Roles," in *Readings in Introd. Sociology*, pp. 3–19; Paula Fass, *The Damned and the Beautiful: American Youth in the 1920s* (New York, 1977).

92.   Firestone, *Dialectic of Sex*, pp. 126ff.; Nancy Henley and S. Freeman, *The Sexual Politics of Interpersonal Behavior* (New York, 1971).

93.   Zeldin, *France, 1848–1945,* I, pp. 285–314.

94.   Anthony Pietropinto and Jacqueline Simenauer, *Beyond the Male Myth: A Nation-wide Survey* (New York, 1977), pp. 49ff.

95.   Zweig, *Worker.*

96.   Albert Ellis, *The American Sexual Tragedy* (New York, 1962); Lester W. Dearborn, "The Problem of Masturbation," *Marriage and Family Living* 14 (1952): 46–55.

97.   B. Glassberg, "The Quandary of a Virginal Male," *Family Coordinator* 19 (1970): 82–87; E. Kanin, "Male Aggression in Dating-Courtship Relations," *American Journal of Sociology* 63 (1957): 197–204.

98.   This would produce genetically inferior children if production of children were involved.

99.   Merrill, *Courtship.*

100.   A. C. Kinsey et al., *Sexual Behavior in American Females* (Philadelphia, 1953), and idem, *Sexual Behavior in the Human Male* (Philadelphia, 1948); Louis Terman, *Psychological Factors in Marital Happiness* (New York, 1938).

101.   C. Kirkpatrick and E. Kanin, "Male Sexual Aggression on a University Campus," *American Sociological Review* 22 (1957): 52–58; John Scazoni, *Sexual Bargaining: Power Politics in the American Marriage* (Englewood Cliffs, N.J., 1972).

102.   Carl Degler, "What Ought To Be and What Was: Women's Sexuality in the Nineteenth Century," *American Historical Review* 79 (1974): 1469–1490; Pietropinto and Simenauer, *Beyond the Male Myth*; Shere Hite, *The Hite Report* (New York, 1976).

103.   Ferdinand Lundberg and Maryna Farnham, *Modern Woman: The Lost Sex* (New York, 1947), p. 144ff.

104.   Hite, *Report*; William H. Masters and Virginia Johnson, *Human Sexual Response* (Boston, 1966).

105.   Hite, *Report.*

106.   Pietropinto and Simenauer, *Beyond the Male Myth.*

107.   Mirra Komarovsky, *Dilemmas of Masculinity: A Study of College Youth* (New York, 1976); G. Ginsberg et al., "The New Impotence," *Archives of General Psychiatry* 26 (1972): 218–20. See, also, on another problem of male sexuality, J. Balswick, "Attitudes of Lower-Class Males toward Taking a Male Birth Control Pill," *Family Coordinator* 21 (1972): 195–201.

108.   Pietropinto and Simenauer, *Beyond the Male Myth*, p. 150ff.

109. Ibid.

110. Lionel Gendron, *L'Amour après 50 ans* (Montréal, 1969).

111. Masters and Johnson, *Human Sexual Response*; see also, William H. Masters et al., *The Pleasure Bond* (Boston, 1975).

112. Pietropinto and Simenauer, *Beyond the Male Myth*, p. 68 et passim.

113. Komarovsky, *Blue-Collar Marriage*; Young and Wilmott, *Symmetrical Family*; Zweig, *Worker*.

114. Zweig, *Worker*.

115. Heer, "Measurement"; Russell Middleton and Snell Putney, "Dominance in Decisions in the Family: Race and Class Differences," *American Journal of Sociology* 65 (1960): 605–609.

116. Lasch, *Haven*.

117. L. W. Hoffman, "Effects of the Employment of Mothers in Parental Power Relations and the Division of Household Tasks," *Marriage and Family Living* 22 (1960): 27–35.

118. Martin, *Battered Wives*, p. 103. There is an increasing reminder that a good bit of family mutuality may be due to the sociologist's firm belief that this is what should exist, and his determination to find the same.

119. Rosser and Harris, *Family*; Wilmott and Young, *Family and Kinship*, passim, note how often wives turn to their mothers instead of their husbands as family referents.

120. Hoffman, "Effects"; K. F. Geikon, "Expectations Concerning Husband and Wife Responsibilities in the Home," *Journal of Marriage and the Family* 26 (1964): 349–352.

121. Komarovsky, *Blue-Collar Marriage*; Rosser and Harris, *Family*; Zweig, *Worker*.

122. Hoffman, "Effects"; Geilson, "Expectations."

123. E. R. Mowrer, *The Family, Its Organization and Disorganization* (Chicago, 1932); H. R. Lantz and E. D. Snyder, *Marriage* (New York, 1962); Dyer and Urban, "Institutionalization"; Burgess and Locke, *Family*.

124. Lasch, *Haven*, p. 215, fn. 16, claims that the outside world turned nasty first, spoiling the family.

125. Komarovsky, *Blue-Collar Marriage*; see, also, Wilmott and Young, *Kinship and Family*, for a British analogue.

126. Komarovsky, *Blue-Collar Marriage*, p. 133ff.

127. Philip Slater, *The Pursuit of Loneliness; American Culture at the Breaking Point* (Boston, 1970).

128. Komarovsky, *Blue-Collar Marriage*; L. Holmstrom, *The Two-Career Family* (New York, 1972); Rhona Rapoport and Robert Rapoport, *Dual-Career Families* (London, 1971).

129. May, "Pressure to Provide."

130. Jeanne Binstock, "Metamorphosis of the Mother," *Dissent* 25 (1978): 413; this is not, however, to fall back into the postwar analytical patterns; the traditional levels can and must be reduced, and the prospects can be exciting.

131. Chafe, *American Woman*, p. 170ff.; *Fortune*, August 1946, pp. 5–6; see, also, Patai, *Women*, particularly the essay by Helge Pross.

132. Otto Pollack, "The Outlook for the American Family," *Journal of Marriage and the Family* 29 (1967): 193–205.

133. But A. S. Rossi, "A Biosocial Perspective on Parenting," *Daedalus* 107 (1977): 1–33, reminds us, in a fascinating but largely male-less essay, of the continuing, and possibly prospective, limitations, as she forecasts a new surge of motherhood. Lasch, *Haven*, pp. 167–189, differs greatly, but in stressing passive fathers and an irremediable family/social nexus he offers still less help to interested fathers. For pathological results of paternal passivity, see William McCord, Judith Porter, and Joan McCord, "The Familial Genesis of Psychoses,"

Psychiatry 25 (1962): 70; Victor D. Sanua, "Sociocultural Factors in Families of Schizophrenics: A Review of the Literature," *Psychiatry* 24 (1961): 247ff.

134. Rossi, "Biosocial Perspective"; Zweig, *Worker*; R. J. Tasch, "The Role of the Father in the Family," *Journal of Experimental Education* 20 (1952): 319–361; Carl Levett, "A Paternal Presence in Future Family Models," in *The Family in Search of a Future*, ed. H. Otto (New York, 1970).

135. Carole Klein, "The Single Parent—Male," *The Single Parent Experience* (New York, 1973), pp. 43–59; Robert Miner, *Mother's Day* (New York, 1978); Zweig, *Worker*.

136. Lasch, *Haven*; Seeley et al., *Crestwood Heights*, p. 116ff.

137. Komarovsky, *Blue-Collar Marriage*; Zweig, *Worker*.

138. Levett, "Paternal Presence"; Green, *Fathering*.

139. Ariès, "Family and the City," p. 227ff.

Chapter 8

1. Carolyn Heilbrun, *Toward a Recognition of Androgyny* (New York, 1973); June Singer, *Androgyny: Toward a New Theory of Sexuality* (New York, 1977). On the basis of female change, Jeanne Binstock, "Metamorphosis of the Mother," *Dissent* 25 (1978): 413, argues that "women inevitably must be liberated to enjoy the fruits of other occupations—whether they want to or not." See, also, Chafe, *Women and Equality*.

2. Maccoby, *Gamesman*.

3. Komarovsky, *Dilemmas of Masculinity*, passim; Ross Firestone, ed., *A Book of Men: Visions of the Male Experience* (Boston, 1976); Max Gunther, *Virility: A Celebration of the American Male* (Chicago, 1975); Harvey Kaye, *Male Survival* (New York, 1974).

4. Laurel Galana, *The Violent Sex* (New York, 1978); Beata Bishop and Pat O'Neill, *The Eggshell Ego: An Irreverent Analysis of Today's Male* (New York, 1977); see, also, Jon Snodgrass, ed., *For Men Against Sexism* (New York, 1977).

5. G. Ginsberg et al., "The New Impotence," *Archives of General Psychiatry* 26 (1972): 218–220.

6. Firestone, *Dialectic of Sex*.

7. Young and Wilmott, *Symmetrical Family*; Alice Rossi, "A Biosocial Perspective on Parenting" *Daedalus* 106 (1977): 1–33.

8. Lasch, *Haven in a Heartless World*; Riesman, *Lonely Crowd*.

9. Erica Jong, *Fear of Flying* (New York, 1973); Bishop and O'Neill, *Eggshell Ego*; Hennessey, *I, B.I.T.C.H.*; Alice Rossi, "Equality between the Sexes: An Irreverent Proposal," *Daedalus* 93 (1964): 607–652.

10. Rosaldo and Lamphere, *Woman, Culture, and Society*.

11. Goldberg, *Inevitability of Patriarchy*.

12. Barbara Polk, "Male Power and the Woman," in Cox, *Female Sexuality*, p. 401; Chafe, *Women and Equality*; Miller, *Towards a New Psychology*.

13. de Beauvoir, *Second Sex*; Vern L. Bullough, *The Subordinate Sex: A History of Attitudes toward Women* (Urbana, Ill. 1974).

14. June Wayne, "The Male Artist as a Stereotypical Female," *Art Journal* 33 (1973): 414–416.

15. See fn. 4. Male liberation is more a term than a developed concept; we have popularized literature in the field before we have literature. But see Jack Nichols, *Men's Liberation*; Fasteau, *Male Machine*; Pleck and Sawyer, *Men and Masculinity*; Farrell, *Liberated Man*; Goldberg, *Hazards of Being Male*.

16. Sidney Jourard, "Some Lethal Aspects of the Male Role," *The Transparent Self* (New York, 1964), pp. 34–41; Alan Booth, "Sex and Social Participation," *American Sociological Review* 37 (1972): 183–192; J. Balswick and C. Peek, "The Inexpressive Male: A Tragedy of American Society," *Family Coordinator* 20 (1971): 363–368; Henley and Freeman, *Sexual Politics*. Women, in fact, worry about their own ability to maintain healthy emotionality; see Helena Lopata, *Occupation: Housewife* (New York, 1971), p. 208.

17. On raising androgynous children, see Barbara Spring, *Education for Young Non-Sexist Children* (New York, 1975); Clarice Brown, *Female and Male: Socialization, Social Roles and Social Structure* (New York, 1978); Carrie Carmichael, *Non-Sexist Childraising* (Boston, 1977); see, also, Arlene Skolnick, ed., *Rethinking Childhood* (Boston, 1976).

18. Goldberg, *Inevitability*; Robert A. Johnson, *He: Understanding Masculine Psychology* (New York, 1977).

19. This is notably the case in Nichols, *Men's Liberation*.

20. Mead, *Male and Female*; Rosaldo, "Woman, Culture, and Society;" in *Woman, Culture, and Society*, pp. 17–42.

21. Lasch, *Haven*; René Dubos, *The Mirage of Health: Utopias, Progress, and Biological Change* (New York, 1959); Ivan Ilich, *Medical Nemesis: The Expropriation of Health* (New York, 1976).

22. Gail Sheehy, *Passages: Predictable Crises of Adult Life* (New York, 1975); Daniel Levinson, "The Male Mid-Life Decade," in *Life History Research in Psychopathology*, ed. David Ricks (Minneapolis, Minn. 1974); Daniel Levinson, *The Seasons of a Man's Life* (New York, 1978).

23. George Sheehan, *Doctor Sheehan on Running* (New York, 1975); Thaddeus Kostrobala, *The Joy of Running* (New York, 1977).

24. It will be interesting to see more complete histories of modern male friendship in contrast to the images now being tossed about without empirical reference save for women's impressions and individual male experience. See Fasteau, *Male Machine*; Tiger, *Men in Groups*. At present, novels provide an excellent source; see, for example, C. P. Snow's *Strangers and Brothers* series, particularly the novel of the same name and *Homecoming*. On women's worries concerning their sisterhood, see Joan Cassell, *A Group Called Women: Sisterhood and Symbolism in the Feminist Movement* (New York, 1977).

25. Weiss, *Marital Separation*; Hunt, *World of the Formerly Married*; Stearns, *Old Age in European Society*; Statistique de France, *Mouvement général de la population*, pp. 1856ff.

26. Magee—Women's Hospital, *A New Generation* (Pittsburgh, 1978), pp. 5–6.

27. For an interesting comment on the utility of an updated paternalism as a larger social style, see Rothman, "The State as Parent," pp. 67–98.

28. Green, *Fathering*, passim.

29. I am indebted to Carol Stearns for this subtle notion; we have both recently decided to waive our rights and greatly enjoy the outcome.

30. See Ernest Becker: "Man can expand his self-feeling not only by physical incorporation but by any kind of triumph or demonstration of his own excellence." *Escape from Evil* (New York, 1975), pp. 11–12.

Selective Bibliography

There are really no existing histories of men, though all sorts of studies bear on the topic. For biological, psychological, and anthropological aspects, see: Michelle Zimbalist Rosaldo and Louise Lamphere, eds., *Woman, Culture, and Society* (Stanford, Calif., 1974); Lionel Tiger, *Men in Groups* (New York, 1969); Desmond Morris, *The Naked Ape* (New York, 1968); Dorothy Dinnerstein, *The Mermaid and the Minotaur* (New York, 1976); Eleanor Maccoby and Carol Jacklin, *The Psychology of Sex Differences* (Stanford, Calif., 1974); Herb Golberg, *The Hazards of Being Male* (New York, 1976).

On the Western tradition and preindustrial society, see: Peter Laslett, *The World We Have Lost* (Boston, 1965); idem, *Family Life and Illicit Love in Earlier Generations* (Cambridge, Eng., 1977); Philip J. Greven, Jr., *Four Generations: Population, Land, and Family in Colonial Andover, Massachusetts* (Ithaca, N.Y. 1970); idem, *The Protestant Temperament* (New York, 1978); Robert W. Malcolmson, *Popular Recreations in English Society, 1700–1850* (Cambridge, Mass., 1973); Lawrence Stone, *The Family, Sex and Marriage in England, 1500–1800* (New York, 1977); Randolph Trumbach, *The Rise of the Egalitarian Family: Aristocratic Kinship and Domestic Relations in Eighteenth-Century England* (New York, 1978); Natalie Z. Davis, *Society and Culture in Early Modern France* (Stanford, Calif., 1975); J. G. Peristiany, ed., *Honour and Shame: The Values of Mediterranean Society* (Chicago, 1968).

The following histories of women are useful: Renate Bridenthal and Claudia Koonz, eds., *Becoming Visible: Women in European History* (New York, 1977); Patricia Branca, *Women in Europe Since 1750* (London, 1978); idem, *Silent Sisterhood: Middle-Class Women in the Victorian Home* (Pittsburgh, 1975); Joan W. Scott and Louise Tilly, *Women, Work and Family* (New York, 1978); Mary Hartman and Lois Banner, eds., *Clio's Consciousness Raised* (New York, 1974); Nancy Cott, *Bonds of Womanhood* (New Haven, 1977); William Chafe, *Women and Equality* (New York, 1977);

Martha Vicinus, ed., *Suffer and Be Still* (Bloomington, Ind., 1972); idem, *A Widening Sphere* (Bloomington, Ind., 1977).

The impact of industrialization on men can be traced in various ways. See: E. P. Thompson, *The Making of the English Working Class* (New York, 1964); Peter N. Stearns, *Lives of Labor: Work in Maturing Industrial Societies* (New York, 1975); John R. Gillis, *Youth and History: Tradition and Change in European Age Relations* (New York, 1974); Herbert G. Gutman, *Work, Culture and Society in Industrializing America* (New York, 1976); Edward Shorter, *The Making of the Modern Family* (New York, 1976); Michael Gordon, ed., *The Family in American History* (New York, 1974); Michael Anderson, *Family Structure in Nineteenth-Century Lancashire* (Cambridge, Eng., 1971); Theodore Zeldin, *France, 1848–1945: Ambition, Love, and Politics,* 2 vols. (Oxford, 1973–1977).

On the twentieth century, see: Peter Filene, *Him/Herself: Sex Roles in Modern America* (New York, 1975); Mirra Komarovsky, *The Unemployed Man and His Family* (New York, 1940); idem, *Dilemmas of Masculinity: A Study of College Youth* (New York, 1976); Maureen Green, *Fathering* (New York, 1976); Ferdynand Zweig, *Worker in an Affluent Society* (New York, 1962); Anthony Pietropinto and Jacqueline Simenauer, *Beyond the Male Myth: A Nationwide Survey* (New York, 1977); Peter Wilmott and Michael Young, *Family and Class in a London Suburb* (New York, 1965); idem, *Family and Kinship in East London* (London, 1957); idem, *The Symmetrical Family* (London, 1973); Christopher Lasch, *Haven in a Heartless World: The Family Beseiged* (New York, 1977); Alice S. Rossi, Jerome Kagan, and Tamara Harven, *The Family* (New York, 1978); George H. Sage, ed., *Sport and American Society* (Boston, 1974); J. H. Goldthorpe, *The Affluent Worker in the Class Structure* (Cambridge, Eng., 1976); Marc Fasteau, *The Male Machine* (New York, 1974); Sar S. Levitan, ed., *Blue-Collar Workers* (New York, 1971); Steven Goldberg, *The Inevitability of Patriarchy* (New York, 1973); Joseph Pleck and Jack Sawyer, eds., *Men and Masculinity* (Englewood Cliffs, N.J., 1974); Daniel Levinson, *The Seasons of a Man's Life* (New York, 1978); Jack Nichols, *Men's Liberation: A New Definition of Masculinity* (New York, 1975).

Index

accounting 39, 99
adolescence 21, 62, 63, 146, 149, 157, 158
Africa 28
agricultural society 7, 13, 19ff., 52, 182
alcoholism 66, 112, 144–45
alienation 71, 129, 131
androgyny 179ff., 192
anthropology 2, 14, 173, 181
anti-Semitism 41
apprenticeship 66, 97
aristocracy 25, 36, 82, 86, 188
Asia 21, 25, 28
assembly line 71
Atlas, Charles 8
automobile 128, 143

Balzac, Honoré de 82
bars 40, 66, 74, 123, 145, 147
baseball 110
Bavaria 63
Bebel, August 73
Belgium 76
berdaches 21
bestiality 46
bicycles 75, 76, 107
biological attributes 3ff., 14–15, 100, 174
birth control 53, 67, 88ff., 98, 106, 114,
  146, 161, 172
Boccaccio, Giovanni 30
bonding (male) 18, 145, 164, 188–90, 195–
  96
Boone, Daniel 51
brawls 63
breadwinning 45, 47, 72, 102, 139, 172,
  177
Britain 48, 54, 60, 65, 67, 80, 88, 91, 101ff.,
  106, 131, 142–43, 147, 150, 152, 154
Bromme, Moritz 64–65
Bruce, Robert 15
budgets 68, 75, 101

building trades 21, 41, 42, 67
bureaucracy 41, 82, 97, 109, 112, 130
Burton, Robert 30

Calamity Jane 52, 74
Calvinism 33
Canada 6
capitalism 30, 47, 80, 86, 118, 143
Carnegie, Andrew 96
Catholicism 50, 106, 154
Chaucer 30
Chicago 105
chivalry 31
Christ 27
Christianity 14, 23ff., 84, 86, 87, 103
chromosomes 2–3
Cincinnati 100, 103
classical society 14
clubs 40, 83
coitus interruptus 67, 89
college 90–91, 101ff., 119, 135
communism 138
Comte, Auguste 82
condoms 68
Congress (U.S.) 116
costume 37, 38, 40, 46, 107, 156
courage 15, 16ff., 19, 37, 74
courtship 10, 65–66
cowboys 2, 51
crafts 21, 33, 36–37, 45, 59, 61, 66, 73,
  142, 149
Crimean War 50
Crockett, Davy 51
custody (child) 57, 108, 147, 152

Daimler 65
dancing 75
daughters 57, 107
death 50, 112
demography 42, 53, 88, 115, 146

Depression (1930s)   116, 122, 127–28, 150
Dinlock   66
divorce   57, 108, 154, 163, 180
dockwork   41
doctors   80, 91, 99, 134, 176–77
Douglass, Frederick   45
drinking   18, 24, 53, 60, 63, 66, 75, 76, 77, 94, 110, 120, 144, 176
duels   25

emotions (emotionality)   29, 36, 81, 94, 98, 163, 178–79, 191ff., 195
engineering   34, 42
Enlightenment   36, 89, 103
Erikson, Erik   26
Eve   23, 87

family   3ff., 36, 60, 127, 145ff., 189ff.
fathers and sons 3, 16, 19, 33, 43, 44–45, 48ff., 54, 61, 66–67, 75, 95, 97, 123, 149, 164ff., 192ff.
feminism   1, 4, 9–10, 37, 57–58, 87, 97, 107, 116ff., 134, 135, 136, 139, 158, 170ff., 195–96
flappers   107
football   76, 102, 142
Ford, Henry   71
France   6, 24, 28, 32, 40, 50, 60, 64, 74, 80, 85, 88, 102, 106, 108, 131, 136, 138, 150, 154, 190
fraternities   83, 123, 176
Freud, Sigmund (Freudianism)   3, 157
frontier   20, 51, 54

Galveston, Tex.   100
gambling   76
gardening   36, 76
Gaskell, Mrs. Hugh   85
Germanic tribes   20, 25
Germany   6, 51, 60, 62, 64–65, 67, 68, 69, 73, 92, 102, 131, 137
God   13, 24ff., 35, 47, 50, 85, 87, 92, 103
golf   141
grade inflation   136
Greece   14, 23–24, 99, 188
Greek-Americans   75
guilds   32, 144

Hamburg   56
Harvard University   38
health   31, 133, 135, 183, 187
Hegel, Georg Wilhelm Friedrich   80
Henry VIII   31

Henry, John   59–60
hobbies   142
homosexuality   5, 11, 21, 28–29, 37, 50, 61
hunting   13, 16ff., 18

illegitimacy   44, 63, 158
imperialism   57, 115
impotence   173
India   13
Indians (American)   14, 20, 21, 26, 28
"Indian Princesses"   151
inflation   68, 70
insanity   50, 180
instrumentalism   72, 109, 129
intellectuals   82
Islam   28
Italy   25, 28, 32

Japan   21
Judaism   24

Keats   82
kinship   48, 75, 161
Komorovsky, Mirra   162
Ku Klux Klan   121

Landers, Ann   171
Lasch, Christopher   140, 149
Latin America   143
lawyers   82
leisure   5, 34, 40, 52, 60, 75, 93ff., 102, 111, 127ff., 140ff., 171, 187ff.
Lille   75, 83
London   56, 69, 91, 142
longevity   3, 10, 53–54, 183–84, 190
love   30, 36, 55, 60, 67, 108, 122, 152ff., 194
Low Countries   6
Luder, Hans   33
Luther, Martin   33

marriage age   33–34, 55, 56, 63, 88, 147
marriage manuals   90, 157
marriage rates   44, 55, 146
Mary, Virgin   27, 28, 32, 50
Masai   15
masturbation   5, 34, 46, 65
mathematics   176
Mead, Margaret   4
medicine   87, 119
men's liberation   2, 122, 174ff., 195
metals   40, 41, 45, 62
Michelet, Jules   82

Middle Ages   7, 25, 188
middle class   39ff., 52, 57, 59, 78, 79ff., 115, 129ff., 157ff., 164ff.
mid-life crisis   185–86
military service   20, 34, 51, 54, 101ff., 115, 119, 170
Mill, John Stuart   49, 56
mining   8, 39, 41, 42, 62, 66, 67
ministers   84–85
mobility   43, 66–67, 72, 109, 129
modernization   7, 10, 38
monks   31
morris dance   75
motherhood   17, 18–19, 54, 98, 106, 163ff., 171, 174, 175, 192
Mother's Day   116
Mulhouse   88
music hall   65
mutuality (marital)   160ff.

narcissism   149
nazism   116
New England   26, 33
New Jersey   163
nurturing   15
nutrition   43, 63, 114

old age   71, 76
Old Testament   24, 26
orgasm   90, 157, 158
Osgood, Samuel   84
ovariotomy   55

Pandora   23
Paris   91
paternalism   79, 94, 109, 194ff.
patriarchalism   1, 16, 26, 35, 37, 40, 44, 45, 47, 48ff., 57, 86, 93ff., 105ff., 113, 151, 154, 160, 164, 170ff., 181, 185, 190, 194–195, 196
peasantry   21, 25, 32, 45, 60
pedestal image   80
Pericles   23
Pestalozzi, Johann Heinrich   95
phrenology   49
politics   18, 58
pornography   65, 157
Pound, Ezra   24
power   14, 23, 32, 179ff.
priesthood   21, 31
primates   14, 16
primitive society   4, 14ff.
Princeton University   38

printers   70–71
professional men   81ff., 97, 119, 134
Prohibition   110
Prometheus   24
prostitution   64, 91, 156
protest   73ff., 135, 136–38, 186
Protestantism   32ff., 106, 181
psychological attributes   3ff., 15ff., 184
psychologists   135, 151, 180
puberty   7, 29, 63, 90
puddling   41

Quakers   89

railroads   40, 45, 71
rationalism   23, 42, 80, 82, 99ff., 119, 134, 173
Reformation   32
religion   23, 100, 106, 181
Renaissance   32
retirement   133, 186
Rheims   64
Rhodes scholarships   102
romanticism   50
Rome   23–24

Samoa   182
savings   94
Scandinavia   6, 137
Schlumberger, Camille   88
schools   51, 52, 61, 77–78, 94, 97, 98ff., 119, 136, 144, 171
Schopenhauer, Arthur   82
scientific management   71
scouting   51
servants   90, 94
sexuality   3ff., 29, 34, 44, 45–46, 55, 60, 63–65, 66, 75, 77, 79ff., 89ff., 108, 156ff., 171, 196
Social Darwinism   66, 80, 83, 94
socialism   11, 61, 92
Spain   25
Sparta   23
sperm   3
sports   18, 23, 51, 60, 76, 77, 101ff., 110, 120, 140ff., 188
strikes   73ff., 137
suburbia   128–29
suicide   53, 112, 180
Switzerland   88, 95

Tarzan   112
technology   40–42, 67, 71, 110, 113ff., 129

territoriality   22
textiles   40, 42, 52, 62, 73, 75, 88, 90
Tiger, Lionel   3, 18
time, sense of   82–83
trade unions   7, 55, 62, 73, 109
transvestism   21, 38
Tristan, Flora   85

United States   6, 24, 51, 60, 80, 88, 91–92,
    101ff., 106, 113, 115, 116ff., 131, 133,
    136, 137, 142–43, 147, 152, 154, 163, 165
urination   3

vacations   94
Victoria (Queen)   94
Victorianism   7, 9, 71ff., 114, 117, 121, 156
Vietnam War   113, 180
violence   60, 142–43, 169

Wales   76
Watergate   180
Wayland, Francis   95, 96
Western civilization   4, 6, 9, 13, 16, 23ff.,
    41, 57, 80, 85, 173, 180, 196
white-collar work(ers)   43, 97, 109, 132,
    136–37
wife-beating   69, 117, 120, 150
wigs   37
witches   28
womb envy   14
work   5, 53, 109, 113, 127ff., 185ff.
working class   7, 44, 54, 59ff., 104ff., 129ff.
World War I   51, 73, 114, 115
World War II   15, 100, 123, 128, 138, 147,
    150

YMCA   151